# SELF-REGULATION AND THE COMMON CORE

The Common Core State Standards for English Language Arts created new challenges for teachers and pre-service instructors. Self-regulated learning, using one's thoughts, feelings, and behaviors to reach goals, can help students become independent, self-directed learners. This book provides educators the support they need to apply the principles of self-regulated learning in their teaching for success with the Common Core. In this book, Marie C. White and Maria K. DiBenedetto present information on how to apply academic self-regulation by integrating two models: one which addresses how students develop self-regulatory competence, the other which focuses on the various processes within the three phases of self-regulated learning. In addition, *Self-Regulation and the Common Core* provides specific lesson plans for grades K-12, using the standards and the integrated framework to promote higher order thinking and problem-solving activities.

**Dr. Marie C. White** is Associate Professor of Educational Psychology and Chair of Childhood and Adolescent Education at Nyack NYC.

**Dr. Maria K. DiBenedetto** is a high school science teacher in North Carolina. Both authors have extensive experience in teacher education and are experts in self-regulated learning.

# SELF-REGULATION AND THE COMMON CORE

## Application to ELA Standards

Marie C. White and Maria K. DiBenedetto

NEW YORK AND LONDON

First published 2015
by Routledge
711 Third Avenue, New York, NY 10017

and by Routledge
2 Park Square, Milton Park, Abingdon, Oxon, OX14 4RN

*Routledge is an imprint of the Taylor & Francis Group, an informa business*

© 2015 Taylor & Francis

The right of Marie C. White and Maria K. DiBenedetto to be identified as author of this work has been asserted by them in accordance with sections 77 and 78 of the Copyright, Designs and Patents Act 1988.

All rights reserved. No part of this book may be reprinted or reproduced or utilised in any form or by any electronic, mechanical, or other means, now known or hereafter invented, including photocopying and recording, or in any information storage or retrieval system, without permission in writing from the publishers.

*Trademark notice*: Product or corporate names may be trademarks or registered trademarks, and are used only for identification and explanation without intent to infringe.

*Library of Congress Cataloging-in-Publication Data*
White, Marie C.
 Self-regulation and the common core : application to ELA standards / by Marie C. White and Maria K. DiBenedetto.
   pages cm
 Includes bibliographical references and index.
 1. Self-culture.  2. Motivation in education.  3. Metacognition.
4. Language arts (Elementary)—United States.  5. Language arts (Secondary)—United States.  6. Education—Standards—United States  I. DiBenedetto, Maria K.  II. Title.
   LC32.W55 2015
   371.39'43—dc23
   2014034706

ISBN: 978-0-415-71419-8 (hbk)
ISBN: 978-0-415-71420-4 (pbk)
ISBN: 978-1-315-88284-0 (ebk)

Typeset in ApexBembo
by Apex CoVantage, LLC

Printed and bound in the United States of America by Publishers Graphics, LLC on sustainably sourced paper.

# CONTENTS

Foreword by Barry J. Zimmerman and Dale H. Schunk     *vii*
*Preface*     *xi*
*Acknowledgments*     *xv*

## PART I
## Linking the Common Core and Self-Regulation     1

1  Spirals and Crosswalks     3

2  Theory-Based Instruction: Self-Regulation of Learning     8

3  Self-Regulation in a Classroom Context     17

## PART II
## Elementary School     27

4  The Road to Independence Begins With Strategic Help Seeking: Kindergarteners and First Graders     29

5  Writing From Informational Text: Grades 2 and 3     66

6  Building Academic Language: Grades 4 and 5     107

## PART III
## Middle School        155

7  The Self-Regulated Writer Reads Like a Writer: Grades 6, 7, and 8        157

## PART IV
## High School        209

8  A Dimensional Crosswalk: From the Common Core to Self-Regulation        211

9  A Strategic Approach to Research Projects: Grades 9 and 10        220

10  Beginning a Research Paper: Grades 11 and 12        246

*Index*        *281*

# FOREWORD

Over the past thirty years, self-regulation has gone from a topic viewed as relevant in clinical contexts to one embraced by educational researchers and practitioners. *Self-regulation* refers to individuals' self-generated cognitions, affects, and behaviors that are systematically oriented toward attainment of their goals (Zimmerman, 1998). Because education involves learning, there is a great deal of current interest in *self-regulated learning*, or self-regulation processes applied during a learning experience, where the goal is a desired level of achievement (Sitzmann & Ely, 2011).

Research on self-regulated learning in education has grown dramatically, in no small part because of the belief that many student learning difficulties stem from poor academic self-regulation skills. Researchers have addressed many facets of self-regulated learning. The earliest educational research focused on identifying key processes involved in self-regulated learning, such as goal setting, self-efficacy, metacognitive monitoring, and time management. Subsequently, a great deal of research was conducted on the effectiveness of interventions designed to teach students self-regulatory processes and motivate them to use these processes to improve their academic learning. Currently, an active area of research is determining how self-regulatory processes change over time as students learn and improve their skills.

What has not been well researched are ways to build self-regulation instruction into regular classroom practices such that teachers can implement these in the context of their normal instruction. In other words, despite the relevance of self-regulated learning to classroom practices, the gap between theory and research on the one hand and practice on the other remains wide.

This text is explicitly designed and written to help bridge that gap and make self-regulated learning an integral component of instructional practices. The text is well grounded in theory and research, and clearly shows how educational practitioners can use what we know about self-regulatory processes to help students become better self-regulated learners.

Throughout this text, the authors integrate two key aspects of self-regulated learning shown by theory and research to be critical: phases of self-regulated learning and levels of self-regulatory skill development. Zimmerman's (2000) three phases of self-regulated learning encompass learner actions before, during, and after task engagement. The *forethought* phase precedes actual performance and includes self-regulatory activities that set the stage for action, such as identifying goals, deciding which strategies to use, establishing favorable social and environmental conditions, and feeling self-efficacious for learning. The *performance control* phase includes task engagement activities that affect attention and action. Learners implement task strategies and monitor their performance outcomes. During the *self-reflection* phase, which occurs during pauses and after tasks are completed, learners respond evaluatively to their efforts. They may persist if they believe their strategies are working or modify their strategies or seek assistance if they believe their learning progress is inadequate. Self-reflections return learners to the forethought phase.

The four levels of self-regulatory skill development reflect the idea that learning begins with social (external) sources and shifts to self (internal) sources (Schunk & Zimmerman, 1997; Zimmerman, 2000). At the initial *observation* level, learners acquire basic skills and strategies from social sources such as modeling and coaching, although learners may not be able to perform those skills and strategies. With practice, feedback, and encouragement during the *emulation* level, learners' performances approximate those of the models. The major difference between these two levels is that learning occurs through instruction and observation at the observation level and at the emulation level, learners can perform the behaviors, although perhaps in rudimentary ways. Both levels primarily are social because learners require exposure to models, real or symbolic (e.g., televised). Learning is not yet internalized, or part of their self-regulatory systems, so they need assistance to perform.

At the third level, *self-control*, learners can employ the skills and strategies on their own when performing the same or similar tasks. They continue to pattern their actions after those of their teachers (models). They have not yet developed the capability to modify their performances based on adaptations they deem necessary in given situations. At the final level, *self-regulation*, learners can adapt their skills and strategies based on what alterations they believe may be needed to deal with changing personal and environmental conditions. At this level, students have internalized skills and strategies, which means they can transfer them beyond the learning setting; adjust them to fit new contexts; and maintain their motivation through goal setting, perceived goal progress, and self-efficacy. The progression from social to self sources is complete.

*Internalization* is a critical component of this progression (Schunk, 1999). When knowledge and skills are internalized, they are under the learner's self-regulatory control. Although learning can occur without internalization, as when learners are directed what to do, internalization is needed for maintaining self-regulated learning over time and transferring it beyond the original learning context. Internalization yields learners with such self-influences as goal setting, progress monitoring and self-evaluations, task strategies, and self-efficacy, which they can self-regulate to promote their motivation and learning.

This text shows educators how to apply these ideas in K–12 settings. The opening chapter describes the underlying theory in depth so that readers are firmly grounded in the conceptual framework before learning how to apply it. The second chapter then links this framework with the Common Core standards to further establish its validity for use in contemporary educational settings. The third chapter discusses attributes of self-regulated teachers and learners as substantiated by research evidence. Beginning with Chapter 4, the authors discuss detailed applications of self-regulated learning in educational contexts ranging from kindergarten to grade 12. These chapters illustrate how different self-regulatory processes can be developed in students in various content areas (e.g., reading, writing) across grade levels. Illustrations of the levels and phases of self-regulated learning are provided so practitioners can understand how the theoretical ideas can translate into practice.

The authors of this text—Marie C. White and Maria K. DiBenedetto—are professional educators with extensive experience at both the K–12 and higher education levels. Thus, they knowledgeably speak to both teacher educators who want their students to learn how to use self-regulated learning themselves and help their students become better self-regulated learners, and to practicing teachers who want to use self-regulatory processes in their teaching and help students develop those skills. The credibility of the authors with the content of this text and with the intended audiences will resonate well with researchers and practitioners alike.

The field of self-regulated learning has made tremendous advances in education over the past three decades. The direction that the field needs to take now is captured in this book: applying the theory and research findings to settings where teaching and learning occur. This book has great potential to not only advance the field of self-regulated learning, but also improve the learning skills of countless students. In short, this text underscores a point made repeatedly by self-regulated learning researchers—that self-regulation instruction can make a real difference in people's lives.

Barry J. Zimmerman<br>and Dale H. Schunk

## References

Schunk, D. H. (1999). Social-self interaction and achievement behavior. *Educational Psychologist, 34,* 219–227.

Schunk, D. H., & Zimmerman, B. J. (1997). Social origins of self-regulatory competence. *Educational Psychologist, 32,* 195–208.

Sitzmann, T., & Ely, K. (2011). A meta-analysis of self-regulated learning in work-related training and educational attainment: What we know and where we need to go. *Psychological Bulletin, 137,* 421–442.
Zimmerman, B. J. (1998). Academic studying the development of personal skill: A self-regulatory perspective. *Educational Psychologist, 33,* 73–86.
Zimmerman, B. J. (2000). Attaining self-regulation: A social cognitive perspective. In M. Boekaerts, P. R. Pintrich, & M. Zeidner (Eds.), *Handbook of self-regulation* (pp. 13–39). San Diego: Academic Press.

# PREFACE

The Common Core standards initiative encourages learners to take charge of their learning. Whether in a rural school, a suburban educational setting, or an urban learning environment, the Common Core provides a framework to equalize the learning opportunities for students of diverse backgrounds. In reality, we now have guidelines useful for helping students become independent, self-directed learners and to provide them with the tools needed for lifelong decision making and success. Teachers are the implementers of the standards, making decisions every day regarding classroom pedagogy while assessing individual students' prior knowledge, learning development, and learning differences. The implementation of these standards is the foundation to ensuring that all students, regardless of where they live and attend school, will be prepared for success in postsecondary education and the workforce. However, we need to find ways to increase teacher efficacy, specifically related to understanding how the Common Core standards can increase student learning and achievement. This book describes how teachers empowered with efficacy beliefs could align their teaching with the standards using a well-established theory of self-regulated learning. Students' self-regulated learning involves three features: use of learning strategies such as self-monitoring, responsiveness to their self-evaluations about how effective their learning is, and insightful assessments of their motivational processes.

At first glance, the standards can appear too complex for implementation in diverse learning environments. For that reason, this book provides educators with practical knowledge and tools to use self-regulated learning processes to guide instruction in the context of meeting the requirements set by the Common Core standards in grades K–12. Daily, educators are all making efforts to transform education and to make college and career readiness a reality for our students. We recognize the value of having consistent standards and regard the transition into implementing the Common Core standards as both a challenge and a major step forward for educators and students.

The Common Core standards are challenging educators to prepare a more diverse population of students for the world beyond K–12 classrooms. Through modeling, educators can promote self-regulated learning for their students. Utilizing self-regulated learning strategies shifts the focus of instruction to nurturing strategic and motivated students rather than delivering curriculum or managing classroom behavior.

## Structure of the Book

The book addresses the gap between the requirements put forth by the standards and classroom instruction designed to produce college- and career-ready learners. The chapters provide teachers with crosswalks that incorporate metacognitive training with reading, writing, speaking and listening, and language standards. This crosswalk links specific Common Core standards to strategic teaching methods that include explicit instruction in self-regulated learning. Traditional models of professional development have not yet linked the relationship of self-regulated learning to the Common Core standards. Each chapter provides teachers with teaching methods that can provide students with the tools to regulate their own learning, setting the stage to aid students in self-regulated learning through adulthood.

The first chapter aligns the Common Core standards with self-regulated learning using the concept of the crosswalk. The second chapter presents an overview of self-regulated learning describing and integrating the self-regulatory competence and phases of self-regulated learning models. Chapter 3 introduces the learning context, describing how a self-regulated teacher uses instruction in the classroom and how students who are self-regulated engage in processes that are part of both the Common Core and self-regulated learning. Chapter 4 begins the lesson plans, starting with grades K–1, in which through modeling, students are taught about self-efficacy, help seeking, and self-monitoring while reading and speaking about informational texts. Chapter 5 describes the process in which second and third graders observe the teacher modeling self-efficacy, goal setting, task analysis, strategic planning, and self-monitoring to gather evidence from informational texts for writing tasks. In Chapter 6, fourth and fifth graders engage in deliberate practice to apply strategies that include using morphemes and context clues to increase academic language. Chapter 7 focuses on middle school students learning to use mentor texts as models of good writing to help them produce clear and coherent essays based on research and reflection.

Chapter 8 explores the connections between self-regulation dimensions and the Common Core for grades 9–12. It addresses college and career readiness at the high school level by focusing on time management skills, self-monitoring, environmental structuring, goal setting, self-efficacy, self-evaluation, and help-seeking in the context of preparing to write a research paper. Chapter 9 focuses on preparing ninth and tenth graders to do short- and long-term research projects, beginning with the writing of the research question. The students are taught how to use a study log to self-monitor while working this one component of a research project. In the final chapter, the teacher guides students through the process of synthesizing sources and includes strategies to structure their final research paper.

# ACKNOWLEDGMENTS

We began writing this book with the intention to communicate that self-regulated learning, as a teaching approach, could facilitate educators', learners', and parents' understanding of the significant benefits of the Common Core standards for learning. Throughout this process, we have benefited by a number of individuals who have been instrumental in shaping our thoughts and understanding of the importance of the links between self-regulation and the Common Core standards. Dr. Barry J. Zimmerman, our mentor, has influenced our knowledge and understanding of the important role of self-regulation for instruction. We are grateful for his mentorship and guidance throughout our doctoral studies and even during the present time as we worked on this book. We are also indebted to Dr. Dale H. Schunk and Dr. Héfer Bembenutty for their advice, consistent availability, and encouragement throughout this project. We thank our families, friends, colleagues, teachers, and students for their patience, feedback, generosity of time, and invaluable support.

# PART I
# Linking the Common Core and Self-Regulation

# 1
# SPIRALS AND CROSSWALKS

"Why is my first grader preparing for college?" This question reflects a significant misunderstanding of the Common Core initiative by many parents, and it is a question teachers should be able to answer. Some school districts have ignored the question, while others have partnered with parents to respond to it. The Common Core State Standards (CCSS) were designed to provide teachers and parents with a clear understanding of what students are expected to learn and how they can help their students achieve success in academics. The standards are intended to serve as a guide towards attaining the knowledge and the skills required for success in college and careers. The establishment of consistent state standards offers educators and parents novel opportunities in developing and sharing curriculum and instructional best practices that include training in self-regulation.

As more states uniformly adopt the Common Core, decisions about curriculum and teaching methods continue to be made by local communities. According to Reeves (2012), the hierarchy of standards implementation is not generally understood, and this misunderstanding contributes to much of the confusion surrounding the Common Core. Standards decisions are made at the state level, curriculum decisions are made by local districts, and local teachers and principals make instructional decisions. Federal and state agencies set the standards, and superintendents, principals, and teachers choose the best curriculum and methods to meet the required learning goals for their specific student population.

As learners grow and develop physically, mentally, and emotionally, they can also mature towards becoming proactive learners and eventually take charge of their learning. It makes common and educational sense to link the standards to strategies that enable students to "spiral up," aligning their progress with the Common Core standards for text complexity. As students navigate what is known as the "staircase of complexity," they remain in an upward progression towards more complex texts, secure in their prior knowledge and proficiency in literacy skills from previous years of learning. It is educationally appropriate to prepare students for the complexity of college- and career-ready texts. When we consider each grade level to be a "step" of growth and development towards acquiring the necessary skills to reach specific goals for all readers, we are equipping students to develop the language skills and the conceptual knowledge they need for success beyond the academic setting and helping them shift their focus to lifelong learning. Teachers are given the opportunity to scaffold and support learners as they set proximal goals, monitor performance, and reflect on their progress towards becoming college and career ready.

## Standards for All Students

In learning environments where Common Core standards are aligned with self-regulated learning (SRL), teachers, students, and parents could have a better understanding of the expectations and the processes to meet them. The National Governors Association (NGA) and the Council of Chief State School Officers (CCSSO) set attainable goals by providing a pathway to college and career readiness for students. There is evidence that prior to the governors taking action, four out of every ten new college students, including 50 percent of those enrolled in two-year institutions, were taking remedial courses. In addition, feedback from employers has reflected inadequate preparation of high school graduates for success in the workplace (Bautch, 2013).

The College and Career Readiness anchor standards complement grade-specific standards, with the former providing broad standards and the latter providing specific goal-related skill development. Taken together, they define the skills and understanding that all students must demonstrate to be college and career ready as they progress from simple to complex skill development. For example, becoming college and career ready requires more than students entering the postsecondary arena having the ability to fully participate in their career training without remediation. It requires sustained motivation and attention to take charge of one's learning processes. *Ready for college* means that a high school graduate will not require remediation in English and mathematics and they will have the knowledge and the skills necessary to qualify for and succeed in entry-level, credit-bearing college courses. *Career ready* means that high school graduates have the English and mathematics knowledge and skills needed to qualify for and succeed in the postsecondary job training and/or supplemental education necessary for their chosen career. Whether preparing for college or a career, academic learning must become a proactive activity, requiring self-initiated, motivational, and behavioral processes as well as metacognitive ones, all of which make up Self Regulated Learning (SRL). Self-initiated processes enable students to become controllers rather than victims of their learning experiences (Zimmerman, 1998). Self-regulation is not an academic skill, such as the literacy skills outlined in the Common Core; rather, it is the self-directed process by which learners *transform their mental abilities into academic skills.*

Learning is a multidimensional process involving personal, behavioral (both cognitive and emotional), and contextual components (Zimmerman, 1998). Therefore, the academic standards that make up the Common Core can only serve as a guide for the content and skills our students are required to learn, and that is insufficient college- or career-ready preparation. Learners must be able to apply cognitive strategies to a task within the context of a specific setting. Building and using a toolbox of effective strategies that change over time as skills are developed is how one becomes self-regulated. The standards are common, but the attainment of each standard is an individualized quest dependent on the diverse and changing interpersonal, contextual, and environmental conditions experienced by the learner. As a result, learners must be taught to constantly reassess the effectiveness of the strategies that work in one academic subject and do not transfer to others.

Self-regulated learners will know when to shift from methods of understanding a text using a strategy to memorize key words to using an organizational strategy for more complex texts to enhance integration of knowledge and reading comprehension (Zimmerman, 1998). Self-regulated learners will seek help and use resources appropriately to attain their goals if they see they cannot persist on their own to complete the task. We propose that if students are trained at the kindergarten and first-grade level to use the self-regulatory strategy of help seeking, then the stigma our culture associates with seeking help will be removed from the academic setting in the early grades (Karabenick & Newman, 2006; Nelson-Le Gall, Gumerman, & Scott-Jones, 1983; White & Bembenutty, 2013). This acquired skill could provide the learner from an early age with significant strategies to use when in need of resources or assistance to complete a specific task, study for an exam, or do homework.

At the middle and high school level, our teachers are working with a population (67 percent of eighth graders and 76 percent of twelfth graders) that is writing below grade level (Salahu-Din, Persky, & Miller, 2008). Promoting students from elementary to middle school without obtaining mastery of the literacy skills needed to perform adequately at the next level has negatively impacted college and career readiness. As a result, the Common Core standards make writing an equal partner to reading, and more importantly, writing is assumed to be the vehicle through which a significant amount of reading proficiency will be accomplished and evaluated.

There is a need for explicit and systematic instruction that emphasizes writing strategies. At the earliest grades, the Common Core provides the framework to introduce young writers to self-regulatory strategies for planning, revising, paragraph and sentence construction, and word processing. Studying, collaborating with, and emulating models of good writing is a self-regulatory instructional method that has shown significant results in gaining writing proficiency over time.

High school graduates need the foundational skills to enable them to learn not only at the entry-level jobs, but also throughout their careers. With this in mind, training in self-regulated learning becomes the center of the Common Core. Standards for achievement have been set and reset, yet actual training in the metacognitive processes required to meet the standards has not yet been instituted. Shifting the focus to becoming self-regulated learners while ascending the "spiral staircase of complexity" can provide students with strategies that, when developed over time, make them lifelong learners.

Explicit instruction in SRL is rarely reported, yet is practiced in many classrooms daily. We propose that there are many teachers who might not realize they are integrating explicit segments of SRL instruction into their lesson plans that can be more effective if done systematically and consistently. Classroom practices in general require the consideration of students' individual differences, and so is the case with the ability to self-regulate. Contrary to some beliefs, it does not take several years of experience before teachers can begin to consider students' needs and abilities when planning and implementing instruction. We believe that pre-service and in-service teachers can be trained and mentored to implement tasks that encourage proactive learning and nonthreatening peer and self-evaluations, all characteristics of classrooms that support SRL.

## Taking the Crosswalk: From the Common Core to Self-Regulated Learning

There are crosswalks from city, state, subject, and grade-level standards aligning the Common Core with standards that already exist. Each section of the book introduces a crosswalk from the Common Core standards to SRL. Standards-based education shares many commonalities with SRL theory. Standards-based classrooms are places where the focus is on student-centered learning through critical thinking, problem solving, cooperation, and individual achievement. Both sustain the belief that student performance can be raised when specific goals are established, monitored, and reflected upon while carrying out a specific task.

The Common Core standards invite students to use higher-order thinking skills and employ all of the dimensions of learning using metacognitive awareness. Self-regulation is a vital component to the metacognitive processes (Zimmerman, 2000). Instruction in SRL serves as a framework for metacognitive knowledge and skill acquisition, which in turn builds secondary scholars who are college and career ready. There are pedagogical approaches, curriculum choices, and student learning processes evident in learning environments that support self-regulation and that are helping teachers and teacher educators transition successfully into adopting the Common Core standards. The standards encourage students to seek help, to practice accurate self-monitoring, and to apply metacognitive skills within various learning contexts, all of which are self-regulatory strategies that encourage proactive learning and independent evaluation.

The benefits of exploring both SRL and the Common Core standards is that SRL provides a toolkit for teachers to help their students become motivated to learn, to engage in productive performance strategies, to self-reflect upon the feedback they receive, and to use this feedback to guide future efforts and performance. By aligning the Common Core standards with self-regulation training, teachers can empower their students to become independent agents of their own learning and in turn increase the efficacy to transfer and adapt the skills they have obtained to life events beyond the classroom. In addition, the proposed integrated framework is dynamic and fluid; it provides the skilled teacher with a framework for constantly adapting teaching methods to meet the diverse needs and learning differences of students in the classroom setting.

## References

Bautch, B. (2013). *Reforming remedial education.* Washington, DC: National Conference of State Legislatures.

Karabenick, S. A., & Newman, R. S. (Eds.). (2006). *Help seeking in academic settings: Goals, groups and contexts.* Mahwah, NJ: Erlbaum.

Nelson-Le Gall, S., Gumerman, R. A., & Scott-Jones, D. (1983). Instrumental help-seeking and everyday problem-solving: A developmental perspective. In B. M. DePaulo, A. Nadler, & J. D. Fisher (Eds.). *New Directions in Helping* (Vol. 2, pp. 265–283). New York, NY: Academic Press.

Reeves, D. B. (2012). The myths of Common Core. *American School Board Journal, 199*(3), 36–37.

Salahu-Din, D., Persky, H., & Miller, J. (2008). *The nation's report card: Writing 2007.* Washington, DC: National Center for Education Statistics, Institute of Education Sciences, U.S. Department of Education.

White, M. C., & Bembenutty, H. (2013). Not all avoidance help seekers are created equal: Individual differences in adaptive and executive help seeking. *SAGE Open,* 1–14. doi:10.1177/2158244013484916

Zimmerman, B. J. (1998). Academic studying and the development of personal skill: A self-regulatory perspective. *Educational Psychologist, 33*(2–3), 73–86.

Zimmerman, B. J. (2000). Attainment of self-regulation: A social cognitive perspective. In M. Boekaerts, P. R. Pintrich, & M. Zeidner (Eds.), *Handbook of self-regulation* (pp. 13–39). San Diego, CA: Academic Press.

# 2
# THEORY-BASED INSTRUCTION
## Self-Regulation of Learning

Social cognitive theory relies upon the belief of the human agency, where the person, behavior, and the environment work in a reciprocal fashion (Bandura, 1997). Instructional applications of social cognitive theory involve models, self-efficacy beliefs, and self-regulated learning (SRL) (Schunk, 2001; Zimmerman, 2013).

This book describes how SRL develops and demonstrates how it can be applied to the context of twenty-first-century learning. The theory of SRL explains and describes how individuals with diverse social backgrounds and qualities of education are able to learn and achieve competence on designated tasks (Zimmerman & Schunk, 2011). Social cognitive theorists frame self-regulation as highly context dependent, and not linked to a general trait or level of development (Schunk, 2001). Personal, behavioral, and environmental factors form an interdependence, called triarchic reciprocal causality, from which learners can derive feedback and adapt their approach to specific learning tasks (Bandura, 1989). Figure 2.1 depicts the interactions of the three *interdependent strategic feedback loops* that regulate personal (covert), behavioral (action), and environmental processes adjusted to include examples related to student learning (Zimmerman, 1989).

Self-regulatory development goes hand in hand with students' self-efficacy; progress towards and attainment of goals also have a positive influence on learner's self-efficacy. Self-efficacy, as defined in Chapter 1, is the degree of beliefs one has about the ability to successfully perform a certain task (Bandura, 1997). It influences choice of activities, effort, and persistence. Self-efficacious students participate more readily, work harder, persist longer, and have fewer adverse emotional reactions when they encounter difficulties than do those who doubt their capabilities (Bandura, 1997). Social cognitive theorists make the case that self-regulatory systems are open, meaning that goals and strategic activities can

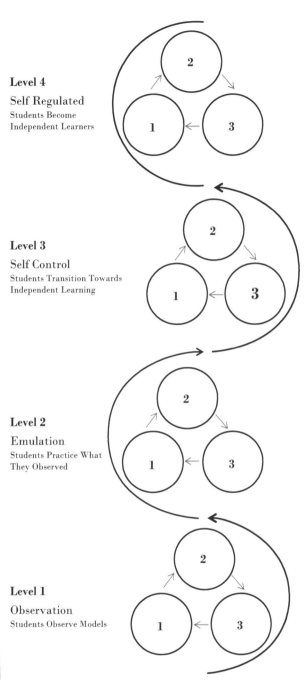

**Level 4**

Self Regulated

Students Become Independent Learners

**Level 3**

Self Control

Students Transition Towards Independent Learning

**Level 2**

Emulation

Students Practice What They Observed

**Level 1**

Observation

Students Observe Models

**Phase 1: Forethought**
Teacher provides worthwhile opportunities for students to independently integrate strategic planning and self-regulatory strategies. Students are encouraged to take charge of challenging assignments and evaluate their self-efficacy prior to beginning a task.

**Phase 2: Performance**
Students independently apply sel-regulatory strategies such as focusing attention, using imagery, self-instruction and help seeking to assignments beyond the classroom setting. Homework becomes an opportunity to engage in learning proactively rather than just getting it done.

**Phase 3: Reflection**
Students recognize their work is a result of strategic behaviors. Teachers monitor students use of self-regulatory strategies in and out of the classroom and support their efforts with praise and attributional connections to successful performance in class.

**Phase 1: Forethought**
Students are guided to set realistic goals and choose strategies; the teacher monitors and provides feedback as needed.

**Phase 2: Performance**
Students are engaged in small groups or individually working on a task with less teacher supervision than provided in previous levels. They are prompted to implement strategic behaviors to accomplish their goals.

**Phase 3: Self-Reflection**
Students incorporate teacher feedback into self-evaluations of their performance. They evaluate their strategy choices when reflecting on which choices led to attaining their goals.

**Phase 1: Forethought**
Teacher prompts students to set goals; together they analyze the task and choose strategies based on levels of competency and self-efficacy ratings.

**Phase 2: Performance**
Teacher encourages students to practice applying strategies to the task, discuss challenges, and monitor progress and self-efficacy to complete the task successfully.

**Phase 3: Self-Reflection**
Teacher helps students evaluate their strategy choices, task performance, and make attributions to specific behaviors that increased self-efficacy and performance.

**Phase 1: Forethought**
Teacher models goal setting, activates prior knowledge, analyzes tasks engaging students in planning strategies and assessing self-efficacy

**Phase 2: Performance**
Teacher models task engagement and self-regulated learning behaviors engaging students in using strategies to work towards attaining goals set during forethought phase.

**Phase 3: Self-Reflection**
Teacher models self-evaluation by evaluating performance and making attributions engaging students in checking progress against the goals set during the forethought phase.

**FIGURE 2.1**

*Sources*: Concept Marie White and Maria K. Dibenedetto/Design Erin White Demster

be changed when self-evaluations are a result of credible feedback. Students are motivated to attempt new and challenging tasks if they have experienced success with similar tasks. Building self-efficacy in learners is a significant factor of SRL development.

## Becoming a Competent, Independent, Self-Regulated Learner

### *Levels of Development*

Students can become competent, independent, and self-regulated as teachers systematically follow the four levels of development posited by Zimmerman (Schunk & Zimmerman, 1997; Zimmerman, 2000, 2002; Zimmerman & Kitsantas, 1997, 2002). The predicted outcome of attaining self-regulatory competency is accomplished when the learner can work on a task independently. Concurrently, training in the self-regulatory cyclical phases of forethought, performance, and self-reflection is necessary at each level, as students are becoming independent learners to reinforce the practice of self-regulatory strategies for specific tasks. In this book, we integrate both the developmental and cyclical approach to self-regulatory training by situating the cycles of self-regulation within the levels of attaining self-regulatory competency.

Educators can set the pace for learning according to their students' level of academic development in their classrooms using the cyclical phases to sequence instructional practices and promote mastery learning. Situating instructional practices within Zimmerman's (2000, 2002) levels of SRL development, which are observation, emulation, self-control, and self-regulation, recognizes that in order for instruction to support SRL development, one must attend to the interaction between these two models as students slowly progress toward self-regulation. The Common Core standard for English language arts is designed with a staircase of complexity that spirals up while reinforcing skills not mastered in prior grades. Similarly, self-regulation encourages students to reflect on their performance on a specific task and reset goals they come up short of attaining.

### *Self-Regulatory Competence*

In order to develop *self-regulatory competence*, teachers guide their students through four levels of SRL development: (1) *observation*, (2) *emulation*, (3) *self-control*, and (4) *self-regulation* (Zimmerman, 2000, 2002). The teacher models the desired behavior while supporting the students to engage in the behavior, gradually shifting to student-initiated self-control and self-regulation (Pape, Bell, & Yetkin-Ozdemir, 2013).

### *Level 1: Observation*

Self-regulatory competence begins with students observing teachers, peers, or a knowledgeable individual (Kitsantas, Zimmerman, & Cleary, 2000; Schunk & Zimmerman, 1997; Zimmerman, 2000; Zimmerman & Kitsantas, 2002). At this level, teachers control the *pacing* of the learning because students are dependent on them to demonstrate and provide verbalizations of their thoughts, actions, and reasons for their actions. Teachers set up classroom environments that will help build students' self-efficacy. To illustrate, young students may not initially feel capable of editing their written work, but upon observing a peer self-edit using the interactive whiteboard or observing their teacher think aloud as she edits a writing sample, they are able to understand what is needed to perform the task.

## Level 2: Emulation

Actually performing the task involves being able to *emulate* or attempt to approximate what they have observed the model do (Zimmerman, 2000). The teacher remains present, providing students with support, encouragement, and feedback on the accuracy of their attempts to emulate the model, or align their performance to the set standard. The student's self-efficacy, while still beginning to form, is reinforced by the teacher's feedback and the student's own sensory feedback from motoric activities. The teacher paces the instruction and feedback according to students' abilities to replicate what has been observed. Students who are learning how to edit their writing, for example, will first observe their teacher demonstrate how she edits a writing sample by thinking aloud and verbalizing each step. The teacher then asks the students to edit similar writing samples so that they can perform the same task, using self-talk to guide their editing. The teacher provides feedback as to the accuracy of each edit, and students begin to feel self-efficacious as they see the similarities between their performance and the teacher's even though they are still dependent on her guidance and feedback. Eventually, their edited work corresponds to the teacher's model, laying the foundation to move on to the next level.

## Level 3: Self-Control

Entering the third level indicates *self-control* as students continue to practice what was learned and reinforced in the first two levels, performing the task without input from the teacher (Schunk & Zimmerman, 1997). Teachers at this level provide opportunities for students to work on the processes involved to accomplish the task, rather than on outcomes. Teachers manage the pace of learning as they intentionally and gradually shift the responsibility for learning and performing to students. As students practice editing their writing samples, the teacher provides opportunities for them to use their newly acquired editing skills independently. As the students complete an editing assignment for homework, they demonstrate evidence of *self-control* by using their editing skills independently to perform the task. During this level, students begin to internalize the skill or strategy, but they are not yet ready to make adjustments to their performance based on what they believe will be most effective. Mastering the use of the skill at the self-control level requires extensive deliberate practice on new tasks independently (Zimmerman, 2013). At this level, the learner executes learning strategies in structured settings with some automaticity, which is the ability to complete a task without conscious thought, relying on internalized representations of the model's performance.

### Level 4: Self-Regulation

The final level, *self-regulation*, is reached when learners are capable of making adjustments to their actions in response to the environment and when they feel self-efficacious in their ability to regulate their feelings, thoughts, and behavior (Zimmerman, 2000). At this level, students are able to monitor their own behavior and adapt their skills and strategies systematically to changing personal and contextual conditions. The learner becomes the initiator, having internalized what has been learned so they can perform without teacher supervision. The teacher provides the students with opportunities to edit writing samples for homework and only provides assistance if requested. In turn, students adapt editing strategies to various writing samples and maintain their motivation to complete the task independently. This level is especially characterized by strong self-efficacy beliefs and the consistent use of self-regulatory processes (Pape et al., 2013).

## Phases of Self-Regulated Learning

Attainment of self-regulation skills can also be explained from a cyclical structure of self-regulatory processes with phases that show causal relationships between SRL processes and both key motivational beliefs and learning outcomes (Zimmerman, 2000, 2013). Researchers have identified individual behaviors, cognitions, and key processes in which self-regulated learners engage during three phases of SRL: *forethought, performance,* and *self-reflection* (Zimmerman, 2000). Forethought-phase processes are for learning preparation; performance-phase processes are to focus students on their learning efforts while on task; and the self-reflection phase is when the task is completed, at which time students can evaluate their performance. The information gained from self-evaluations during the self-reflection phase can guide the forethought processes and beliefs for future learning efforts, making this process cyclical (Zimmerman, 2013). The process requires the learner to actively participate and become fully engaged in each part of the cycle.

Motivational variables such as *self-efficacy, outcome expectations* (beliefs about the ultimate benefits), *intrinsic interest* (engaging in designated tasks for the sake of learning), and *goal orientation* (the general reason for learning or studying, either to attain mastery of the material or to perform at a certain level) are important motivators for students to engage in learning activities during each phase. There is a great deal of research to support the importance of how students address the subprocesses of self-regulation in various learning situations. A high school student with low self-efficacy beliefs about her capability to complete a research project and who does not see the value of the research process in her everyday life, for example, is likely to be less motivated than the student who believes she will perform well and is preparing for both college and career readiness.

*Forethought.* The forethought phase occurs with the initial efforts to learn taking place. Learners set the stage for the performance phase by engaging in a detailed task analysis to break down a learning task into the steps required to complete the task successfully. They set proximal and attainable goals based on their evaluation of their own self-efficacy, task requirements, and outcome expectations. Students who are highly motivated and self-efficacious are more likely to set realistic and attainable goals than those who are not. In addition, the more motivated students are likely to develop plans consisting of strategies to track performance using self-monitoring and self-evaluation methods (Zimmerman, 2000).

*Performance.* The performance phase occurs once the student begins the learning task. During the performance phase, students engage in two types of processes, self-control and self-observation, to direct their learning and guide their efforts as they monitor their progress. Self-regulated students are active during this phase, measuring their progress against the standard and adjusting their strategies when required. *Self-control* processes such as self-instruction, imagery, attention focusing, task strategies, environmental structuring, and help seeking are considered in the forethought phase but implemented in the performance stage.

Help seeking is a self-regulatory strategy known to be positive and significantly associated with academic achievement (Karabenick & Newman, 2006). During this phase, students engage in delay of gratification for the sake of completing designated tasks. Systematic *self-observation* includes metacognitive monitoring and self-recording. Self-recording involves keeping track of specific aspects of one's performance in real time or while it is occurring (Zimmerman, 2000). Metacognitive monitoring involves being aware and mentally tracking the processes learners engage in while performing a specific task. Study logs have been successfully used to assist students of all ages with keeping track of the progress towards the attainment of self-set goals. During this phase, learners' performance can benefit from credible feedback that assists them with attributing their efforts to specific practices.

*Self-Reflection.* The self-reflection phase occurs *after* the task has been completed. At this point, students use information gained from self-monitoring records to compare their performance with self-set goals. By forming *self-judgments* about their progress, they are able to adjust their behaviors to meet their goals and attribute success or failure to a specific behavior. *Self-reactions* are formed during this phase. Zimmerman (2000) suggests that learners will *react* by either being *satisfied* or not, or by making *adaptive* or *defensive responses.*

Self-satisfaction refers to the level of contentment students feel about their performance. An *adaptive* response occurs when a student reacts to his or her performance by attributing it to a strategy or a behavior, whereas a *defensive* response would suggest the performance was due to something uncontrollable, such as luck or an innate ability. Students and teachers who employ study logs as a means of tracking progress and communicating feedback collect credible data from which they can learn more about the strengths and weaknesses of their performances. Self-reactions, then, are based on information gained from self-monitoring, and can be trusted to make adjustments to the way students approach similar tasks. Information gathered during the self-reflection phase is interpreted and applied when setting goals and choosing strategies for future assignments.

### *An Integrated Framework: Self-Regulated Learning for Teachers and Students*

Phases (i.e., forethought, performance, and self-reflection) situated in levels of self-regulation (i.e., observation, emulation, self-control, and self-regulation) provide a framework for SRL in the twenty-first-century classroom (Bembenutty, Cleary, & Kitsantas, 2013; Pape, Bell, & Yetkin-Ozdemir, 2013; Zimmerman & Schunk, 2011). For instance, Pape and colleagues (2013) argued that teachers should be more explicit with modeling and discussion of mathematical thinking and strategic behavior during early stages of learning. They propose a framework for teaching literacy skills across grades and within content areas that take students' SRL development into consideration when making pedagogical shifts. Building knowledge through text complexity using academic vocabulary and writing from sources all require teachers to identify both levels and phases of self-regulation for individual students. The integrated model initially gives teachers control of the learning environment by carefully *pacing* students according to their status at each level while guiding them individually through the three phases of SRL.

In the first level, *observation*, the main objective of each lesson is to provide students with opportunities to observe others who serve as "models." The three phases (forethought, performance, and self-reflection) will ultimately be modeled but not performed by the students. Research has shown that modeling is a powerful way for students to learn how a task is completed, the ways of thinking about solving a problem, how to not give up when one gets the wrong answer, and to remember what was observed long after the model is no longer present (Bandura, 1997). Teachers model through each of the three phases by thinking out loud, demonstrating, and having fellow students who are also competent display a behavior or thought in the classroom. Research has also shown that when students observe models fail and then succeed, they learn how to cope with failure and not give up (Moylan, 2013). At this level, teachers want students to learn by observing others, not through trial and error, which takes a great deal of time and often does not result in performance achievement. In addition, trial and error without proper scaffolding often results in a lack of self-efficacy for future similar academic tasks. This builds frustration and anxiety in students rather than a sense of competency and optimism for future success (Schunk & DiBenedetto, 2014).

In the second level, *emulation*, teachers provide students with opportunities to practice what was demonstrated in level one, thereby beginning a gradual movement through the phases. The three phases are scaffolded by the teacher to set up a model for the self-regulation cycle as the student moves through the subsequent levels. The teacher is still controlling the learning context by closely monitoring and providing feedback on each of the three phase processes and on performance. Teachers create a "safe" environment whereby students can replicate what they observed, which helps them to feel more self-efficacious. Students here will work with the teacher to set appropriate goals, which should be attainable and specific. They discuss strategies for completing the tasks and should be guided and prompted by the teacher to monitor and reflect during each of the three phases. Research shows that teachers who allow students ample time to practice a strategy with support from them are able to fade this support as students move to the next level (Harris, Graham, & Santangelo, 2013).

In the third level, *self-control*, students begin to feel a sense of autonomy and practice with less teacher supervision, allowing the three phases (forethought, performance, and self-reflection) to be developed more fully by students, and for the teacher to be phased out of the scaffolding process even though the students may still be looking for support. Teachers, for example, may ask students to complete homework or classwork independently or to work with their peers. Students are beginning to internalize what they observed and pattern their behaviors after the model's performance. The difference in this level from the previous two is that here students can repeat what they have learned without having the teacher close by. Teachers at the self-control level gradually shift the responsibility of pacing of the learning from themselves to their students, encouraging them to work more independently. At this level, students are not yet able to adapt or regulate their learning entirely on their own yet; however, being able to accomplish the learning tasks continues to build their self-efficacy to the point at which they feel they are capable of meeting the challenges of completing the tasks on their own.

It is in the fourth level, *self-regulation*, that students regulate their own learning by making alterations to their goals, strategies, and effort in response to the task demands, thereby fully developing the three phases that allow them to become independently self-regulated learners. They adapt and reflect as to whether their goals were realistic, their strategies appropriate, and their attention to the task adequate. Students at this level transfer what they have learned to other learning situations that share some similarities and do so with the beliefs and feelings about their capability for success. They deal with unanticipated events and make adjustments needed to complete the task. The ultimate goal of the Common Core standards is to prepare students to be college ready and to enter the workforce. In order to do this successfully, students must be able to learn and adapt successfully to new and more complex learning experiences beyond the context of high school. Students who reach the fourth level of SRL are ready to independently apply their skills to the demands of the twenty-first century.

## References

Bandura, A. (1989). Human agency in social cognitive theory. *American Psychologist, 44*, 1175–1184.

Bandura, A. (1997). *Self-efficacy: The exercise of control*. New York, NY: Freeman.

Bembenutty, H., Cleary, T. J., & Kitsantas, A. (2013). *Applications of self-regulated learning across diverse disciplines: A tribute to Barry J. Zimmerman*. Charlotte: NC: Information Age Publishing.

Harris, K.R., Graham, S., & Santangelo, T. (2013). Self-regulated strategies development in writing: Development, implementation, and scaling up. In H. Bembenutty, T. J. Cleary, & A. Kitsantas (Eds.), *Applications of self-regulated learning across diverse disciplines: A tribute to Barry Zimmerman* (pp. 59–88). NC: Information Age Publishing.

Karabenick, S. A., & Newman, R. S. (Eds.). (2006). *Help seeking in academic settings: Goals, groups and contexts*. Mahwah, NJ: Erlbaum.

Kitsantas, A., Zimmerman, B. J., & Cleary, T. J. (2000). The role of observation and emulation in the development of athletic self-regulation. *Journal of Educational Psychology, 92*, 811–817.

Moylan, A. (2013). Cyclical feedback approaches for enhancing academic self-regulation in postsecondary mathematics classrooms. In H. Bembenutty, T. J. Cleary, & A. Kitsantas (Eds.), *Applications of self-regulated learning across diverse disciplines: A tribute to Barry Zimmerman* (pp. 125–151). NC: Information Age Publishing.

Pape, S. J., Bell, C. V., & Yetkin-Ozdemir, I. E. (2013). Sequencing components of mathematics lessons to maximize development of self-regulation: Theory, practice, and intervention. In H. Bembenutty, T. J. Cleary, & A. Kitsantas (Eds.), *Applications of self-regulated learning across diverse disciplines: A tribute to Barry J. Zimmerman* (pp. 29–58). Charlotte, NC: Information Age Publishing.

Schunk, D. H. (2001). Social cognitive theory and self-regulated learning. In B. J. Zimmerman & D. H. Schunk (Eds.), *Self-regulated learning and academic achievement. Theoretical perspectives* (pp. 125–152). Mahwah, NJ: Lawrence Erlbaum Associates.

Schunk, D. H., & DiBenedetto, M. K. (2014). Academic self-efficacy. In M. J. Furlong, R. Gilman, & E. S. Huebner (Eds.), *Handbook of positive psychology in schools* (2nd ed., pp. 115–130). New York, NY: Routledge.

Schunk, D. H., & Zimmerman, B. J. (1997). Social origins of self-regulatory competence. *Educational Psychologist, 32*(4), 195–208.

Zimmerman, B. J. (1989). A social cognitive view of self-regulated academic learning. *Journal of Educational Psychology, 81*(3), 329.

Zimmerman, B. J. (2000). Self-efficacy: An essential motive to learn. *Contemporary Educational Psychology, 25*(1), 82–91.

Zimmerman, B. J. (2002). Becoming a self-regulated learner: An overview. *Theory into Practice, 41*(2), 64–70.

Zimmerman, B. J. (2013). From cognitive modeling to self-regulation: A social cognitive career path. *Educational Psychologist, 48*, 1–13.

Zimmerman, B. J., & Kitsantas, A. (1997). Developmental phases in self-regulation: Shifting from process goals to outcome goals. *Journal of Educational Psychology, 89*, 29–36.

Zimmerman, B. J., & Kitsantas, A. (2002). Acquiring writing revision and self-regulatory skill through observation and emulation. *Journal of Educational Psychology, 94*, 660–668.

Zimmerman, B. J., & Schunk, D. H. (Eds.) (2011). *Handbook of self-regulation of learning and performance*. New York, NY: Routledge.

ontextual factors of the learning environment can provide support for even
# 3
# SELF-REGULATION IN A CLASSROOM CONTEXT

Contextual factors of the learning environment can provide support for even young learners to develop the ability to self-regulate their learning. The classroom context is filled with challenges that can easily become overwhelming. Statistics of teacher retention, especially in the urban schools, have led to a total overhaul of teacher education (Feistritzer, 2011). Present and future teachers are required to immerse themselves in the context of real school life to experience the interactive dynamics of teaching and learning all the way from the classroom to the principal's office and out into the community. Although the Common Core standards do not readily address context, they do require administrators, teachers, and instructors to consistently evaluate how their beliefs, goals, values, perceptions, behaviors, classroom management, social relations, and arrangement of physical space impact the student's understanding of the classroom.

Social cognitive theory raises our awareness of the influence of contextual factors on learning and any attempt to self-regulate (Bandura, 1986). Learning environments that promote self-regulated learning (SRL) are instructional settings where teachers and learners are not powerless victims of context, but rather proactive managers of their learning. The Common Core standards guide instruction, but they do not define or suggest an instructional or social context. Considering the complex makeup of our diverse classrooms and the challenge of meeting all the needs of every student, educators need to find a common ground with parents, peers, technology, and the students themselves. A context in which models of instruction focus on the student's use of specific processes to guide their learning diminishes the differences in personal talent and skill and enhances motivation in every learner.

According to Bandura (2006), "Self-regulation is the capability of interest. The issue is not whether one can do the activities occasionally, but whether one has the efficacy to get oneself to do them regularly in the face of different types of dissuading conditions" (p. 311). Few students naturally self-regulate, which means they do not know how to plan, monitor, and assess their learning. In order to promote better learning habits and strengthen study skills, educators who encourage self-regulation provide opportunities for students to take charge of their learning. In order for teachers to encourage SRL processes in their students, they themselves must be self-regulated in their emotions, behaviors, and teaching and learning. The self-regulated teacher is essential to a well-managed instructional setting; how he or she sets the stage, directs the performance, and provides feedback are essential components of an SRL environment.

## What Does a Self-Regulated Teacher Look Like?

*Teachers who focus on their own self-regulated learning skills are increasingly aware of their own teaching practices.*

### The Teacher Self-Monitors During Instruction

One of the indicators of the teacher's self-regulation is a proactive, rather than a reactive, approach to instruction. The teacher uses metacognitive strategies to monitor and regulate his or her own behavior to improve the teaching and learning processes. This strategic use of self-monitoring is different from changes that result from reflecting, in that the teacher learns to think before he or she acts in the planning or forethought phase. Early on, the teacher recognizes when goals are set too high, is aware of student disinterest, and observes the results from effective efforts. Knowing that it is appropriate to change the course of direction because students are not responding to an instructional segment is the mark of a self-regulated teacher. As he or she moves from forethought to performance, the teacher consistently guides and directs his or her behavior through self-direction, making changes that increase learning and motivation not only in his or her students, but in the teacher as well.

### The Teacher Is a Model

The most important factor affecting student learning and achievement is the teacher (Marzano, Pickering, & Pollack, 2001). Teachers guide classroom practice and have a significant influence on student learning through *modeling* both effective and ineffective strategies. Student-centered instruction has been shown to be superior to traditional methods and requires the presence of an effective and competent model. The educator whose personal beliefs incorporate the impact of vicarious or observational learning, the reality of contextual influences, and the effectiveness of consistent modeling of self-regulatory strategies can regulate his or her own learning and that of the students. In addition, the self-regulated teacher pays close attention to the observational behaviors of students, making sure students are trained in observational learning strategies prior to modeling instructional segments.

## *The Teacher Has High Self-Efficacy*

The self-regulated teacher is not a super teacher; yet, he or she exhibits high levels of teacher efficacy. Bandura (1997) noted, "Teachers' beliefs in their efficacy affect their general orientation toward the educational process as well as their specific instructional activities" (p. 241). He or she is a work in progress, a lifelong learner who makes adjustments to personal beliefs when they are challenged by changing pedagogies, such as with the Common Core standards. A dominant definition of teacher efficacy (Tschannen-Moran, A. Hoy, & W. Hoy, 1998) includes the way teachers view the resources and strategies at their disposal to influence student behavior and learning outcomes. Subsequently, the teachers' "I Can Do It" is derived from their self-evaluations of their capabilities in a specific teaching and learning context. A teacher might feel very strongly that he or she is highly effective in one area of teaching and weak in others, and therefore he or she would look for areas that require improvement. Teacher efficacy is related to student achievement, so it is critical to the success of the Common Core that teachers feel confident they can successfully execute the behaviors necessary to produce the desired outcomes (Bandura, 1977). Overall, teachers who have confidence that their students will benefit from their teaching are more effective in working with a diverse population of students (Dembo & Gibson, 1985; Moos & Ringdal, 2012).

## *The Teacher Builds Self-Efficacy in Students*

Yes you can! The teacher builds self-efficacy in even the youngest learners by helping students acquire the necessary skills and beliefs that they can do the assigned tasks (Bembenutty, 2011). More importantly, the teacher helps students examine their self-efficacy beliefs accurately, making realistic evaluations of their abilities specific to the task at hand. Asking students to rate their own self-efficacy is one way to raise their awareness of the importance of knowing their capabilities prior to beginning a task. Reminding students of their past successes with a similar task helps engage them in attempting a more difficult version of the same type of task. In addition, when the teacher takes on the attributes of a coping model by admitting to and correcting errors as a model for their students, the students then observe that those who have authority are capable of making and correcting errors (Schunk & Zimmerman, 2007).

## *The Teacher Gives Choices*

The teacher knows that both self-regulation and self-efficacy require learning environments where student autonomy and choice are factors (Tonks & Taboada, 2011). Most researchers agree that choice of tasks that include students' level of interest is a strong indicator of how motivated the student will be to complete the task. The teacher recognizes that when students perceive some control over their own learning, their persistence and effort are increased, and they structure choices that are meaningful in relation to the goals for the specific task. Across grade levels, the teacher couples choice of topic for both reading and writing exercises with direct instruction of strategies as a key motivational tool for accomplishing difficult tasks.

## *The Teacher Knows SRL Is a Process*

The teacher prepares students to handle the responsibilities of becoming self-regulated learners by teaching them *how* to learn. He or she knows that promoting SRL in the classroom is a long-term process that requires instruction in metacognitive strategies situated in learning environments that enable use of these strategies (Dignath-van Ewijk & van der Werf, 2012). The teacher uses a variety of instructional elements for SRL training and consistently provides extensive opportunities for exercising self-regulation with supervision and support for as long as necessary for students to become proficient.

His or her role in the development of SRL in the classroom is to recognize that not all of the students are at the same level of self-regulatory competency, and to provide differential support for individuals for whom the process might take more time. By controlling the instructional patterns of the classroom, as well as the expectations for each learner, the teacher focuses on each level of learning to become self-regulated as a process and not just as an outcome. Therefore, the teacher pays close attention to the development of self-regulatory competency within the context of specific instructional segments. He or she pays more attention to the impact of explicit modeling and individual learning during supervised practice during the early stages of learning (*observation* and *emulation*) before slowly withdrawing support from his or her students in a scaffolded process.

## *The Teachers Is an Agent of Change*

The teacher who is intentional about removing the all-knowing "authority figure" image from the classroom and integrating student-centered activities into their instructional contexts believes that students should be active participants in their own learning. The discomfort in moving away from lecture and direct instruction is a reality that most teachers face when moving from a teacher-centered to a student-centered learning environment, especially in a high-stakes testing era. Personal beliefs about students' capabilities will influence the supporting of SRL in the classroom. Examination of these beliefs is most challenging to traditional teachers and teacher educators who want to create classroom contexts that foster SRL. Experienced teachers who readily experiment with new teaching methods and closely monitor the outcomes are more likely to promote SRL in their classrooms (Hoekstra, Brekelmans, Beijaard, & Korthagen, 2009).

## The Teacher Is Self-Reflective

A self-regulated teacher will not resist self-evaluation; in contrast, he or she will consistently reflect on performance and make the necessary adjustments to teaching strategies or seek help when learning outcomes are not satisfactory. The teacher who knows how to best support students' SRL focuses on his or her own SRL skills and teaching practices. Self-monitoring and evaluation of specific teaching practices in light of individual student performance reveal adjustments that can be made to increase student performance. Training teachers in reflective teaching strategies has become a significant part of teacher education and professional development. The introduction of the Common Core standards with ongoing curriculum revisions requires teachers to be flexible, innovative, and adaptable. Reflective thinking helps instructors to embrace adaptations, challenge personal beliefs, and adjust instructional pedagogy to meet the needs of individual students (Schraw & Olafson, 2002).

## The Teacher Sets Realistic and Attainable Goals

The challenge of setting realistic and attainable goals requires the teacher to focus on strategy and skill development, not on the high-stakes testing results. The self-regulated teacher gives students the opportunity to dissect broad goals into smaller subgoals in order to raise each student's self-efficacy and to promote and retain interest in the task (Bandura & Schunk, 1981). In addition, students are invited to participate in goal setting and to help set the performance standard. Partnering with students to set measurable, proximal, and achievable goals helps students gauge their progress along with the teacher. Formative assessment has a stronger influence on learning when both the teacher and the student share the responsibility of determining whether or not goals have been reached or if they need to be reset.

## The Teacher Encourages Help-Seeking

The self-regulated teacher recognizes strategic help-seeking is a sign of academic resourcefulness that leads to successful completion of difficult tasks. Although others in our Western culture might see it as a weakness, self-regulated teachers are known for their willingness to seek help and to create a learning environment that facilitates such strategic help-seeking (Karabenick & Newman, 2006). The teacher recognizes that young students come to participate in regulating their own learning and development by learning how to obtain assistance from others at times of need (Newman, 2000). A level of personal involvement can make students facilitate student–teacher communication and mitigate the difference between the role of the authority figure and the role of the submissive student when it comes to seeking assistance with a difficult task (Moos & Ringdal, 2012).

When not dismissed, feelings of respect influence both social and behavioral engagement early on, and students will recognize the teacher or other's involvement in the completion of a difficult task as a strategy instead of a weakness (Newman & Goldin, 1990).

### *The Teacher Provides Corrective Feedback*

The Common Core standards have stressed the need for formative assessment, a practice strongly advocated by self-regulation theorists. Zimmerman (2013) stressed the influential role of feedback as the means by which self-regulated learners have their attention drawn to components of the social and physical environments, the results of their actions, and the thinking processes about a given task. Consistent and constructive feedback provides the learner with opportunities to adapt their performance during the completion of a difficult task rather than to persist to an unsuccessful completion of the task. The self-regulated teacher provides corrective feedback by reteaching and leading students to correct answers and, as a result, increases students' motivation to complete the task. In addition, feedback that leads to students' self-evaluation and correction increases self-efficacy (Pape et al., 2013).

> How can a high school teacher work to increase self-efficacy through corrective feedback when implementing the Common Core?
>
> I teach and model strategies for my students; then, I ask them to use the strategies to complete tasks independently. I equip them with strategy charts in handout form, which has detailed explanations of each step written out for them. Students refer repetitiously to the charts throughout tasks until they memorize the steps and no longer need the charts. Even so, with all of this, I'm constantly moving around the classroom looking for opportunities to give feedback, asking students questions of redirection, which guides them in self-correction.
>
> Andre Hayes (Teacher, High School)
> Grades 9–12, English Language Arts, Brooklyn, New York

### *Summary*

The role of the self-regulated teacher in the classroom context goes far beyond the scope of the specific components outlined in the chapter. The behaviors that identify teachers who create and maintain a learning environment that promotes self-regulation are acquired over time, and often as a result of frustrating attempts to manage a classroom before a realistic self-evaluation. Teachers are lifelong learners drawing on resources in their teaching environments to inform their work and professional growth (Little, 2007). Self-regulated teachers take charge of their own learning and through modeling, encourage their students to do the same (Rényi, 1996). Research provides a substantial amount of evidence that self-regulation assists students in taking charge of their own learning; consequently, SRL strategies ought to be valuable for teachers as well.

## What Does a Self-Regulated Student Look Like?

### What Is a Self-Regulated Learner?

> At one time or another, we all have observed self-regulated learners. They approach educational tasks with confidence, diligence, and resourcefulness. Perhaps most importantly, self-regulated learners are aware when they know a fact or possess a skill and when they do not . . . . self-regulated students proactively seek out information when needed and take the necessary steps to master it. When they encounter obstacles such as poor study conditions, confusing teachers, or abstruse textbooks, they find a way to succeed. Self-regulated learners view acquisition as a systematic and controllable process, and they accept greater responsibility for their achievement outcomes.
>
> —Zimmerman, 1990, p. 4

There are clear indicators of self-regulation in students' behavior, both social and nonsocial. Zimmerman and Martinez-Pons (1986) identify students whose use of specific SRL strategies in and out of the classroom are also the students who get the highest grades. Subsequent research has supported these findings, along with the important link to self-efficacy as related to a specific task. It is important to note that self-regulation does not cross domains; evidence of a learner's use of self-regulatory strategies in math does not mean the same behaviors will be applied in reading.

### The Student Is Proactive

Self-regulated students view learning as an activity that they can do for themselves in proactive ways rather than as something that happens to them as a result of someone's teaching (Zimmerman, 2001). A student takes charge of task conditions using self-regulatory processes to sustain motivation. He or she closely monitors self-efficacy by using self-monitoring tools. The self-regulated student recognizes when a strategy choice is not working and changes it during task performance rather than sticking with the initial choice and failing to complete the task successfully, ultimately lowering self-efficacy.

> How can an elementary school teacher help students self-monitor while preparing for the state exams?
>
> As part of our fourth-grade test preparation, we give students practice tests in January, February, and March. After they take the practice test, they record their scores on a graph and create a realistic goal to aim for a higher score on the next test. Several of my students were highly motivated by the graphing strategy because they saw numbers and knew that they wanted to aim for a higher score. They worked very hard by attending tutoring sessions, asking for additional practice, and asking questions. As a result, the students saw their growth and felt extremely proud of their progress, lessening their anxiety for the test. All of my students passed the state exams (NYS 2014). Not only did our class have the highest scores in the school, but not one of them failed! Setting short-term, realistic goals is one way to motivate elementary school students!
>
> Arleen Rodriguez (Elementary School Teacher)<br>Grade 4, Bronx, New York

## *The Student Manages the Environment*

The self-regulated student plans and sets goals for specific learning tasks, keeping in mind that the environment will bring distractions that will challenge the ability to focus on a task and may result in poor performance. Therefore, the student will carefully manage the challenges of how, where, when, and with whom studying will be done in order to complete the task successfully. He or she knows how to say "no" to peers, siblings, or others who can interfere with studying and still maintain healthy relationships.

## *The Student Manages Time*

The self-regulated student sets aside time each day for regular study periods. He or she knows that time management is key to successful task completion and overestimates how much time a given task will take, allowing for interruptions. In order to complete his or her work within a specific time frame, the self-regulated student is careful to prioritize the most difficult tasks to be completed first.

## *The Student Sustains Motivation*

The self-regulated student knows when something is not working and makes adjustments to choices he or she has made so a task can be completed successfully. If during the performance phase the student notices the strategy, environment, level of interest, or study partner is not going to lead to successful task completion, he or she will not hesitate to make adjustments and begin the task again.

## The Student Benefits From Feedback

The self-regulated student applies feedback from peers and instructors in order to improve performance. Rather than respond to corrective feedback with diminished self-efficacy or fear of failure, the reflective student will use constructive feedback to review his or her performance and find ways to improve future performances. He or she incorporates the feedback when attributing the specific actions that led to the success or failure of a given assignment.

> How can a teacher inspire the self-regulatory strategy of help-seeking in all students?
>
> A straight-A student came to me with an assignment he was nervous about. Though he excelled in most subjects without breaking a sweat, he was always looking to improve. He was also afraid of public speaking and needed to recite a speech in front of the school. He brought his ideas to me and knew that his essay needed desperate work. He trusted my help and did not get offended when I suggested multiple changes. He was very concerned about giving a good speech and it was obvious he knew he needed help. We worked on the essay together and he was quite thankful for the time. His delivery might still need work, but the text of his speech was very good!
> Damien Garafolo (Social Studies High School Teacher)
> Nutley, New Jersey

## References

Bandura, A. (1977). Self-efficacy: Toward a unifying theory of behavioral change. *Psychological Review, 84*(2), 191–215.

Bandura, A. (1986). *Social foundations of thoughts and action: A social cognitive theory.* Englewood Cliffs, NJ: Prentice Hall.

Bandura, A. (1997). *Self-efficacy: The exercise of control.* New York, NY: Erlbaum.

Bandura, A. (2006). Adolescent development from an agentic perspective. *Self-Efficacy Beliefs of Adolescents, 5,* 1–43.

Bandura, A., & Schunk, D. H. (1981). Cultivating competence, self-efficacy, and intrinsic interest through proximal self-motivation. *Journal of Personality and Social Psychology, 41*(3), 586–598.

Bembenutty, H. (2011). Meaningful and maladaptive homework practices: The role of self-efficacy and self-regulation. *Journal of Advanced Academics, 22*(3), 448–473.

Dembo, M. H., & Gibson, S. (1985). Teachers' sense of efficacy: An important factor in school improvement. *The Elementary School Journal, 86,* 173–184.

Dignath-van Ewijk, C., & van der Werf, G. (2012). What teachers think about self-regulated learning: Investigating teacher beliefs and teacher behavior of enhancing students' self-regulation. *Education Research International, 2012,* 1–10.

Feistritzer, C. E. (2011). *Profile of teachers in the US 2011.* Washington, DC: National Center for Education Information.

Hoekstra, A., Brekelmans, M., Beijaard, D., & Korthagen, F. (2009). Experienced teachers' informal learning: Learning activities and changes in behavior and cognition. *Teaching and Teacher Education, 25*(5), 663–673.

Karabenick, S. A., & Newman, R. S. (2006). *Help-seeking in academic settings: goals, groups, and contexts.* Mahwah, NJ: Lawrence Erlbaum Publishers.

Little, J. W. (2007). Teachers' accounts of classroom experience as a resource for professional learning and instructional decision making. In P. Moss (Ed.), *Evidence and decision-making* (pp. 217–240). Chicago, IL: University of Chicago Press.

Marzano, R. J., Pickering, D., & Pollock, J. E. (2001). *Classroom instruction that works: Research-based strategies for increasing student achievement.* Alexandria, VA: Association for Supervision and Curriculum Development.

Moos, D. C., & Ringdal, A. (2012). Self-regulated learning in the classroom: A literature review on the teacher's role. *Education Research International, 2012.*

Newman, R. S. (2000). Social influences on the development of children's adaptive help-seeking: The role of parents, teachers, and peers. *Developmental Review, 20*(3), 350–404.

Newman, R. S., & Goldin, L. (1990). Children's reluctance to seek help with schoolwork. *Journal of Educational Psychology, 82*(1), 92–100.

Pape, S. J., Bell, C. V., & Yetkin-Ozdemir, I. E. (2013). Sequencing components of mathematics lessons to maximize development of self-regulation: Theory, practice, and intervention. In H. Bembenutty, T. J. Cleary, & A. Kitsantas (Eds.), *Applications of self-regulated learning across diverse disciplines: A tribute to Barry J. Zimmerman* (pp. 29–58). Charlotte, NC: Information Age Publishing.

Rényi, J. (1996). *Teachers take charge of their learning: Transforming professional development for student success.* Washington, DC: National Foundation for the Improvement of Education.

Schraw, G., & Olafson, L. J. (2002). Teachers' epistemological world views and educational practices. *Issues in Education, 8,* 99–148.

Schunk, D. H., & Zimmerman, B. J. (2007). Influencing children's self-efficacy and self-regulation of reading and writing through modeling. *Reading & Writing Quarterly, 23*(1), 7–25.

Tonks, S. M., & Taboada, A. (2011). Developing self-regulated readers through instruction for reading engagement. In B. J. Zimmerman & D. H. Schunk (Eds.), *Handbook of self-regulation of learning and performance* (pp. 173–186). New York: Routledge.

Tschannen-Moran, M., Hoy, A. W., & Hoy, W. K. (1998). Teacher efficacy: Its meaning and measure. *Review of Educational Research, 68*(2), 202–248.

Zimmerman, B. J. (1990). Self-regulated learning and academic achievement: An overview. *Educational psychologist, 25*(1), 3–17.

Zimmerman, B. J. (2001). Theories of self-regulated learning and academic achievement: An overview and analysis. In B. J. Zimmerman & D. H. Schunk (Eds.), *Self-regulated learning and academic achievement: Theoretical perspectives* (2nd ed., pp. 1–37). Mahwah, NJ: Erlbaum.

Zimmerman, B. J. (2013). From cognitive modeling to self-regulation: A social cognitive career path. *Educational Psychologist, 48,* 1–13.

Zimmerman, B. J., & Martinez-Pons. M. (1986). Development of a structured interview for assessing student use of self-regulated learning strategies. *American Educational Research Journal, 23,* 614–628.

# PART II
# Elementary School

# 4

# THE ROAD TO INDEPENDENCE BEGINS WITH STRATEGIC HELP SEEKING

Kindergarteners and First Graders

SRL Theory and the Common Core Applications for Early Literacy Strategy Training

> *Keywords: help-seeking, literacy, monitoring, comprehension, social, teacher, adaptive, text, close reading, metacognitive modeling, annotating, coping model, speaking and listening, self-regulation skills: modeling, observational learning, self-monitoring, logs, self-efficacy, help seeking*

## Speaking and Listening

This strand of the Common Core refocuses learning, teaching, and formative assessment in the K–5 classrooms on oral language to better prepare learners for their future as fully literate participants in their world. Emergent literacy learners can thrive in a supportive classroom where listening and speaking experiences are planned around opportunities for exploring language and interacting with peers, adults, and quality literature (American Speech-Language-Hearing Association, 2001). As depicted in Table 4.1, we place the speaking and listening strand at the kindergarten and first-grade level on the crosswalk in association with the standard that requires students to *ask and answer questions in order to seek help,* get information, or clarify something that is not understood (SL.CCR. 1–3.K3, 1.3).

We focus on the speaking and listening standards first, having determined that the literature supports focusing on the development of oral language as a foundation for literacy skills. According to the American Speech-Language-Hearing Association (2001), oral and written language are intricately connected because:

**TABLE 4.1** Crosswalks From Common Core Standards to Self-Regulated Learning

| College- and career-ready preparation | Common Core State Standards for speaking and listening | Self-regulated learning target (kindergarten and grade 1) |
|---|---|---|
| Anchor: Kindergarten and grade 1 | Strand and standard | Self-regulation strategy training |
| **Integrate and evaluate information presented in diverse media and formats, including visually, quantitatively, and orally (CCSS. Ela-Literacy. CCRA.Sl.2)** | Speaking and Listening (strand) Comprehension and Collaboration (Standard) **Kindergarten** CCSS.ELA-Literacy.Sl.K.3 Ask and answer questions in order to seek help, get information, or clarify something that is not understood | Learning how to use strategies of asking and answering questions that lead to adaptive help-seeking and task comprehension through monitoring text |
| | **Grade 1** CCSS.ELA-Literacy.Sl.1.1.C Ask questions to clear up any confusion about topics and texts under discussion | Learning how to use strategies of asking and answering questions that lead to adaptive help-seeking and task comprehension through monitoring text |
| | CCSS.ELA-Literacy.Sl.1.2 Ask and answer questions about key details in a text read aloud or information presented orally or through other media | |
| | CCSS.ELA-Literacy.Cl.1.3 Ask and answer questions about what a speaker says in order to gather additional information or clarify something that is not understood | |

- Spoken language is the basis for the development of reading and writing
- Spoken and written language work together to develop language and literacy competence from childhood through to adulthood
- Children who struggle with oral language often have difficulties with reading and writing
- Children who struggle with reading and writing often have problems with oral language
- Instruction in written language can develop oral language

The similarities in the Common Core requirements for kindergarteners and first graders are depicted in Table 4.2, noting comprehension of what is being said is a significant part of any discussion, conversation, or instruction.

**TABLE 4.2** Kindergarten and First Grade Speaking and Listening Strand and Standards Similarities

| *Comprehension and collaboration: Kindergarten* | *Comprehension and collaboration: Grade 1* |
| --- | --- |
| SL.K.1. Participate in collaborative conversations with diverse partners about kindergarten topics and texts with peers and adults in small and larger groups.<br>• Follow agreed-upon rules for discussions (e.g., listening to others and taking turns speaking about the topics and texts under discussion).<br>• Continue a conversation through multiple exchanges. | SL.1.1. Participate in collaborative conversations with diverse partners about grade 1 topics and texts with peers and adults in small and larger groups.<br>• Follow agreed-upon rules for discussions (e.g., listening to others with care, speaking one at a time about the topics and texts under discussion).<br>• Build on others' talk in conversations by responding to the comments of others through multiple exchanges.<br>• Ask questions to clear up any confusion about the topics and texts under discussion. |
| SL.K.2. Confirm understanding of a text read aloud or information presented orally or through other media by asking and answering questions about key details and requesting clarification if something is not understood. | SL.1.2. Ask and answer questions about key details in a text read aloud or information presented orally or through other media. |
| SL.K.3. Ask and answer questions in order to seek help, get information, or clarify something that is not understood. | SL.1.3. Ask and answer questions about what a speaker says in order to gather additional information or clarify something that is not understood. |

## *Developing Adaptive Help-Seeking: The Social Dimension of Self-Regulation*

The self-regulatory strategy of help-seeking can be successfully integrated into teaching and learning practices through collaborative learning in the early grades, when children tend to be less competitive and more intrinsically motivated to learn. It is not a surprise that the authors of the Common Core emphasize that learning will come from social collaborations within the context of a classroom. In the past, American kindergarten classrooms were intent on shifting early educational experiences away from children's social and emotional skills towards a heavy focus on academic skills (Kagan & Kauerz, 2007). However, raising a young learner's awareness of when and how to ask for assistance when faced with a difficult task or text can lead to a significant increase in independent learning and academic success (Karabenick & Newman, 2006).

Self-regulation is a key factor in early development and a precursor to literacy acquisition (Hulit, Howard, & Fahey, 2010). The Common Core recognizes that the youngest learners need to gain comprehension through collaborating with others by asking and answering questions in order to get information or to clarify something that is not understood (CCSS.ELA-Literacy.SL.K.3). This particular English Language Arts (ELA) standard opens the door to introducing the social strategy of adaptive help-seeking in kindergarten and first grade, which is a self-regulated learning strategy.

Self-regulation is not learned in isolation; the youngest learners can be encouraged to work together to translate literacy-learning experiences into behaviors they can use to regulate their thoughts, emotions, and actions (Blair & Diamond, 2008). In addition, training in self-regulatory strategies, such as adaptive help-seeking, can connect speaking and listening behaviors with the goals of processing and understanding what is being heard and said. Training the youngest students to ask for clarification can erase many misconceptions that often accompany early learning experiences. Instead of being passive listeners, young students can become engaged and responsive participants in their learning by monitoring their own comprehension.

## Beyond Speaking and Listening

The standard involves more than speaking and listening; it requires the youngest elementary school students to participate in collaborative conversations with peers and with adults that go beyond the simple acquisition of receptive and expressive language. Within the context of speaking and listening, students are expected to ask and to answer questions to seek help, or to clarify an idea they do not comprehend using strategies characteristically associated with literacy acquisition. In the earliest stages of literacy skills acquisition, attaining this particular Common Core standard strongly links oral and written language development with speaking and listening. It also sets the stage for close reading in kindergarten and the first grade.

- Substantial emphasis placed on reading and writing informational texts in grades K–5 calls for specific instruction in "deliberate efforts by a reader to better understand what is being read," a behavior associated with stronger reading comprehension skill (Duke & Block, 2012, p. 60).
- Common Core standards integrate learning how and when to ask and to answer questions that indicate seeking help for clarification of something that is not understood in order to ensure each student's engagement in the process.
- Conversations during close reading are centered upon kindergarten and first-grade texts and topics that introduce and reinforce the acquisition of academic vocabulary (content specific).
- Facilitators of such conversations encourage them to follow rules for discussion, such as listening to others and taking turns speaking.

## Shifting to Be College Ready

Students in the early grades are devoting more time to reading informational texts. They will require training in asking questions that clarify any ideas they do not comprehend when engaged in reading a difficult passage of a text or a literacy piece. At all levels of literacy instruction, exemplary teachers routinely offer direct and explicit demonstrations of the cognitive strategies used by good readers when they read. In other words, they model the thinking that skilled readers engage in while they attempt to decode a word, self-monitor for understanding, summarize while reading, and edit when composing.

Close reading practices that have been utilized most commonly at the secondary and college levels are being introduced in kindergarten and the first grade by training students to encounter a text many times and inviting them to become engaged in critical thinking. Young readers who metacognitively process what they are reading will be easier to engage and have a better understanding of what they are reading (Fisher & Frey, 2012).

- *ELA standards* shift to reading a true balance of informational and literary texts, turning elementary school classrooms into places where students access the world, science, social studies, the arts, and literature through text.
- *Kindergarten students* are introduced to equal amounts of content-rich nonfiction and informational texts.
- *Informational texts in the primary grades* provide opportunities for students to build social studies and science knowledge through diagrams, maps, tables, and glossaries, as well as text.
- *Shifts in literacy instruction* require that teachers be prepared to teach comprehension strategies.
- *Kindergarten and the first-grade teachers* should offer choice in the topics and texts that are read and provide opportunities for students to work together to achieve a goal or complete a task (Duke & Block, 2012).
- *Metacognitive modeling during close reading* can train students to examine the text through multiple readings, identifying deep structures within the text that might be confusing and may slow down fluency and comprehension.

## Adaptive Help-Seeking—Why Doesn't Everyone Do It?

Learning to cope with academic difficulty through training in adaptive help-seeking provides young learners with strategies that can help them maintain task involvement, avoid the unpleasantness of repeated failure, and develop as an independent learner (Corno, 2008).

- Classroom teachers have observed students who were inquisitive and curious learners in the early grades become disinterested as they progress through elementary to middle school.

- Motivation to learn can be undermined, perhaps due to frequent and significant setbacks while striving to meet the academic demands of the changing learning environments. Setbacks lower self-efficacy during a time when young learners should have experiences that increase self-efficacy for all areas of learning and development.
- Early inquisitive years are when the development of cognitive self-regulation is highly influenced by adults; teachers can put rules of engagement in place that invite and support academic help-seeking.

Students can be instructed regarding what to do when a text becomes confusing instead of struggling in isolation and eventually giving up. Rather than persisting towards failure, young learners can be trained in help-seeking strategies specifically for comprehending informational texts:

- Research that spans over thirty-five years provides evidence that the ability to utilize adults and peers appropriately as resources to cope with difficulties encountered in learning situations is one of the most important skills children can cultivate (Nelson-Le Gall, 1981; Nelson-Le Gall, Gumerman, & Scott-Jones, 1983).
- *Self-regulated students* are independent learners who are not self-sufficient and isolated. They are comfortable with asking for help when necessary, mainly because in their experience, the effort has been an integral part of their academic development and has been rewarded with successful completion of difficult tasks.
- Students from all age groups frequently do not take charge of their own learning, particularly when they face challenging or difficult schoolwork. Even though assistance is available, they often give up prematurely, sit passively, or persist unsuccessfully on their own without asking for help (Newman, 2000). Students as early as the second grade do not want to appear "dumb" if they ask for help (Newman, 2000; Newman & Goldin, 1990). As students enter the age where peer and teacher approval is more important than seeking help, they are less likely to seek help, and will often weigh the costs of social embarrassment against academic success and allow their thoughts and fears to compete with their beliefs about the benefits of obtaining help when needed (Newman & Goldin, 1990).
- *Classrooms* in which teachers share their time, energy, and nurturance tend to have students who are more attentive, put in more effort, are more self-expressive, and are more engaged in learning.
- *Teacher involvement* is critical to encouraging adaptive help-seeking because of two mediating processes: teacher–student intersubjectivity and students' personal beliefs. Teacher–student intersubjectivity is characterized by how in tune the teacher is with the student's purpose, focus, and affect—in other words, when all are on the "same page" (Newman, 2000). Preschoolers,

kindergarteners, and first graders willingly approach their teacher for assistance due to the "niceness and kindness," or the affective traits, of the teacher. As they mature as learners, students begin to evaluate teachers as helpful based on how aware they are of the students' problems.

The Common Core standards alert teachers, instructors, and parents that seeking help for a hint or clarification of a misunderstood concept is a good thing, and we need to train our young learners on how to do it effectively. Asking for the answer is not something that will lead to future academic growth and development, but effective help-seeking will promote independent learning (White & Bembenutty, 2013).

## Application of the Integrated Framework to Language Arts (Close Reading)

### What Does Adaptive Help-Seeking Look Like to Young Learners During Close Reading Read-Alouds?

We chose *close reading* for this section because it is a key requirement of the Common Core and it directs the reader's attention to the text itself (Burke, 2013). Kindergartners and first graders are provided with time and instructional support to learn how to thoughtfully focus on significant details or patterns in a text in order to develop a deeper and more precise understanding of the text's form, craft, and meaning.

One comment often made about kindergartners is that they ask so many questions. Their innate curiosity should be encouraged and shaped into learning experiences. Appropriate instructional supports, such as training in adaptive help-seeking, maximizing the intent of close reading, and providing a structure for questioning, should be part of classroom instruction.

### Teacher Modeling: An Essential Practice of Close Reading

Teacher modeling should reflect a familiarity with close reading as it is practiced in the elementary school classroom (Fisher & Frey, 2012). Teacher modeling should include repeated interactive read-alouds—a systematic method of reading aloud that allows the teacher to demonstrate her own understanding of the passage (McGee & Schickedanz, 2007). This method helps teachers scaffold children's understanding of the passages as they are guided through levels of attaining self-regulatory competency (observation, emulation, self-control, and self-regulation) in this specific area of instruction.

- The teacher models, guides, and promotes questioning practices to assist students with reading and gleaning information from texts. Establishing

specific patterns of adaptive help-seeking discourses in the classroom can train even the youngest students to value the strategic usefulness and skills of questioning.
- Teacher feedback during close reading can motivate children to know when they need help. Directing children to ask for help in specific situations, with appropriate motives and questioning strategies, helps them distinguish between adaptive and excessive help-seeking.
- Comprehension begins as texts are reread and analyzed to unearth complex structures, themes, and insights for even the youngest learners.
- Revisiting a text offers the possibility that as young readers develop their literacy skills over time and into high school, they will be challenged to think more deeply about texts that they are already able to comfortably and fluently decode and understand at a surface level.
- Reading aloud requires the instructor to scaffold student understanding by discussing the text. However, read-alouds should have accompanying expression, pausing at important points and pointing to pictures to support student understanding.

### *How Can Close Reading Literacy Experiences Be Used to Instruct Monitoring Strategies and Adaptive Help-Seeking?*

- The teacher encourages students to use help strategically—for example, revisiting misread passages and trying to figure out the author's intended meaning. This teaches them to monitor their work to determine their need for more assistance.
- The teacher models how to question and probe while reading informational texts to help students learn to ask intelligent questions, both of themselves and of others, when they are no longer understanding what they are reading (Newman, 2008).

### *How Can Self-Monitoring Logs Be Useful to Increase Adaptive Help-Seeking and Self-Efficacy?*

The learning experience described in this chapter, from beginning to end, includes the use of self-monitoring logs to focus young learners on their own thoughts, feelings, and behaviors while engaged in planning and doing difficult tasks. Both help-seeking and self-efficacy are two critical areas of learning and development that require kindergarten and first-grade teachers to spend more time monitoring how their students feel about their developing skills and capabilities regarding a specific task. In addition, monitoring self-reactions—the way a student feels about a completed task—provides the teacher and student with information that can guide future task planning and performance. These types of assessments provide the teacher with insights into young students' perception of their academic abilities while they are developing.

Kindergarteners and first graders can be introduced to monitoring self-efficacy and help-seeking with logs that illustrate facial expressions such as *"I can't do it!"* or *"I think I need some help!"* Logs with pictures of models whose facial expressions most represent the facial expressions of the young learner are motivators for them to enter a rating for their levels of self-efficacy, help-seeking, and reactions to learning (Bandura, 1986).

Three types of self-monitoring logs are used in this chapter (see Table 4.3). Monitoring logs of self-efficacy, help-seeking, and self-reactions are collected at various checkpoints during the process. First, students practice with the self-monitoring logs by doing exactly what their teacher does during the observation level as the teacher self-evaluates with input from the students. Afterwards, during emulation and self-control, students maintain and enter information independently into their own set of logs.

## Materials:

- All displayed materials written on large pad (3 × 3 feet surface), interactive whiteboard, or overhead transparency
  - Short passage from informational text with illustration. (The passage must be written on a surface that can be easily read by students and markings easily detected.)
- Markers, sticky notes, highlighters
- Self-monitoring logs (see Table 4.3)
  - Teacher report (self-efficacy, help-seeking)
  - Teacher report (self-reactions–self-reflection phase)
  - Student report (self-efficacy, help-seeking)
  - Student report (self-reactions)

**TABLE 4.3** Self-Monitoring Logs Distribution

**Teacher monitoring: The logs are for the student to fill out along with the teacher as the teacher models how to rate her self-efficacy and help-seeking and how to identify self-reactions following a task.**

| Log | Level | *Forethought* | *Performance* | *Self-Control* |
|---|---|---|---|---|
| **Self-efficacy** | Observation | ✓ | ✓ | ✓ |
| **Help-seeking** | Observation | ✓ | ✓ | ✓ |
| **Self-reactions** | Observation | ✓ | ✓ | ✓ |

*Continued*

**TABLE 4.3** (Continued)

| \multicolumn{5}{l}{Student self-monitoring: Students self-monitor their self-efficacy, help-seeking, and self-reactions while they are doing a reading activity.} |
|---|---|---|---|---|
| Log | Level | Forethought | Performance | Self-Reactions |
| **Self-efficacy** | Emulation | ✓ | ✓ | ✓ |
|  | Self-control | ✓ | ✓ | ✓ |
|  | Self-regulation | ✓ | ✓ | ✓ |
| **Help-seeking** | Emulation | ✓ | ✓ | ✓ |
|  | Self-control | ✓ | ✓ | ✓ |
|  | Self-regulation | ✓ | ✓ | ✓ |
| **Self-reactions** | Emulation |  |  | ✓ |
|  | Self-control |  |  | ✓ |
|  | Self-regulation |  |  | ✓ |

- Red and green cards (teacher distributes two cards to each student post-observation of forethought phase)★
- Individual reading passages

**Prior Knowledge Assessment.** Before students begin observing how to seek help, the teacher should assess the students' levels of ability to understand when they need to seek help and the type of help they should be seeking. Teachers should spend time first explaining to students that asking for help is done not to find the answers to questions, but to obtain information on how to understand something that is confusing. In addition, students need to learn how to make appropriate choices on whom or what they seek help from.

### The Plan: The Road to Independence Begins with Strategic Help-Seeking: Comprehension of Informational Text

**Objective:** Students will increase their awareness of what to do when texts become confusing using the self-regulatory strategy of adaptive help-seeking during the reading of a complex text. Students will ask the teacher to stop reading and then ask questions to clarify the meaning of the text.

**Sessions:** The suggested time frame for the lessons is divided into sessions that can be shortened or lengthened using the teacher's professional judgment. Throughout the three phases of self-regulated learning, the teacher must capture and maintain students' interest by closely monitoring their attention span and motivation. The planning processes for students in kindergarten and grade one take into account that levels of self-efficacy and help-seeking are dependent upon developmental levels of the students. Therefore, teachers must set short-term, easy-to-reach (proximal) goals for each session.

## Observation Level

## Watch It!

### Sessions 1–7

**Observation:** Teacher models how to read and reread a text while demonstrating adaptive help-seeking strategies. The teacher thinks aloud and models self-questioning in an attempt to differentiate what parts of the text are clear and what parts are confusing. While observing the teacher stop, reread, and ask specific text-related questions, students "look and listen" to observe how and when the teacher stops reading, asks for help, and receives help.

## Observation of Forethought

### Getting Ready to Read!

### Sessions 1–2

**Forethought:** Students observe the teacher prepare to read a selected passage from an informational text. Throughout the entire forethought phase processes, which are outlined later, students are instructed and reminded to pay close attention to the teacher and to observe what the teacher is saying and doing. In this phase, the teacher carefully describes the plans she has for how to read and comprehend a challenging passage from an informational text.

### Modeling: What Is the Teacher Doing?

Modeling involves the teacher demonstrating a series of strategies to the students as they observe the teacher's behavior. In reading a challenging informational text, the teacher thinks aloud, contemplating the difficulty of the passage that needs to be read in order to learn more about a specific topic and to answer specific questions. This is the teacher's and the students' first encounter with the text as a group and should provide substantial opportunities for speaking and listening.

### What Is Self-Efficacy?

- Self-efficacy should be explained to students using specific examples in order for them to become familiar with the term as well as its application to themselves. The teacher can provide many examples of self-efficacy and engage students in a discussion about their own feelings of self-efficacy for particular tasks.

- In the lesson on adaptive help-seeking, the teacher models how to assess one's own self-efficacy to read a complex passage. The teacher does this by thinking aloud. The teacher thinks aloud as she surveys the book by verbalizing statements about her feelings of capability to comprehend the passages in the book in order to be able to respond correctly to questions. For example:
- *"This passage looks very hard and very complicated. I have never read a passage like this before all by myself."*
- *"Maybe I can do this by myself; after all, it is supposed to be a great book and it has a lot of pictures."*

As the teacher contemplates these questions, she identifies strengths and weaknesses in completing the task and emphasizes the weaknesses. This is done in order to help students understand that not feeling capable of completing a task does not mean that one will not complete the task correctly. It is essential for students to realize that this is a targeted point in which the strategy of help-seeking will lead to success rather than failure.

The teacher rates her self-efficacy by placing a check in the box beneath the appropriate diagram on the following self-monitoring log. Students copy what the teacher did onto their own identical log.

### What Is Help Seeking?

- The teacher demonstrates the behavior of a coping model—someone who has doubts about her ability to complete a task independently. The teacher thinks aloud about her doubts, explaining why it is important not to ignore or become anxious about these doubts.

  Thinking aloud, the teacher emphasizes the following:
  - *"What if I cannot do this task by myself? Is it okay to ask for help?"*
  - *"Who would I ask for help if I could not understand what I am reading?"*
  - *"How will I know when and if I really need help?"*

The teacher rates herself by placing a check in the appropriate box on help-seeking on the following self-monitoring log while the students copy what the teacher did onto their own identical log.

**TABLE 4.4** Forethought Phase: Self-Monitoring of Self-Efficacy. Illustrations by Jeremiah Demster

| Teacher thinks: "I can't do it!" | Teacher thinks: "I'm not sure I can do it!" | Teacher thinks: "I can do it!" |
|---|---|---|
| | | |

**TABLE 4.5** Forethought Phase: Self-Monitoring of Help-Seeking

| Teacher thinks: "It's not ok to get help! No way!" | Teacher thinks: "I guess it's ok to get help! Not sure!" | Teacher thinks: "I think it is ok to get help! Oh yes, please help!" |
|---|---|---|
| Teacher thinks: "I don't need any help!" | Teacher thinks: "I think I need some help!" | Teacher thinks: "I need a lot of help!" |
| Teacher thinks: "No one I know can help me." | Teacher thinks: "I am not sure who can help me." | Teacher thinks: "I know who can help me." |

## Post-Observation of Forethought

### Do You Think Your Teacher Can Do It?

★ After observing the teacher, the students receive two cards, one red and one green.

**Teacher:** Poses a question to the students, asking them to hold up the green card if they think the teacher can read the passage independently and the red card if they think the teacher will need help. The teacher tallies the responses and displays them on a scorecard for all to see.

**Students:** Each student is asked to respond to the question posed by the teacher, predicting the teacher's performance on the passage about to be read. Based on what they have observed, holding up the green card indicates their belief that the teacher will do the task independently. Holding up a red card indicates their belief the teacher will need help.

## Observation of Performance

### Listen!

### *Sessions 3–4*

**Performance Phase:** Students observe the teacher begin to read a short passage from the chosen informational text with at least one illustration.

### *Modeling: What Is the Teacher Doing?*

Students are reminded to pay close attention to the teacher. The teacher makes sure that students are engaged as she models what to do when reading a passage becomes difficult or confusing. The teacher demonstrates how to reread the passage and to ask for help when things become unclear and self-efficacy begins to drop.

### *Why Do We Monitor Self-Efficacy?*

Teachers should be careful to choose an illustrated, grade level–appropriate, complex passage that is challenging, but not too difficult to be discouraging. Thinking aloud, she reads all the way through the passage, calling attention to any words, ideas, or illustrations that are confusing by annotating each one by underlining, highlighting, or circling. By the end of the passage, the teacher models her doubts that this task can be done independently, demonstrating low self-efficacy for the task.

- As the teacher continues to think aloud, she shares how sometimes working independently can lead to frustration and lower self-efficacy; however, with help, the teacher feels confident that the task would be completed successfully.
- It is important for the teacher to emphasize that low self-efficacy might lead one to give up, and she pays close attention to those feelings that make her want to quit rather than ask for help.

### *Rate Your Teacher's Self-Efficacy!*

Students are asked to put a check mark in the box that is most like what they think the teacher feels about reading the difficult passage.

**TABLE 4.6** Performance Phase: Self-Monitoring of Self-Efficacy

| Teacher thinks: "I can't do it!" | Teacher thinks: "I'm still not so sure." | Teacher thinks: "I know I can do it!" |
|---|---|---|
| 😟 | 😕 | 😃 |

## What Is Help-Seeking?

Thinking aloud, the teacher models what a reader should do when confused and the questions the reader should ask in order to move along with her reading. The teacher emphasizes that when a text becomes confusing, good readers *stop* reading and then seek help.

- Teacher expresses frustration at not being able to work quickly and independently.
- Teacher verbalizes the struggles that can be encountered during a close reading exercise and how to obtain a better understanding of the passage with hints, not answers.
- Teacher invites students to give hints, not answers, to clarify the confusing parts of the text, stressing the goal as being able to complete this type of task independently.
- Students come to the teacher's aid by using prior knowledge and text and illustration cues. The teacher uses the hints and provides feedback, identifying the most helpful hints as well as other responses that might have been blurted out in the form of an answer.

## Rate Your Teacher's Help-Seeking Strategies!

Students are asked to rate their observations of the teacher's help-seeking strategies while reading the passage by placing a check mark in the appropriate box.

**TABLE 4.7** Performance Phase: Self-Monitoring of Help-Seeking

| Teacher thinks: "It's not ok to get help! No way!" | Teacher thinks: "I guess it's ok to get help! Not sure!" | Teacher thinks: "I think it is ok to get help! Oh yes, please help!" |
|---|---|---|
| | | |
| Teacher thinks: "I don't need any help!" | Teacher thinks: "I think I need some help!" | Teacher thinks: "I need a lot of help!" |
| | | |
| Teacher thinks: "No one I know can help me." | Teacher thinks: "I am not sure who can help me." | Teacher thinks: "I know who can help me." |
| | | |

## Observation of Self-Reflection

### Looking Back to Move Forward!

#### Sessions 5–6

**Self-Reflection:** Students observe the teacher reflect on her ability to read and comprehend the passage. The teacher forms evaluations and indicates changes in self-efficacy and attitudes towards help seeking.

### Modeling: What Is the Teacher Doing?

The teacher thinks aloud while reflecting on the process of annotating, stopping when confused, and seeking help as the means towards a successful outcome for the literacy task.

### Reflecting on Self-Efficacy

The teacher rereads aloud the same passage, stopping and thinking aloud as she calls attention to confusing words, ideas, or illustrations. The teacher describes how the hints enabled a better understanding of the passage and raised self-efficacy. The teacher attributes an increase in self-efficacy to specific hints or behaviors that increased the likelihood that the task would be completed successfully.

### Rate Your Teacher's Self-Efficacy

Students are asked to rate their observations of the teacher's self-efficacy now that the reading task is complete by placing a check mark in the appropriate box.

### Reflecting on Help-Seeking

The teacher thinks aloud while reflecting on the task performance, specifically focusing on what she did when confused and whether or not the behavior led to a successful completion of the task.

**TABLE 4.8** Self-Reflection Phase: Self-Monitoring of Self-Efficacy

| Teacher thinks: "I couldn't do it!" | Teacher thinks: "I did ok." | Teacher thinks: "I did great!" |
|---|---|---|
| | | |

**TABLE 4.9** Self-Reflection Phase: Self-Monitoring of Help-Seeking

| Teacher didn't want help. "No way!" | Teacher asked for a little help. "Not sure!" | Teacher asked for help. "Oh yes, please help!" |
|---|---|---|
| | | |
| Teacher said: "I didn't need any help!" | Teacher said: "I thought I needed a little help!" | Teacher said: "I knew exactly how much help I needed!" |
| | | |
| Teacher said: "No one I knew could help me." | Teacher said: "I didn't know who could help me." | Teacher said: "I knew who could help me." |
| | | |

- The outcome is observed by the students as the teacher rereads the passage for a third time, showing a higher self-efficacy and identifying the specific areas that are no longer confusing as a result of seeking the appropriate help.

## Rate Your Teacher's Help-Seeking Strategies

Students are asked to rate their observations of the teacher's help-seeking strategies now that the reading task is completed.

## Self-Reactions

- Self-reactions involve evaluating what one has done in terms of set standards of what one believes to be success. The teacher, for example, will evaluate her ability to comprehend the difficult passage and to respond to the challenging questions in ways in which she feels satisfied.
- If one is not satisfied, or if one encounters unanticipated challenges, the self-evaluation provides the opportunity to make adjustments or revisions so that in the future, performance will result in success. In the instance of close reading, the teacher will evaluate how the reading sessions went and whether or not the help-seeking strategies were helpful.

**TABLE 4.10** Self-Reflection Phase: Self-Monitoring of Reactions

| Teacher thinks: "It did not go so well." | Teacher thinks: "It went ok." | Teacher thinks: "It went great!" |
|---|---|---|
| The teacher thinks: "I could never do well; I am not good at this!" | The teacher thinks: "I did ok, but I could do better." | The teacher thinks: "I did great, but I can do even better." |

The teacher writes her responses for all students to view. Students are instructed to copy the ratings of her performance evaluation and what her feelings are about doing similar future tasks.

## Post-Observation Challenge!

### What Have We Done So Far?

#### Session 7

A **post-observation challenge** can determine which of the students are ready to move on to the emulation level where they will be asked to replicate what they observed the teacher doing. The teacher will present the option to move forward or repeat the observation by asking, *"Who is ready to stop when they are reading and ask questions when things become confusing the way I just did? Raise your green card!"*

Students who feel ready will raise the green card, and those who feel that they need more observation time will raise the red card. The teacher tallies the responses and displays them on a scorecard for them all to see. The teacher engages in a few short discussions with the students to gauge their understanding and self-regulatory level of competency. The teacher encourages students to talk about their observations and their feelings and other thoughts about what they observed.

## Emulation Level

### Work Together!

#### Sessions 8–14

**Emulation:** The teacher guides students through tasks that require individual learners to emulate how to read a challenging text, while demonstrating adaptive help-seeking strategies. Students now will interrupt the teacher to stop, request a reread, and ask questions when the text becomes confusing. The students will attempt to imitate how and when the teacher asked for and received help. Students can work on the task as a whole group or can be divided into small groups. Careful attention is given to allotting time for students to self-monitor their self-efficacy and help-seeking using the logs.

### Emulation of Forethought

#### Planning Together!

#### Sessions 8–9

**Forethought:** Students attempt to imitate the planning behaviors they observed their teacher perform as they observed her preparing to read aloud a selected passage from an informational text. The teacher gives students the opportunity to participate by speaking about what they observed the teacher say as she prepared to read the passage. Students are encouraged by the teacher to focus their discussions on the strategies they heard while listening to the teacher describe what she did when the passage became hard to read. Students are asked to rate their self-efficacy and create help-seeking questions for clarification prior to beginning the task.

### *Modeling: What Is the Teacher Doing?*

The teacher makes her actions and, while closely guiding students through a reread of the same passage (or a new one), reminds students to repeat the observed forethought behaviors. Students should remain in a group (or small groups) and be closely monitored as they approximate a successful imitation of the modeled forethought think-alouds. The teacher thinks aloud, repeating specific behaviors until each student has shown a clear understanding of the process.

### *Thinking about Self-Efficacy*

- The teacher reads through the passage, inviting students to identify confusing parts of the text by raising a red card.

**48** Elementary School

- Following the read-aloud of the passage, the teacher asks students to verbalize their thoughts of being able to complete this reading task.
- Students are instructed to record on their self-monitoring logs their own self-efficacy ratings on their beliefs about their ability to complete the task independently.

**TABLE 4.11** Forethought Phase: Self-Monitoring of Self-Efficacy

| "I can't do it!" | "I'm not sure I can do it!" | "I can do it!" |
|---|---|---|
| 😟 | 😕 | 😃 |

## Thinking about Help-Seeking

- Following the read-aloud of the passage, the teacher asks the students to work in groups to discuss what types of questions they would pose when seeking help to clarify a confusing part of the passage.
- Students are then asked to share their groups' questions. Doing this helps students make observations about each other's thinking as they brainstorm in their groups.
- The teacher asks students in each group to share with the class the questions the group generated. The teacher provides guidance and feedback, and scaffolds students to help refine the questions and to provide more clarity. The questions are written on the board for the class to see.
- The teacher circulates around the room and asks students to place a check in the appropriate box on the self-monitoring log (see Table 4.12). The teacher is monitoring students' completion of the log and provides assistance when students have questions.

**TABLE 4.12** Forethought Phase: Self-Monitoring of Help-Seeking

| "It's not ok to get help! No way!" | "I guess it's ok to get help! Not sure!" | "I think it is ok to get help! Oh yes, please help!" |
|---|---|---|
| 😟 | 😕 | 😃 |

| "I don't need any help!" | "I think I need some help!" | "I need a lot of help!" |
|---|---|---|
| | | |
| "No one I know can help me." | "I am not sure who can help me." | "I know who can help me." |
| | | |

## Emulation of Performance

### Practicing

### *Sessions 10–11*

**Performance phase:** Students attempt to imitate behaviors they observed their teacher perform when reading aloud a selected passage from an informational text. The teacher gives students the opportunity to participate by imitating the actions they observed their teacher do when parts of the passage became confusing. For this age group, students will remain in groups and be closely monitored as they try to replicate with their peers what they observed their teacher do when reading.

*Modeling: What Is the Teacher Doing Now?*

- The teacher distributes individual passages for students to follow and reads aloud the same passage displayed on a large surface.
- The teacher can model while closely guiding students through a reread of the same passage, or a new one, requiring them to emulate the observed behaviors. The teacher continues to think aloud if she observes common questions or stumbling blocks among the students. The teacher guides the students to think aloud during this phase.

*Can Self-Efficacy Be Monitored?*

- The teacher reads aloud through the passage, asking students to closely follow and raise their red cards each time they come across words, ideas, or illustrations that are confusing.
- The teacher scaffolds as she continues to model annotating and asks students to do it themselves when they come across challenging material by underlining, highlighting, or circling.

- Each time a student raises a red card, the teacher asks her to think aloud about the confusing part of the passage and encourages other students to help with the difficult content by also thinking aloud.
- Students are asked to rate their self-efficacy for completing the task successfully, accounting for the level of difficulty and their confidence in their skills now that they are actually doing the task.

**TABLE 4.13** Performance Phase: Self-Monitoring of Self-Efficacy

| "I can't do it!" | "I'm not sure I can do it." | "I can do it!" |
|---|---|---|
| | | |

## *Can Help-Seeking Be Monitored?*

- The teacher reminds students what a reader should do when confused (STOP) and how to phrase questions when seeking help.
- The teacher invites students to reread the text aloud and to stop to ask for help when the text becomes confusing.
- The teacher invites students to pose questions to seek clarification of the confusing parts of the text.
- The teacher invites students to give hints, not answers, to clarify the confusing parts of the text.
- The teacher reminds students to use prior knowledge as well as text and illustration cues.
- The teacher uses hints and provides feedback, identifying the most helpful hints as well as other responses that might have been blurted out in the form of an answer.

Students are instructed to rate their feelings about their own help-seeking by placing a check in the appropriate box as the teacher had done during the observation level.

**TABLE 4.14** Performance Phase: Self-Monitoring of Help-Seeking

| "It's not ok to get help. No way!" | "I guess it's ok to get help. Not sure!" | "I think it is ok to get help. Oh yes, please help!" |
|---|---|---|
| | | |

| "I don't need any help!" | "I think I need some help." | "I need a lot of help!" |
|---|---|---|
| | | |
| "No one I know can help me." | "I am not sure who can help me." | "I know who can help me." |
| | | |

## Emulation of Self-Reflection

### Reflecting and Reacting!

### *Sessions 12–13*

**Self-Reflection:** Students are guided by the teacher to evaluate what it was like for them to stop and interrupt the reading flow when the material became challenging. Students reflect on what it was like to engage in help-seeking behavior.

### *Modeling: What Are My Teacher and Peers Doing?*

The teacher instructs students to think aloud in their groups as they reflect on the process of annotating, stopping when confused, and seeking help as the means towards a successful outcome for the literacy task. The teacher circulates about the room, listening carefully and scaffolding as necessary.

### *Does Monitoring Self-Efficacy Make a Difference in Doing a Challenging Task?*

- The teacher rereads aloud the same passage, stopping and asking students what was positive about stopping when coming across confusing words, ideas, or illustrations.
- The students think aloud as they reflect on whether they stopped enough to help themselves understand the confusing passage.
- The teacher asks the students to discuss whether they can attribute increases in self-efficacy and performance to the specific help-seeking strategies used.

**52** Elementary School

Now that the reading task has come to an end, under close teacher supervision, students are asked to rate feelings of self-efficacy by placing a check mark in the appropriate box.

TABLE 4.15 Self-Reflection Phase: Self-Monitoring of Self-Efficacy

| "I couldn't do it!" | "I did ok." | "I did great!" |
|---|---|---|
|  |  |  |

## Reflecting on Help-Seeking

- Students are asked to recite the questions they asked that led to completing the task successfully. The teacher helps students structure the questions to ask for a hint rather than an answer.
- Both students and teacher discuss their performance, specifically focusing on the types of questions they asked when confused and if they led to clarification.
- The teacher rereads the passage for a third time to determine if students can identify the specific areas that are no longer confusing as a result of seeking the appropriate help.

Students are asked to rate their thoughts about their help-seeking strategies now that the reading task is completed.

TABLE 4.16 Self-Reflection Phase: Self-Monitoring of Help-Seeking

| "I didn't want help. No way!" | "I asked for a little help. Not sure." | "I asked for help. Oh yes, I really needed help!" |
|---|---|---|
|  |  |  |

| "I didn't need any help." | "I thought I needed a little help." | "I knew exactly how much help I needed." |
|---|---|---|
| | | |
| "No one I knew could help me." | "I didn't know who can help me." | "I knew who could help me." |
| | | |

## What Do Self-Reactions Tell Me About My Performance?

- The teacher and students discuss evaluating their ability to comprehend the difficult passage and to respond to the challenging questions in terms of satisfaction levels.
- If one is not satisfied, or if one encounters unanticipated challenges, the self-evaluation provides the opportunity to make adjustments or revisions so that in the future, the performance will result in success. In the instance of close reading, the students will evaluate how the reading sessions went and whether or not the help-seeking strategies were helpful.

The teacher asks students to evaluate their performance and to place a check mark in the box that best describes her feelings about doing similar future tasks. The teacher reminds students that the teacher did this in the past and that the students should do this following the teacher's model.

**TABLE 4.17** Self-Reflection Phase: Self-Monitoring of Reactions

| "It did not go so well." | "It went ok." | "It went great!" |
|---|---|---|
| | | |
| "I could never do well because I am not good at this." | "I did ok, but I could do better!" | "I did great, but I can do even better!" |
| | | |

## Post-Emulation Review

### Take a Moment . . . What Have We Done So Far?

#### Session 14

A **post-emulation challenge** can determine which of the students are ready to move on to the self-control level, where they will be asked to replicate what they observed the teacher doing, this time with much less scaffolding. The teacher will present the option to move forward or to repeat the practice sessions by asking, *"Who is ready to stop when they are reading and ask questions when things become confusing on their own? Raise your green card!"*

Students who feel ready will raise the green card, and those who feel that they need more practice time will raise the red card. The teacher tallies the responses and displays them on a scorecard for them all to see and rewards each student for making good choices. The teacher engages in a lengthy discussion with the students to gauge their understanding and self-regulatory level of competency. The teacher encourages students to talk about their observations and their feelings and thoughts about what they practiced. At the next level, the teacher continues to pace the learning, but with less scaffolding. The teacher needs to be sure students are ready to advance towards more independence before beginning the self-control level.

## Self-Control Level

### It's Your Turn!

#### Sessions 15–21

**Self-Control:** The teacher observes and remains available to students as they work in small groups on a task that requires them to be actively engaged in understanding a passage being read aloud from an informational text. Students are now pacing their own learning with support from the teacher as needed. Students are expected to replicate what they observed and practiced, but with less instruction from the teacher. At this level, students are not yet able to read and comprehend different informational texts entirely on their own.

## Self-Controlled Forethought

### Planning it!

### *Sessions 15–16*

**Forethought:** Students are provided with a reading passage identical to the teacher's and directed to read along with the teacher as the new passage is being read aloud. The teacher recommends they make plans about what they will do when the text becomes confusing, as the teacher had done during the observation and emulation levels. Students are encouraged to not deviate from what they observed and practiced.

### *Modeling: Who Is the Model?*

The teacher encourages students to work independently or with each other as she reads aloud a new passage. Students are instructed to rely on their own self-monitoring of their comprehension; in other words, they should be using annotations in areas where the text is confusing or unclear to them. The teacher is now available as needed and remains observant until the students request help. While quietly monitoring the students' group discussions as they work on their plans for how to comprehend the text, the teacher remains available to provide feedback and monitor students' progress.

### *Rating Self-Efficacy*

- Teacher reads aloud through the entire passage, stopping intermittently so students can discuss with each other how they plan to identify areas of confusion.
- Teacher asks students to discuss with each other and then rate their ability to identify parts of the passage that are confusing and to ask questions that will help them complete the task successfully.

**TABLE 4.18** Forethought Phase: Self-Monitoring of Self-Efficacy

| "I can't do it on my own!" | "I'm not sure I can do it on my own." | "I can do it on my own!" |
|---|---|---|
| 😟 | 😕 | 😊 |

**56** Elementary School

**TABLE 4.19** Forethought Phase: Self-Monitoring of Help-Seeking

| "I have no plans to get help. No way!" | "I plan to get some help if I need it. Not sure." | "I have plans to get help. Oh yes, please help!" |
|---|---|---|
| | | |
| "I don't need any help!" | "I think I need some help!" | "I need a lot of help!" |
| | | |
| "No one I know can help me." | "I am not sure who can help me." | "I know who can help me." |
| | | |

## *Practicing Help-Seeking Strategies*

- The teacher reminds students it is up to them to stop and ask for a reread or pose a question for clarification when the text becomes confusing.
- Students are asked to share their plans with each other. Doing this helps students make observations about each other's thinking as they brainstorm in their groups. It also forces students to articulate the strategies they plan on using.
- The teacher provides feedback on the help-seeking questions as needed.
- The teacher instructs students to rate their feelings about help-seeking in the log (Table 4.19).

## Self-Controlled Performance

### Doing It!

### *Sessions 17–18*

**Performance Phase:** Students are closely observed as they apply the actions discussed during the forethought phase to a new passage from a challenging informational text. The teacher continues to observe and monitor students' progress as they work through the passage using the strategies previously observed and practiced under her close supervision.

## Modeling: What Are My Peers Doing?

The focus shifts to peer modeling as the teacher directs students to work with each other. The teacher is attentive to the students and will re-model specific behaviors and help students who may still need some guidance and support in using their help-seeking strategies.

## Rating My Self-Efficacy for This Task

After the passage has been read aloud, students rate their self-efficacy on the self-monitoring log, determining their self-efficacy to *stop* the reading and to ask for clarification using appropriate strategies (help-seeking).

- Students use the self-monitoring log as they have in the previous levels, but are instructed to be transparent about their feelings. They are not to be graded on how they rate themselves, but rather on their transparency in describing their feelings. Students should also be told it is appropriate to differ from their group members because each student has individual feelings about her level of self-efficacy to accomplish certain tasks.

## Evaluating My Help-Seeking Strategies

- Students are instructed to focus on listening to the reading of a new passage and to notify the teacher when the text becomes confusing by raising a red card.
- The teacher will read the text slowly and stop whenever a student raises the red card. The students then work in their groups to independently annotate the confusing part of the text and to identify help-seeking questions, even if their group members did not raise the red card.
- Students are instructed to raise their green cards to alert the teacher that their group has finished developing help-seeking questions. The teacher does not review with the students the responses to the help-seeking questions unless the students appear to be genuinely confused and are unable to resolve their questions in their groups.

**TABLE 4.20** Performance Phase: Self-Monitoring of Self-Efficacy

| "I can't do it!" | "I'm not sure I can do it." | "I can do it!" |
|---|---|---|

**TABLE 4.21** Performance Phase: Self-Monitoring of Help-Seeking

| "It's not ok to get help! No way!" | "I guess it's ok to get help. Not sure!" | "I think it is ok to get help! Oh yes, please help!" |
|---|---|---|
| "I don't need any help!" | "I think I need some help!" | "I need a lot of help!" |
| "No one I know canhelp me." | "I am not sure who can help me." | "I know who can help me." |

## Self-Controlled Reflection

### Reflecting and Reacting!

#### Sessions 19–20

**Self-reflection:** The teacher encourages students to reflect on what specific strategies worked and what did not work when it was their responsibility to stop the reading of a confusing text and to ask for clarification. This phase is important to help students recognize what actions they might take in the future when participating in reading groups or reading challenging texts on their own.

### Modeling: Who Is the Model Now?

The teacher and students use role playing to re-model the behaviors that lead to better text comprehension. Students are encouraged to discuss what they did well and what improvements could be made to their use of the listening, speaking, and help-seeking strategies to improve comprehension and raise self-efficacy.

## How Important Is Monitoring Self-Efficacy?

Students are instructed to fill out this section of the self-monitoring log prior to beginning the discussion described next.

- The teacher leads students in a discussion on how they rated their self-efficacy for this particular literacy task in the first two phases (forethought and performance) and points out any changes in self-efficacy ratings over the three phases. Reflecting on moments when self-efficacy was high or low and attributing specific circumstances to those feelings can help young learners gain a better comprehension of the importance of monitoring their feelings of competency for future tasks.

## Why Is Monitoring Help-Seeking Important?

Students are instructed to fill out this section of the self-monitoring log prior to beginning the discussion described next.

- The teacher asks students to discuss whether they believe their ability to stop reading and pose a help-seeking question led to a better understanding of the passage than if they had just finished the reading without asking questions.
- The teacher leads students in a discussion of the most effective means of asking for help. Asking students to refer to their monitoring logs, the teacher asks for examples of how seeking help led to a better comprehension of the task.
- The teacher leads students in a discussion of the appropriate way to phrase an adaptive help-seeking question. Students participate by differentiating help-seeking that wants a hint from help-seeking that wants an answer.

**TABLE 4.22** Self-Reflection Phase: Self-Monitoring of Self-Efficacy

| "I couldn't do it!" | "I did ok." | "I did great!" |
|---|---|---|
| | | |

**TABLE 4.23** Self-Reflection Phase: Self-Monitoring of Help-Seeking

| "I didn't want help. No way!" | "I asked for a little help. Not sure!" | "I asked for help. Oh yes, please help!" |
|---|---|---|
| | | |
| "I didn't need any help!" | "I thought I needed a little help!" | "I knew exactly how much help I needed!" |
| | | |
| "No one I knew could help me." | "I didn't know who could help me." | "I knew who could help me." |
| | | |

**TABLE 4.24** Self-Reflection Phase: Self-Monitoring of Reactions

| "It did not go so well." | "It went ok." | "It went great!" |
|---|---|---|
| | | |
| "I could never do well because I am not good at this." | "I did ok, but I could do better." | "I did great, but I can do even better!" |
| | | |

## What Do My Self-Reactions Tell Me About Future Tasks?

The teacher asks each student to evaluate her performance and to place a check mark in the box that best describes her feelings about doing similar future tasks. The teacher reminds students that their evaluations should be based on how they felt doing the reading on their own with little help from the teacher. These evaluations should be private and used for individual conferencing at the end of the task.

The teacher and students discuss evaluating their ability to comprehend the difficult passage and to respond to the challenging questions in terms of satisfaction levels. In this instance of close reading, the students evaluate how the reading sessions went and whether or not the help-seeking strategies led to a better understanding of the passage.

## Post Self-Control Review

### Take a Moment . . . Can I Do This On My Own?

#### Session 21

A **post self-control challenge** can determine which of the students are ready to demonstrate self-regulated competency. Will they be able to ask for help when assigned challenging informational texts on their own outside of the supervision of the teacher? The teacher will present the option to move forward or to repeat the self-control sessions by asking, *"Who is ready to stop when they are reading and ask questions when things become confusing on their own? Raise your green card!"*

Students who feel ready will raise the green card, and those who feel that they need more practice time will raise the red card. The teacher tallies the responses and displays them on a scorecard for them all to see, rewarding each student for transparency and excellent self-efficacy evaluations. The teacher engages in a lengthy discussion with students to gauge their understanding and self-regulatory level of competency. The teacher encourages students to talk about their observations, their feelings, and their thoughts about what they did in their groups. At the next level, the teacher will no longer be pacing the learning. The teacher will be available as a resource to students, who will be doing the reading independently.

## Self-Regulation

### Doing It On My Own (Does Not Mean Alone)!

#### Sessions 22–27

**Self-regulation:** At this level, the students should be ready to work independently and with some degree of flexibility. Students are able now to pace their own comprehension of difficult text—in other words, through their own self-monitoring, when something is difficult to understand, they will *stop*, annotate, and ask for help. The students will consistently respond to read-alouds by signaling the teacher to stop when the text becomes confusing, rather than sit passively and become disengaged. Questions posed for clarification will seek hints rather than answers to promote critical thinking about difficult content from an informational text.

## Self-Regulation of Forethought

### Making My Own Plans!

### *Sessions 22–23*

**Forethought:** Students are often and consistently given reading passages of increasing complexity. These passages are identical to the teacher's, and students are directed to read along with the teacher as the new passage is being read aloud. The teacher reminds students that every time they encounter a challenging task to carefully plan their actions—what will they do to comprehend this new and challenging passage?

### *Modeling: Who Is Modeling?*

Rather than read aloud, the teacher now has the students read quietly in their groups. One or more members of the group read aloud, modeling the *stop* strategy and asking for help when the text becomes difficult. Students readily share this strategy with peers, parents, and other teachers when they are engaged in reading texts that are too difficult to comprehend without assistance.

### *Independent Ratings of Self-Efficacy*

Students independently assess the difficulty level of reading passages and discuss with their peers and teachers their struggles with specific tasks. For example, the difficulty level of the passage may be more challenging for some rather than others depending on topic and prior knowledge. Whether in a reading group or doing homework, self-regulated students incorporate into their planning the level of difficulty of the task and what type of assistance they will require to complete it successfully.

### *Strategic Help-Seeking Beyond the Classroom*

Help-seeking in the earlier grades needs to be closely monitored. These young students can be impulsive and will often ask for an answer rather than a hint.

The teacher monitors students' phrasing of help-seeking questions in various settings and guides what seems to be seeking answers to asking for just enough information to complete the task independently. Other teachers and school personnel make themselves available to younger learners so they become better acquainted with those in the learning environment who can answer their questions.

## Self-Regulation of Performance

### Doing It On My Own!

#### Sessions 24–25

**Performance:** Self-regulated students apply the self-monitoring strategies discussed during the forethought phase to new passages from a challenging informational text and in other areas of their learning. The teacher consistently provides opportunities for students to check their progress as they work through difficult passages for homework and independent reading activities. The teacher is now observing the students take charge of their learning!

### *Modeling*

The teacher continues to model the strategies in the context of the classroom and encourages parents and other teachers to do the same. When the teacher demonstrates her need for help or shares evidence of her own self-monitoring, students will vicariously adopt those strategies and apply them automatically.

### *Self-Efficacy*

Self-regulated students assess their comfort level with a task before they begin it. The teacher should consistently provide opportunities for young learners to evaluate their feelings of competency prior to beginning a task and then share those feelings with the teacher. Students can be encouraged to work together to assess the difficulty level of reading passages and to discuss how their self-efficacy might influence their ability to complete the task.

### *Help-Seeking*

The teacher consistently listens and observes students' help-seeking questions to ensure that the quality of questions will lead to higher levels of reading comprehension. The teacher provides opportunities for students to assist their peers with challenging tasks.

## Self-Regulation of Self-Reflection

### Future Practices

*Modeling*

Self-reflection is a significant part of any learning environment. Teachers who openly reflect on their own self-regulatory learning and study habits will encourage even the youngest learners to adopt the same habits. Sharing practices of help-seeking and self-monitoring in real life as well as in the classroom can encourage young learners to become proactive and take charge of their learning the way their teacher models it every day.

*Self-Efficacy*

At this level, young learners will learn more from what they observe their teacher doing than what she is teaching. Teachers who are willing to share how they overcome their own learning challenges by using strategies such as help-seeking and self-monitoring encourage realistic evaluations of self-efficacy in their students.

*Promoting the Strategy of Help-Seeking in the Classroom*

Students require an arena where help-seeking is a strategy and, when practiced correctly, leads to growth in learning and development. Teachers who include in lesson planning and daily practices opportunities to ask and give help create a learning environment that removes the stigma still associated with those who have difficulty completing tasks independently.

*Self-Reactions*

The teacher provides opportunities for students to use self-monitoring logs and discuss with her their self-evaluations and reactions to difficult tasks. The teacher congratulates the students on their hard work over the past several weeks and encourages them to think about how to use the strategies and logs across disciplines.

## References

American Speech-Language-Hearing Association. (2001). Roles and responsibilities of speech-language pathologists with respect to reading and writing in children and adolescents [Guidelines]. Retrieved from www.asha.org/policy

Bandura, A. (1986). *Social foundations of thought and action: A social cognitive theory*. Englewood Cliffs, NJ: Prentice Hall.

Blair, C., & Diamond, A. (2008). Biological processes in prevention and intervention: The promotion of self-regulation as a means of preventing school failure. *Development and Psychopathology, 20*(3), 899–911.

Burke, B. A. (2013). Up close with close reading. *Library Sparks, 11*(3), 14.

Corno, L. (2008). On teaching adaptively. *Educational Psychologist, 43*(3), 161–173.

Duke, N. K., & Block, M. K. (2012). Improving reading in the primary grades. In I. Sawhill, R. Murnane, & C. Snow (Issue Eds.), *Future of Children, 22*(2), 55–72.

Fisher, D., & Frey, N. (2012). Close reading in elementary schools. *The Reading Teacher, 66*(3), 179–188.

Hulit, L. M., Howard, M. R., & Fahey, K. R. (2010). *Born to talk: An introduction to speech and language development* (5th ed.). Upper Saddle River, NJ: Pearson.

Kagan, S. L., & Kauerz, K. (2007). Reaching for the whole: Integration and alignment in early education policy. In R. C. Pianta, M. J. Cox, & K. Snow (Eds.), *School readiness and the transition to kindergarten in the era of accountability* (pp. 11–30). Baltimore, MD: Paul H. Brooks.

Karabenick, S. A., & Newman, R. S. (2006). *Help seeking in academic settings: goals, groups, and contexts*. Mahwah, NJ: Lawrence Erlbaum Publishers.

McGee, L. M., & Schickedanz, J. A. (2007). Repeated interactive read-alouds in preschool and kindergarten. *The Reading Teacher, 60*(8), 742–751.

Nelson-Le Gall, S. (1981). Help-seeking: An understudied problem-solving skill in children. *Developmental Review, 1*(3), 224–246.

Nelson-Le Gall, S., Gumerman, R. A., & Scott-Jones, D. (1983). Instrumental help-seeking and everyday problem-solving: A developmental perspective. In B. M. DePaulo, A. Nadler, & J. D. Fisher (Eds.)., *New Directions in Helping* (Vol. 2, pp. 65–283). New York, NY: Academic Press.

Newman, R. S. (1990). Children's help-seeking in the classroom: The role of motivational factors and attitudes. *Journal of Educational Psychology, 82*(1), 71.

Newman, R.S. (2000). Social influences on the development of children's adaptive help seeking: The role of parents, teachers, and peers. *Developmental Review, 20*(3), 350–404.

Newman, R. S. (2002). How self-regulated learners cope with academic difficulty: The role of adaptive help seeking. *Theory into Practice, 41*(2), 132–138.

Newman, R.S. (2008). The motivational role of adaptive help seeking in self-regulated learning. In D. H. Schunk & B. J. Zimmerman (Eds.)., *Motivation and self-regulated learning: Theory, research, and applications* (315–337). New York, NY: Routledge.

Newman, R.S., & Goldin, L. (1990). Children's reluctance to seek help with schoolwork. *Journal of Educational Psychology, 82*(1), 92–100.

White, M. C., & Bembenutty, H. (2013). Not all avoidance help seekers are created equal: Individual differences in adaptive and executive help seeking. *SAGE Open 3*(2), 1–14.

# 5

# WRITING FROM INFORMATIONAL TEXT

## Grades 2 and 3

### Strategies for Goal Setting, Planning, and Self-Monitoring

*Keywords: literacy, production and distribution, feedback, evidence from text, writing from sources, self-monitoring, strategies, goals, "I Can" statements. Self-regulation skills: modeling, observational learning, self-monitoring, logs, self-efficacy, task analysis, strategic planning, goal setting, short-term (proximal) and long-term (distal) goals*

Embedding the study of literacy, specifically writing, into all classroom activities is beneficial to both strong and struggling students. The Common Core standards for English Language Arts (ELA) can be easily aligned with literacy integration, which is what many teachers are already doing. For many years, ELA curriculum planners have requested that all teachers become literacy teachers by integrating reading, writing, speaking/listening, and language development into their lesson planning and curriculum choices (Guthrie, Schafer, & Huang, 2001). The Common Core standards focus on strengthening writing skills during the early elementary grades (second and third grade) by devoting a strand to production and distribution of writing through planning, revising, editing, rewriting, and accepting help from adults and peers.

Young students, particularly those for whom writing can be a significant challenge, need to be instructed in critical self-regulation and composition strategies, skills, and beliefs (Harris, Schmidt, & Graham, 1998). Instruction for writing informational/explanatory sentences that convey information accurately requires active collaboration and strategic planning. Writing is a complex and demanding process that requires writers from the earliest stages of literacy development to become aware of the rules and mechanics, while focusing on other contributing elements such as organization, goals, planning, and integrating feedback from collaborators, all of which can be categorized as metalinguistic awareness.

Self-regulation of the writing process can contribute to the growth and development of skilled writers over time. Self-regulated writers are goal oriented, resourceful, and reflective (Harris, Graham, & Santangelo, 2013). They are able to use powerful strategies to help them reach their writing goals. As depicted in Table 5.1, we focus on second and third graders for our crosswalk from the Common Core standards to a self-regulated learning target. The standards themselves avoid including strategies and processes so teachers can have latitude in choosing from a wide array of instructional tools. Teaching writing with specific research-based self-regulatory strategies can help students take charge of their own learning in spite of the many obstacles to becoming proficient writers.

## Do the Crosswalk!

**TABLE 5.1** Linking the Common Core and Self-Regulation

| *College- and career-ready preparation* | *Common Core standards for writing* | *Self-regulated learning target* |
|---|---|---|
| **Anchor standard for writing**<br>Develop and strengthen writing as needed by planning, revising, editing, rewriting, or trying a new approach (CCSS.ELA-Literacy.CCRA.W.2) | **Strand**<br>Writing K–5<br><br>**Standard**<br>Production and distribution | **Self-regulation strategy training**<br>Strategies for goal setting and planning during prewriting activities to foster self-regulatory practices and motivate reluctant writers. |
| | *CCSS.ELA-Literacy.W.2.5*<br>With guidance and support from adults and peers, focus on a topic and strengthen writing as needed by revising and editing.<br><br>(CCSS.ELA-Literacy.W.3.5)<br>With guidance and support from peers and adults, develop and strengthen writing as needed by planning, revising, and editing. (Editing for conventions should demonstrate command of language standards 1–3 up to and including grade 3.) | **Prior knowledge**<br>Evidence of adaptive help-seeking strategies taught in K–1 can be reinforced for seeking guidance and support from peers and adults during planning, revising, and editing. |

## Writing Requires Planning

The Common Core standards pair reading with writing at the earliest levels of instruction, giving individual learners time to build the prerequisite skills towards becoming proficient writers as they progress from K–12. The decision to make goal setting and planning the focus of this chapter recognizes that skilled writing depends on the amount of time the writer spends on planning what to do and say, which includes setting goals from which they can design a writing plan (Harris, Graham, & Mason, 2006).

We consider prewriting to be a critical component of writing instruction in the second and third grades, in particular, planning, goal setting, and self-monitoring. Prewriting is often a place where students get stuck because they do not know how to determine the purpose of their writing assignment; therefore, they cannot set goals. Early training in how to determine the purpose of a writing task and in how to set performance goals can provide second and third graders with strategies that will keep them from getting "stuck" before they begin.

Writing well involves more than putting down ideas as they come to mind. The process requires the writer to think carefully about the purpose of writing, to set specific goals, to plan what to say, to plan how to say it, and to give the reader necessary information. Teachers can help students become effective writers by placing emphasis on how to carry out the planning phase of writing using self-regulatory learning and by supporting students in applying strategies until they are able to do so independently.

## *Writing Complexity*

The Common Core for K–5 increases the complexity of writing requirements at each grade level to guide instruction, ensuring students gain adequate mastery of a range of skills and applications. Each year in their writing exercises, students are expected to demonstrate increasing ability to plan, revise, and edit their writing with help and guidance from adults and peers. The "Just do it!" generation of students often neglect the critical components of goal setting, planning, and self-monitoring because these actions take time. Teachers who prioritize goal setting and planning often find their students fall short of accomplishing their goals because young students are not yet trained to self-monitor their progress. Writing is a complex and demanding process that requires writers from the earliest stages of literacy development to focus on elements such as organization, goals, planning, and integrating feedback from collaborators, as well as the rules and mechanics of writing.

## Self-Regulation and the Writing Process

Self-regulation recognizes writing as a recursive process that requires proximal goal setting, intricate planning, and close self-monitoring. It is left up to the teacher to figure out the best practices to help young developing learners strategically approach writing tasks so they can track their performance. Young students who have not fully developed their self-regulatory skills might have difficulty activating behaviors to self-regulate. Although second and third graders have foundational academic skills, they are still new to demands encountered in academic settings (Dermitzaki & Kiosseoglou, 2004).

Critical to developing self-regulatory learning at the second- and third-grade level is the presence of both competent and peer models. Peer modeling is one way to increase the likelihood that young learners will pay attention to the model and maintain the level of self-efficacy required to self-regulate during challenging, but not too difficult, grade-level tasks. In addition, providing students with a representation of a completed assigned task can raise self-efficacy and increase motivation.

Self-regulation has subprocesses that can help focus young students on themselves, almost like taking a "selfie" of one's thoughts, feelings, and actions while attaining a self-set goal. Self-observation (what am I doing?), self-judgment (how did I do?), and self-reaction (what did I do?) interact to inform the learner about his performance when compared to the performance of the model (or standard). Both self-observation and self-judgment provide information to the learner regarding how he is progressing towards a goal (Schunk, 2001); however, most critical to these subprocesses is that young learners know how to set and commit to goals.

The challenge when working with young learners to set goals and monitor their progress according to the Common Core is significant. Without a goal, a plan cannot be formulated, and without a plan, a goal cannot be attained. Standards can inform and motivate (Schunk, 2001) when one is able to determine progress in reaching it. Students need to be instructed in setting realistic, attainable, and proximal goals so they can monitor their performance against the standard or expected outcome.

## *Goal Setting and Self-Efficacy*

Goal setting is an important motivational process that can lead to increased self-efficacy (Bandura, 1988, 1997; Schunk, 1989; Zimmerman, Bonner, & Kovach, 1996).

- Successful learners set goals that guide planning and performance of a given task.
- Teachers, educators, and parents who recognize the importance of helping young learners set effective goals will observe an increase in goal attainment for even the youngest learners.
- When both teachers and students monitor progress towards goal attainment, students are able to see progress that is made and make decisions about future task-related actions.

- Goal setting also provides a standard for students to emulate. In research and practice, goal setting has been shown to be an influential and valuable means for improving performance.

## *Goal Properties*

Just having goals will not benefit a student's academic performance Schunk (2001). Bandura (1986) and Locke and Latham (1990) have identified various goal properties and have investigated how different goals link with achievement outcomes. For goal setting to be effective, students must be able to recognize the properties of effective goals:

- **Specific**—Goals should be well defined, providing the student with a clear and detailed understanding of what is expected, making it easier for them to compare their performance with a standard and monitor their progress.
- **Difficulty Level**—Goals are set for individuals, not entire classes or groups. How challenging the goal is for the individual will determine whether or not the goal is worth the effort required to reach it.
  - Levels of difficulty should be determined so that the student has to put forth effort and utilize resources, and can measure progress towards attainment.
  - Goal achievement with little or no effort does not increase a student's motivation; however, setting goals that are too difficult can overwhelm students.
- **Proximal**—Proximal goals must be realistic and attainable in the foreseeable future. For a second and third grader, the time between goal setting and goal attainment would be short. Distal goals are a series of proximal goals that will be attained over a longer period. Proximal goals are more immediately attainable and satisfying.

Goal setting and strategic planning occur when students can analyze a learning task, set specific learning goals, and plan or refine the strategy to attain that goal.

- Learners often find themselves engaged in unfamiliar learning tasks with limited ability to break down the task into manageable components. They fail to set specific goals or develop an effective learning strategy.
- Learners' attachment to setting goals can be noted by their enthusiasm and their determination to achieve it (Pintrich & Schunk, 2002, p. 166).
- Teachers can instruct students how to analyze tasks, set effective goals, and make the correct strategy choice (Zimmerman, Bonner, & Kovach, 1996).
- Task conditions that give the learner choices increase the likelihood of task engagement, motivation, and self-regulated learning behaviors.
- Task conditions that provide the learner a model (in the form of a completed successful task) are critical to helping the learner set goals.

## Shifting to Be College Ready

**TABLE 5.2** Writing From Sources

*Writing from sources: Emphasizes use of evidence from sources to inform or make an argument.*

| Self-regulation strategy | Set goals, plan, self-monitor |
| --- | --- |
| Literacy skills | Develop and strengthen writing as needed by planning, revising, editing, rewriting, or trying a new approach (CCSS.ELA-Literacy.CCRA.W.5) |
| Key ideas and details | Ask and answer questions to demonstrate understanding of a text, referring explicitly to the text as the basis for the answers (CCSS.ELA-Literacy.RL.3.1) |

## It's a Shift, Not a Tug of War!

### Shifting Second and Third Graders to Write From Sources

The writing anchor standards involve more than developing and strengthening writing—they represent a significant shift in the emphasis being placed on writing. Practice and instruction in three types of writing—opinion, informational, and narrative—begin in kindergarten and increase in complexity at each grade level.

- Reading and writing grounded in evidence from text is one of the instructional shifts required by the Common Core.
- Writing from sources begins with instruction in the primary grades in all of the skills that are considered essential for high school students to be able to write successfully (Allyn, 2013; Calkins, Ehrenworth, & Lehman, 2012).
- Writing has a purpose, and teaching young learners to identify that purpose is a significant part of writing instruction.
- Second and third graders are transitioning from the *"What do I do?"* to the *"Why am I doing this?"* question. Often, these novice writers lose track of both the "what" and the "why" of a given task if they are not taught how to monitor the way they approach and carry out their intentions.
- **Example:** One can begin to write a short informative paragraph citing evidence from passages about a whale swimming with a dolphin and end the piece with a creative sentence retrieved from prior knowledge expressing how much fun it would be to swim with whales if you were a mermaid. Although this personalized and creative leap previously would have been applauded in writing classes across elementary grades, it is now evidence of how easily students can lose track of the purpose of the paragraph—that being to convey information using facts found in the article (*writing from sources*), not integrating personal feelings recalled from reading about a mermaid's adventure.

## Informational Writing

- Writing from sources for second and third graders includes explaining illustrations and noting themes and key ideas from the text, but it does not include contributions from creative brainstorming.
- Information is found in the text itself.
- Writing informative/explanatory texts *to examine a topic and convey ideas and information clearly* (CCSS.ELA-Literacy.W.4.2, 5.2) emphasizes the ability to use evidence from the text to accurately convey information.
- Students are asked to synthesize information, report information, and persuade others to their line of thinking in writing while making use of source materials (Allyn, 2013).
- Young learners, who are trained to focus on getting their information from a specified source and not include their imaginary thoughts, will be able to write from a source without too much difficulty.

## Before Writing . . . Plan, Set Goals, Gather Evidence, Write!

Modeling and remodeling are essential when teaching young students how to plan and self-monitor writing tasks. Students observe the thinking processes that guide a good writer through planning and writing. Throughout the self-regulatory phases of the writing task, the teacher helps students monitor their self-efficacy and behaviors that will lead to productive writing sessions. The following elements are essential to planning a series of lessons for second and third graders in self-regulation.

## Self-Regulatory Learning Strategies

### Goal Setting

"I Can" statements are one way of stating Common Core goals and an excellent way for young learners to become acquainted with setting goals for a specific assignment. Instead of setting goals as learning objectives, students become empowered through goal setting, beginning each goal with "I Can" rather than "I Will."

### Self-Efficacy

The teacher's monitoring of self-efficacy ratings throughout the process provides a valuable formative assessment and important insights into a student's level of competence for a specific part of the task.

### Task Analysis

Breaking a task into component parts to facilitate its learning makes it easier for both teacher and students to set goals and monitor performance.

## Planning

Strategic planning requires proximal, not distant, goals. Young learners are more likely to design and follow an action plan that has real observable consequences as a result of their actions.

## Self-Monitoring

Systematic and deliberate observation of specific aspects of one's self-regulatory progress helps young students monitor progress towards goal attainment and evaluate self-efficacy. This can be done using the information map described next.

## Information Map

The information map has two sections, A and B. Section A is used for goal setting, rating self-efficacy throughout the phases and levels of the task development. Section B is a graphic organizer used to assist students with planning as

**TABLE 5.3** Information Map: Includes All Phases Self-Efficacy/"I Can" Checklist

| Part A. Follow your teacher's instructions to fill in the blanks at different checkpoints in our Writing from Sources task. We will read the goals together, and afterwards you will rate how strongly you feel about reaching each goal. |
|---|
| Choose one of the following numbers to score yourself! |
| 1 = "I can't do this!" |
| 2 = "I am not sure if I can do this!" |
| 3 = "I can do this!" |

| Short-term goals | I can... | A<br>Forethought phase<br>Self-efficacy | B<br>Performance phase<br>Self-efficacy | C<br>Self-reflection phase<br>Self-efficacy |
|---|---|---|---|---|
| 1 | Read and comprehend passage A. | | | |
| 2 | Read and comprehend passage B. | | | |
| 3 | Gather evidence from passage A. | | | |
| 4 | Gather evidence from passage B. | | | |
| | Long-term goals | | | |
| 5 | Write a sentence using evidence from passage A. | | | |
| 6 | Write a sentence using evidence from passage B. | | | |
| 7 | Write a short paragraph with evidence from passage A and B. | | | |
| | Self-monitoring goal | | | |
| 8 | Monitor myself by comparing my work to each of the previous goals. | | | |

*(Continued)*

| Part B: Information map/graphic organizer |  |
| --- | --- |
| Name _____ | |
| **My plan** ||
| Purpose: What am I doing? ||
| How: What strategies am I using to get to my goals? ||
| Source A | Source B |
| Fact 1 | Fact 1 |
| From Passage A? | From Passage B? |
| Fact 2 | Fact 2 |
| From Passage A? | From Passage B? |
| Fact 3 | Fact 3 |
| From Passage A? | From Passage B? |
| **Writing** ||
| Sentence | Sentence |
| From Passage A? | From Passage B? |
| **Paragraph** ||
| From A and B? ||

part of the prewriting process and serves as a self-monitoring tool. Students are given a simple sequential process for reaching their goals to complete the writing task successfully by using the map as a guide.

## Prior Knowledge and Lesson Requirements

- Text selected is appropriate to students' reading levels and is not too challenging so that the content can be easily comprehended.
- Students have experience in reading informational text.
- Students have been exposed to writing from sources, specifically informational text.
- Students have been exposed to close reading.

## Standardized Test Relevance

- This lesson plan provides early and consistent preparation for second and third graders preparing for the third-grade ELA testing. The self-regulation training should help young learners self-regulate as they prepare for challenging standardized tests that measure third-grade proficiency in writing from sources. In this task, students will be asked to focus on the evidence needed to support an analysis of an informational topic presented through two passages (or multimedia stimuli if available) for third graders, and one passage for second graders.
- State-generated end-of-year assessments for all third graders ask students to demonstrate their ability to read and comprehend complex informational and literary texts.
- Third graders are required to read passages from two narrative informational texts and respond to questions sequenced in a way that they will draw students into deeper encounters with the texts and will result in more thorough comprehension of the concepts.

## Materials:

- Short, informational passages on specific topics; these passages are written on a large surface and projected using an overhead projector, a whiteboard, or interactive whiteboard. The teacher will have passages varying in text difficulty: easy, moderately easy, and challenging.
    - For example, a passage about two endangered species, the whale and bald eagle, can provide second and third graders with interesting informative texts from which they can easily obtain facts. Or, passages about historical figures who lived a long time ago can also provide easily available factual information.
- Pencils/markers/writing tools
- Individual reading passages (copies of what the teacher uses)
- Student worksheet for observation level only
    - "Teacher Can" Checklist (see Table 5.4). At the observation level, students are asked to rate their teacher's self-efficacy and goal progress following each phase. Students observe the teacher modeling how he used Part A of the Information Map to track goal progress and rate self-efficacy, and Part B, the graphic organizer, to plan and do the writing task. Throughout their observations, they enter the data into their worksheets.
    - *Emulation, self-control levels (forethought/performance/self-reflection)*
        - Information map for students (see Table 5.4). Directions at various checkpoints throughout the lesson.
        - Self-efficacy ratings for "I Can" goals (Part A)
        - Graphic organizer (Part B).

## The Plan: Writing From Sources

### Using Self-Regulation to Write From Informational Passages

**Objective:** Students will use the self-regulatory strategies of goal setting, planning, and self-monitoring to track their performance when asked to write

**76**  Elementary School

**TABLE 5.4** "Teacher Can" Checklist

| Goals | Making Predictions<br>This is what *I think* . . . My teacher can . . . | |
|---|---|---|
| | Teacher self-efficacy: My teacher can . . . | |
| | Choose one of the following numbers to score your teacher:<br>1 = My teacher can't do this.<br>2 = I'm not sure my teacher can do this.<br>3 = My teacher can do this! | |
| | **My teacher can. . .** | **Score** |
| 1 | Read and comprehend passage A. | |
| 2 | Read and comprehend passage B. | |
| 3 | Gather evidence from passage A. | |
| 4 | Gather evidence from passage B. | |
| 5 | Write a sentence using evidence from passage A. | |
| 6 | Write a sentence using evidence from passage B. | |
| 7 | Write a short paragraph with evidence from passages A and B. | |
| 8 | Monitor his (her) self by comparing his (her) work to each of the previous goals. | |

informative and explanatory texts based on evidence from one (second grade) or two (third grade) specific sources.

**Sessions:** Although several sessions are suggested for this activity, teachers will need to use their discretion regarding the prior knowledge required to do this task successfully and pace the lessons according to students' needs. Before students begin observing how to write from informational sources, the teacher should assess the students' understanding of what it means to set goals and to make plans to reach goals. Time spent reviewing the different types of goals and their difficulty levels may help students move through the four levels more easily and will lead to success. For example, an easy-to-reach, proximal (short-term) goal may be to read the first paragraph of a difficult passage followed by writing a brief summary sentence using your own words. A more challenging, distal (long-term) goal would be to write a paragraph describing the information passage for the school newspaper.

## Observation Level

## Watch It!

### Sessions 1–12

**Observation:** The teacher uses think-alouds (verbal modeling) and a graphic organizer, making his thought processes transparent as the teacher discusses self-efficacy for the task, setting goals, designing a plan of action (action plan), and self-monitoring progress. The teacher is constantly comparing his work with the targeted goals, making sure not to divert from the plan to reach the goals. The teacher will also demonstrate how to "cope" with challenges that may interfere with the plans to reach the writing goals. Students are observing the teacher who is demonstrating each of the processes used. Students are actively engaged as they fill out logs based on their observations.

## Observation of Forethought

### Planning

### *A Strategic Approach to Writing From an Informational Text*

### Sessions 1–4

**Forethought:** This phase involves setting goals and closely monitoring the plan to reach those goals. For young learners, this phase represents a time when motivational beliefs such as self-efficacy and strategic planning are developing. At this level, students observe the teacher as he prepares to do a writing activity using evidence from an informational passage. The information map (Table 5.3) is actually a self-monitoring log and consists of "I Can" statements (Part A) and a graphic organizer (Part B). As the teacher follows the sequential guidelines of the information map, the students are instructed to follow along and to complete their checklists exactly as the teacher is modeling.

- The teacher uses the "I Can" portion of the log to set short- and long-term goals and rate his self-efficacy to complete the writing task successfully.
- The teacher uses planning strategies to create an action plan for writing. The action plan is a sequence of closely monitored behaviors aligned with the requirements of the writing task. The writing task requires the students to read two passages and to write a short paragraph responding to writing prompts, following sequential steps. During the forethought phase, the teacher completes the self-efficacy/"I Can" checklist portion of the information map (Part A) as students read along and enter the same information into their copies of the checklist.

### *Modeling: What Is the Teacher Doing?*

The teacher models how to analyze the writing task by thinking aloud and providing details of the task requirements. He continues to think aloud as he discusses what self-efficacy is and why it is important to know your strengths and weaknesses when getting ready to begin a new writing task. The teacher uses "I Can" statements to set goals, and shares his plan for reaching these goals.

He reads aloud the task requirements and breaks them down into sequential steps. He then describes what he will be doing as he prepares to do the task.

Teacher: "*I will read passages about two people who lived a long time ago. In order to do this task correctly, I need*:

- *to read and understand the passages,*
- *to gather information (evidence) from the passage,*
- *to write sentences that can be used to construct a short paragraph for my school newspaper to teach others how these two people made a difference in America.*"

Thinking aloud, the teacher calls the students' attention to the information map (Forethought column) and explains how it can be used as a guide for task preparation.

- The teacher states the purpose for this activity by emphasizing the goal is to "write from sources," which means to gather information only from the passage, not from any other source, even though it might help with the assignment.
- The teacher begins and completes his preparation by reading each passage aloud and working through each step of the information map while the students observe and replicate exactly what they observe the teacher do.

## What Is Self-Efficacy?

The teacher describes examples of how self-efficacy applies to writing tasks. The teacher explains that together they will focus on the section of the information map that includes goals and self-efficacy for reaching his goals. His self-efficacy to read two informational passages and respond to writing prompts might be higher if he had read the passages before. Research shows that self-efficacy must be closely tied to specific tasks in order to predict performance. Therefore, the rating and completion of self-efficacy is described in further detail next.

- Thinking aloud, the teacher assesses his self-efficacy to read and write based on passage complexity and the requirements of the writing task. The following are examples of things the teacher may say as he explains self-efficacy to young learners who might not yet be familiar with the term, but can identify the feelings. The teacher shares what he is thinking regarding how confident he feels about completing the tasks.
    - "*I can do a close reading of this passage! It is at my independent reading level and I am familiar with the content.*"
    - "*I don't think I can write about these passages. Even if I can read them, how can I even begin to answer the writing prompt? There is too much information. I need a way to organize this writing task.*"

- The teacher introduces the students to the information map and the "I Can" statements.
- Thinking aloud, the teacher reviews the "I Can" statements, emphasizing what he can do (strengths) and what potential challenges may occur (weaknesses).
- The teacher demonstrates how to complete the self-efficacy ratings based on his own thoughts and feelings of competence as they relate to specific goals and plans described next. Following the teacher's instructions, the students closely listen to his responses to the "I Can" statements/goals and then copy the teacher's ratings onto their own information maps (Part A).

## *What Are Goal Setting and Task Analysis?*

The teacher thinks aloud while analyzing the task in order to demonstrate how to set goals that align task requirements and the Common Core standards.

- The teacher calls the students' attention to the forethought phase (Table 5.3, Column A) information map that contains a checklist of the task requirements in the form of "I Can" statements, making the goals easier to understand.
- The teacher reads and explains how to use each "I Can" statement as short- and long-term goals, and rates his own self-efficacy to reach the set goals.
- Personalizing short-term goals turns learners into "owners" of the goals rather than passive bystanders. "I Can" statements have become tools teachers use in their planning to help students track their progress and understand expectations.

## *What Is Strategic Planning?*

The teacher thinks aloud while describing how the information map can actually serve as a planning tool by outlining the strategies that need to be used.

- The teacher identifies specific components of the information map (Part B) that will guide him through each step of the writing task preparation, such as gathering facts and examples, and drafting sentences, followed by a short paragraph. The teacher does not fill in any part of his information map, but he describes each item as a strategy for reaching the set goals.

## *What Is Self-Monitoring?*

The teacher models how to complete the section of the information map (Table 5.3, Part A) that tracks self-efficacy and guides the writing-from-sources task for the forethought phase. "I Can" goal 8 is a measurement of one's ability to compare what they are doing with what they are supposed to be doing. "*Am*

*I using the evidence from the text or my imagination?"* would be a good self-monitoring question while working on the writing-from-sources task.

## Post-Observation of Forethought

### Predict: Do You Think Your Teacher Can Do It?

After observing the teacher's think-alouds and accompanying actions, each student receives a "My Teacher Can" rating sheet (Table 5.3) and predicts the teacher's ability to accomplish each goal based on their observations.

**Teacher:** Poses questions to the students, identifying and pointing to the components of the writing task as listed on the "I Can" checklist and asks them to predict if the teacher will be able to meet the set goals.

**Students:** Using a number from 1–3, students predict their teacher's performance based on their observations of the teacher's modeling.

## Observation of Performance

### A Strategic Approach to Writing from Sources

#### Sessions 5–8

**Performance:** The teacher thinks aloud while doing a close reading of two short passages. Students observe the teacher as he works through the "I Can" statements as short- and long-term goals for completing the writing task successfully. The teacher then demonstrates how to use the information map as a guide, and models how it can also be used as a self-monitoring tool. The students are actively engaged as they observe and work along with the teacher, completing each section of the information map along with the teacher. The teacher fills out both Parts A and B during the performance phase (see Table 5.3).

### *Modeling: How Am I Doing?*

Teacher models how Part A, the "I Can" statements (goals), and Part B of the information map (Table 5.3) can be used to keep him on task. Thinking aloud, the teacher demonstrates for students what to do if the passages are too difficult. For example, it may be challenging to write from sources when the passages are filled with facts and unfamiliar vocabulary. The teacher may model asking for a less complex passage to work with, how to review vocabulary ahead of time, or how to paraphrase difficult sections for better comprehension.

### Aligning Self-Efficacy and Goal Attainment

The teacher explains that now that the writing process has begun, self-efficacy will be rated again to see if there are any changes in his feelings about his capability to complete the task successfully. The teacher tells the students to follow along as he rates self-efficacy and instructs students to complete their copies of Part A, Column B in the information map. Students are instructed to observe the teacher carefully, copying the teacher's self-efficacy ratings.

The teacher reads through both passages displayed on a large sheet of paper (interactive whiteboard or overhead projector), thinking aloud about whether or not the passages are easy to read and comprehend. Checking off the first two short-term goals on the displayed "I Can" checklist (Goals 1 and 2), the teacher emphasizes again the importance of being able to read and comprehend the passages as a critical step towards being able to write about the passages.

The teacher thinks aloud about his self-efficacy: *"Did I rate my self-efficacy accurately or did I underestimate (or overestimate) how difficult I would find this task?"* The teacher uses this method of thinking aloud to help students understand how one's feelings of capability may change when actually working on an academic task as opposed to planning to work on one. The teacher reminds students of the possible choices of strategies if the passages are too difficult to read through alone.

### Aligning Goal Progress and Task Performance

As the teacher begins the task, he thinks aloud (pointing to the information map) and identifies the sections that can help him monitor how close he came to reaching his goals. The teacher reads aloud the short-term goals (Goals 3 and 4), followed by the remaining long-term goals, describing what he will do in order to accomplish each one. Students focus on their copies of the information map and fill in the blank sections as instructed by their teacher. Statements such as the following guide his progress as the teacher asks and answers his own questions:

- *"What is my purpose? To write from sources by setting goals, gathering information, and writing."*
- *"What are my goals? To...*
  - *Gather evidence from passages (Goals 3 and 4),*
  - *Use evidence from passages to write a sentence (Goals 5 and 6),*
  - *Write a short paragraph (four sentences) using evidence from passages (Goal 7)."*

- The teacher restates the requirements of the writing task and thinks aloud as he describes how to follow the action plan using the information map as a guide. For example, in using passages focused on the lives of two people who have contributed significantly in history, the teacher thinks:
  - *"I am going to use the information map to organize the information I need to write about these two people who lived a long time ago. The facts and examples will be included in an article written for my school newspaper to teach others how these two people made a difference in America."*
  - *"Writing an article for a school newspaper requires informational writing, and the facts are from the reading passages."*
  - *"My goals indicate that I am ready to gather the evidence from the passages."*

### Following the Plan: Using Task Strategies

- Thinking aloud, the teacher focuses students' attention now on the information map. The teacher thinks aloud about the first section, which requires him to:
- Identify the purpose! *"The purpose of this task is to write a newspaper article using informational passages about the contributions of two great Americans."*
- Identify the how! *"I am gathering and using evidence from passages to write sentences and a paragraph using strategies."*

The teacher answers these two questions and instructs students to copy the same responses onto their information maps.

- Thinking aloud, the teacher continues to focus students' attention on displayed reading passages. The teacher selects one passage at a time, reads the passage aloud, and asks the students to read along.
- After the teacher reads the passage once, he stops and rereads, looking for one key fact from the passage, and writes a sentence that includes one fact. The teacher thinks aloud, explaining why this particular fact was selected as important evidence to be used for informational writing. He repeats these actions for the second passage, inviting students to read along with him.
- The teacher summarizes what he has done so far:
  - *Goals 1 and 2: I can find evidence in passages.*
    - **Find the facts:** Students are engaged in observing how the teacher finds and lists the facts. In a read- and think-aloud, the teacher models how to read a passage and remove a fact, adding it to the information map for *Facts*.

- - *Goals 3 and 4: I can use evidence found in passages.*
    - **Evaluate the facts:** The teacher thinks aloud while comparing the facts entered into the performance phase of the information map with the facts in the reading passages, ascertaining whether facts were accurately copied from the passages.
  - *Goals 5 and 6: I can write a sentence using evidence from passages.*
    - **Write the sentence:** The teacher models how to use the facts from each source to write a sentence about each individual.
  - *Goal 7: I can write a short paragraph using evidence from passages.*
    - **Write a paragraph:** The teacher models how to use the facts and examples from each source to write a short paragraph including both individuals.
- Students are instructed to copy exactly what the teacher has written on their information maps.

## *Self-Monitoring*

- The teacher explains how he checks to see if the statements gathered from the sources are facts from the passages and not from his imagination. Students copy the teacher's rating of Goal 8, gaining a better understanding of self-monitoring and how to use Column B of the information map to track goal progress.

*Note:* The teacher has now completed all but one section of the information map, Parts A and B (Table 5.3). The "I Can" checklist is displayed with the completed graphic organizer so students can observe the teacher comparing the completed task with the goals set during the forethought phase. The students will again rate their teacher's performance and check to see if their predictions were correct. The interaction engages them in the process, and rather than being passive observers, they are participants.

## Post-Observation of Performance

### Evaluate: Do You Think Your Teacher Did It?

**Teacher:** Poses questions to the students about the task requirements as listed on the "I Can" checklist and asks them to rate his performance as he attempted to reach these goals.

**Students:** Each student has a "Teacher Did" rating sheet (see Table 5.5). Using a number from 1–3, students assess their teacher's strategy use based on the progress made towards set goals.

## Doing the Work

This is what *I think* . . . My teacher did . . .

**TABLE 5.5** What My Teacher Did . . . Reflection

|  | Self-efficacy: My teacher did . . . |  |
|---|---|---|
| Goals | Use one of the following numbers to score your teacher:<br>1 = My teacher didn't do this.<br>2 = I'm not sure my teacher did this.<br>3 = My teacher did this! |  |
|  |  | Score |
| 1 | My teacher read and comprehended passage A. |  |
| 2 | My teacher read and comprehended passage B. |  |
| 3 | My teacher gathered evidence from passage A. |  |
| 4 | My teacher gathered evidence from passage B. |  |
| 5 | My teacher wrote a sentence using evidence from passage A. |  |
| 6 | My teacher wrote a sentence using evidence from passage B. |  |
| 7 | My teacher wrote a short paragraph with evidence from passages A and B. |  |
| 8 | My teacher monitored his (her) self by comparing his (her) work to each of the previous goals. |  |

# Observation of Self-Reflection

## Reflecting On

### *A Strategic Approach to Writing from an Informational Text*

### Sessions 9–12

**Self-reflection:** Students observe the teacher transparently share his thoughts about his performance, indicating whether or not the information map (Parts A and B) helped with planning, goal setting, and strategy use. The teacher also solicits feedback from the students as he evaluates both the process and results of writing a short paragraph from text. He also expresses his satisfaction with his work, attributing his success to the self-monitoring tools.

### *Modeling: How Did I Do?*

The teacher thinks aloud, reflecting on the process of using "I Can" statements to set goals and using the information map to plan, organize, and self-monitor an informational writing task.

## Partnering Self-Efficacy and Goal Attainment

The teacher thinks aloud, reviewing the task requirements and performance using the "I Can" statements as a guide, changing the first two words to "Did I." The teacher shares strengths and weaknesses while rating his satisfaction with his performance. Students are instructed to copy the teacher's scores and comments on their self-reflection worksheets (see Table 5.6).

**TABLE 5.6** Self-Reflection

| Self-reflection ||||
|---|---|---|---|
| Choose one of the following numbers to score how well you reached your goals: <br> 1 = "I did it!" <br> 2 = "I'm not sure I did this right." <br> 3 = "I did not do this!" ||| Self-reflect and evaluate the strategies used to reach your goals by giving each one a score. <br> 1 = NOT helpful <br> 2 = OK <br> 3 = VERY helpful |
| **I did** | **Short term** | **Score** | **Score** |
| 1 | I did read and comprehend passage A. | | |
| 2 | I did read and comprehend passage B. | | |
| 3 | I did gather evidence from passage A. | | |
| 4 | I did use evidence from passage B. | | |
| | **Long term** | | |
| 5 | I did write a sentence using evidence from passage A. | | |
| 6 | I did write a short paragraph using evidence from passage B. | | |
| 7 | I did self-monitor my actions by comparing my work to the goals set for this task. | | |
| | **Self-monitoring** | | |
| 8 | I did monitor myself by comparing my work to each of the previous goals. | | |
| **What can I do better next time? Changes in goals and strategies suggested by peers or teacher.** ||||

## Linking Goal Attainment, Planning, and Self-Monitoring

The teacher describes how easy it was to follow the sequential steps outlined in the information map. By closely following the process and not diverting from it, he was able to focus on his goals and the plan to reach them. The teacher also emphasizes how using the information map helped him organize and structure the reading and writing task, in addition to providing a way to self-monitor his efforts to gather and use only the information from the text.

## Evaluating the Plan

The teacher thinks aloud as he reflects on his plan and his evaluations of his self-efficacy and the final outcome. The teacher asks, *"Was I able to reach my goals? Did using a graphic organizer help me reach my goals?"*

- The teacher models by thinking aloud on the ways in which the sections of the information map were helpful. He thinks aloud about ways performance could be improved on similar tasks in the future by asking, *"What can I do better next time?"*
- Upon completion of the information map (Parts A and B), the teacher will make sure each student has a copy of the self-efficacy/"I Can" checklists.
- Students are instructed to make sure they have entered the self-efficacy ratings into the Forethought, Performance, and Self-Reflection columns.
- After thinking aloud, the teacher asks the class for feedback about the task.

## Post-Observation of Self-Reflection

### Predict: Do You Think You Are Ready to Try This on Your Own with Help?

A post-observation student self-efficacy evaluation can help determine which students are ready to move on to the emulation level, where they will be asked to imitate the behaviors they observed. The teacher will ask students to rate their own self-efficacy by filling in the blank sections of the "I Can" statements on the information map for all three phases. The teacher will pace the learning by deciding which students are ready to move ahead, and which need to observe the process again before moving to the next more independent level of learning.

## Emulation Level

### Let's See What We Can Do Together!

#### Sessions 13–24

**Emulation:** The teacher guides students through tasks that require individual learners to emulate how to set goals, plan, and self-monitor their actions to complete a writing task based on information gathered from specific reading passages. Under close teacher supervision, students will use the information map as they had observed the teacher do in previous sessions to gather sources from an informational text to be used in a writing task. Students at this level are not yet working independently. They are following the observed teacher's patterns as closely as possible. The teacher remains close by as the students work, scaffolding and providing extensive feedback to students, remodeling as needed.

**Materials.** *See Materials Master List*

## Emulation of Forethought

### Planning

### *A Strategic Approach to Writing From an Informational Text*

### *Sessions 13–16*

**Forethought:** Students attempt to imitate their teacher's actions and behaviors seen during the observation level as the teacher prepared to do a writing activity using evidence from specific informational passages. Students are provided with information maps and told that they will be working on a similar task: reading two passages and selecting facts and evidence to be used to ultimately write an informational paragraph. The teacher reminds students that planning involves rating one's self-efficacy in addition to setting goals and choosing strategies for reaching the goals. As they continue to advance to more independent learning experiences, students are to keep the teacher's modeling in mind as they attempt to use the information maps the way he did.

- The teacher begins by placing students in small groups of about three to four students to work together.
- The teacher reminds the students to begin reading the "I Can" statements and rate their self-efficacy to complete the writing task by attaining set goals.
- Students are then instructed to work together to design a plan of action using the information map.

### *Modeling: What Should We Do Together?*

The teacher focuses students on the task requirements and asks them to follow along:

> *"We will read passages about two people who lived a long time ago. In order to do this task correctly, we need to read and understand the passages, gather information (evidence) from the text (passages), and write sentences that can be used to construct a short paragraph for a school newspaper to teach others how these two people made a difference in America."*

The teacher instructs students to imitate as closely as possible what they observed their teacher do in the previous sessions as they set goals and develop a plan.

## Thinking About Self-Efficacy and Task Requirements

- The teacher and students together do a close reading of the two short passages. This time, the teacher reads from his own text rather than from the interactive whiteboard or an overhead. The students follow along on corresponding individual printouts of the same passages, making annotations similar to what they observed the teacher do during the observation level.
- Following the read aloud, the teacher asks students to think aloud as they evaluate the complexity of the passages and their self-efficacy to read and comprehend the passages (Goals 1 and 2) well enough to complete the writing task.
- While students should continue to keep the teacher's demonstrations of rating self-efficacy in mind, they should be rating self-efficacy based on their own feelings about reaching the goals. The teacher guides group discussions so they include similar statements from the think-alouds the teacher modeled during the observational level.
- Self-efficacy ratings can help teachers determine which students will require more assistance than others and gives teachers an opportunity to provide scaffolding and feedback to students as they determine their own self-efficacy.

## Thinking About Goal Setting and Task Analysis

- Students are instructed to verbalize how the information from the task requirements and the "I Can" statements are used to set short- and long-term attainable goals (Goals 3–7) for the writing task.
- The teacher reminds students that they need to use the information map (Part A, Column A) and pay close attention to how they evaluate their feelings of competency to attain the remaining goals in the form of the "I Can" statements. He clearly links their self-efficacy to goal attainment. Students are encouraged to discuss their feelings about attaining these goals with their group members as they complete the checklist.

## Strategic Planning

- The teacher reminds students to focus on both parts of the information map (A and B) as they make plans to write.
- The teacher focuses students' attention on their individual copies of the information map, asking them to discuss in their groups the various strategies and whether or not the map provides an adequate plan of action.

## Self-Monitoring

- Together, teachers and students discuss each element of the information map. The teacher encourages each student to become more familiar with tracking their progress when gathering information from specific sources by using the map during each step.

- Students think aloud while completing the self-monitoring of strategic planning (Goal 8).
- The teacher provides constant feedback while students design an action plan.

## Predict: Do You Think You Can Do It?

### Post-Emulation Forethought

After working with the teacher to prepare for the writing task, students are given time to review their "I Can" checklists with goals and self-efficacy ratings in order to receive teacher feedback regarding their readiness to move on to the performance phase.

**Teacher:** Individually reviews self-efficacy ratings and "I Can" statements to determine which students are ready to move ahead to the performance phase and which students require remodeling of specific sections, less complex texts, and the support provided at the emulation level.

**Students:** With the teacher's assistance, students work to complete the "I Can" checklist with goals and self-efficacy ratings, making adjustments to their self-evaluation of their abilities to complete the writing task. The self-efficacy ratings should reveal the level of competency each student feels about approaching the task.

## Emulation of Performance

### Practicing
### A Strategic Approach to Writing From an Informational Text

#### Sessions 17–20

**Performance:** Students attempt to become better acquainted with the action plan by imitating the behaviors they observed their teacher perform. The teacher gives students the opportunity to work together as they proceed through each section of the information map. Students use feedback from the teacher and peers to self-monitor their performance. At the emulation level, students are attempting to replicate exactly what they observed the teacher do during the observation level. The teacher remains close by to provide frequent and constant feedback. The pacing of the learning environment remains in the teacher's charge during this level.

### *Modeling: How Am I Doing?*

- The teacher reminds students that the "I Can" goals and writing strategies can be used to help them stay on task. Students work in groups, reading their individual passages, thinking aloud, and completing the information map.

## *Aligning Self-Efficacy and Goal Attainment*

- Students closely read through both passages on their own and rate their self-efficacy (Goals 1 and 2). If the passages are too difficult, students are asked to discuss with their group members strategies for resolving this issue, such as reciprocal teaching among each other, selecting a different passage, looking up vocabulary words, etc.
- The teacher is closely monitoring students' readings and discussions as they replicate what they saw the teacher do during the observation level.

## *Aligning Goal Progress and Task Performance*

- The teacher directs the students to use the information map (displayed on the board and individually distributed) and guides them in discussing how each section (Goals, Gather, Write) can be useful to monitor goal progress as they begin to fill in the blanks with the information they have so far.
- The teacher and students discuss the components of the information map, referring to the sections that state the purpose and goals. The teacher reminds students to ask themselves the following questions just as the teacher had done during the observation level and to rate their response to the "I Can" statements:
  - *"What is my purpose? To write from sources by setting goals, gathering information, and writing."*
  - *"What are my goals? To. . .*
    - *Gather evidence from passages (Goals 3 and 4)*
    - *Use evidence from passages to write a sentence (Goals 5 and 6)*
    - *Write a short paragraph using evidence from passages (Goal 7)."*
- Together, the teacher and students reread the requirements of the writing task and design an action plan using the information map.
- Students respond to the following questions posed by the teacher, either individually or in small groups:
  - Teacher: *"How can we use the information map to help us organize the information needed to write about two people who lived a long time ago?"*
  - Students: Responses can vary as long as they follow the sequence indicated on the information map.
  - Teacher: *"Where can we find the facts and examples that can be included in the newspaper article we need to write so that others can learn about these two people who made a contribution to America?"*
  - Students: The students should respond that the information is gathered from the reading passages only (no outside sources).

## *Carrying Out the Plan: Using Task Strategies*

The students and teacher focus on the information map and fill in specific details to help complete the writing task. The teacher begins by directing the students to state in their own words how they interpret the purpose of the writing assignment. Students should state and enter the purpose of the task in the correct section of the information map.

- The purpose statements should reflect what the teacher modeled (and re-modeled) during the observation level. The teacher assists students to determine the purpose: to gather information only from the passages so that they are basing their writing on a "source," not their imagination.
- The teacher then directs the students to state in their own words how they interpret the goals for the writing assignment and how they would actually gather and use evidence from texts to write a sentence and then a paragraph.
- The students should gather facts and write a sentence that reflects what the teacher modeled during the observation level. The teacher assists students in focusing on the most important part of each goal—for example, making sure the evidence is from the informational text only.
- Students are encouraged to think aloud in their groups as they continue to work. The students select one passage at a time, read the passage, and make annotations as they observed their teacher do in previous sessions. The teacher continues to closely monitor what the students are doing and intervenes when a student needs assistance.
- As the teacher monitors the students rereading the passage, they are reminded to gather key facts, one at a time, and to write them down in the correct section of the information map. Following each fact, the students identify it as being from the text. For longer passages, they would add the page and section of the text where the fact was found. The students think aloud, explaining why this particular fact was selected. The students then turn to the second passage as the teacher closely monitors their fact gathering.

Together, the teacher and class summarize what they have done so far and identify which goals have been met.

## Goals 1 and 2: I Can Find Evidence in Passages

**Find the facts:** Students are engaged in searching through the text, thinking aloud as they select facts from the passage and add them to the information map. Students imitate the way their teacher modeled how to read a passage and add the facts to the information map.

## Goals 3 and 4: I Can Use Evidence Found in Passages

**Evaluate the facts:** Students compare the facts entered into the information map with facts from the passages. They discuss with the teacher and peers whether or not all of the information came from the passage.

## Goals 5 and 6: I Can Write a Sentence Using Evidence From Passages

**Write the sentence:** Students work with the teacher and their peers to compose one sentence using the facts from each source. The students copy the teacher's demonstration of how to use the facts from each source to write a sentence about each individual.

## Goal 7: I Can Write a Short Paragraph Using Evidence From Passages

**Write a paragraph:** The students copy the way the teacher used the facts and examples from each source to write a short paragraph (four sentences) including information about both individuals.

### Self-Monitoring

Students think aloud, discuss, and rate themselves on Goal 8 regarding self-monitoring. Their discussions are guided by the teacher and focus on determining if the sentences and paragraph use only facts from the sources.

## Post-Emulation of Performance

### How Did We Do?

Following a guided discussion on the value of writing goals in the form of "I Can" statements and using strategies to do a challenging writing task, the students discuss the use of the information map and whether they found it helpful or not. They have now completed Parts A and B of their own information maps and are ready to reflect on the process.

**Teacher:** Poses questions to the students to assess if individually or in small groups they were able to accomplish the short- and long-term goals.

**Students:** With assistance from the teacher, each student assesses the final product to determine if the assignment of writing a short paragraph on two famous Americans was achieved.

## Emulation of Self-Reflection

### Reflecting On

*A Strategic Approach to Writing From an Informational Text*

### Sessions 21–24

**Self-reflection:** Teachers and students work together to evaluate group and individual performances. Students are guided by the teacher to describe task-related experiences that led them to determine whether or not the information map was a good planning and goal-setting tool that helped students monitor goal progress and meet the requirements of the writing task.

### Modeling: Who Is Modeling?

The teacher encourages students to think aloud with him as they examine the outcome of the writing task and discuss the strengths and weaknesses of using the information map to guide their actions. Students think aloud as they individually reflect on the process of setting the "I Can" goals and using the information map as a planning tool to help engage in strategy use and self-monitoring skills during the writing task.

### Partnering Self-Efficacy With Goal Attainment

The teacher instructs students to think aloud, reviewing the task requirements and their performance using the "I Can" statements as a guide, changing the first two words to "Did I." The students share strengths and weaknesses while rating their performance, and the teacher guides students on filling out the Self-Reflection column.

### Linking Goal Attainment, Planning, and Self-Monitoring

The teacher and students discuss how the sequential processes in the information map help one to set goals and plans to reach the goals. The teacher also reemphasizes how using the information map helps organize and structure the work to be done in addition to providing a way to self-monitor one's progress towards the final goal.

**Evaluating the plan:** The teacher encourages students to think aloud, comparing their entries for Parts A and B of the information map, and focusing on their self-efficacy evaluations and the final outcome. Students are encouraged to share their ratings with each other regarding how they feel about the process of writing a paragraph using evidence from an informational text. Students are guided to pose questions such as: *"Was I able to reach my goals? Did the strategies help or hinder me in reaching my goals?"*

- Students think aloud, describing the ways in which the information map was helpful. The students are invited to contribute their ideas of what could be changed to improve their performance for similar tasks in the future.
- Students are reminded to fill in all sections of the information map (Part B, Column C) and the self-reflection checklist (Table 5.7), similar to the way the teacher modeled.

## Self-Reflection Checklist

TABLE 5.7 Self-Reflection Checklist: How Did I Do?

<table>
<tr><td colspan="5">How did I do? Self-reflection checklist.<br>
Column A: Choose the rating that best describes how you feel about reaching your goals and enter a score.<br>
Column B: Think about the strategies—were they helpful? Choose a number that describes how you feel and enter a score.</td></tr>
<tr><td colspan="4">A</td><td>B</td></tr>
<tr><td colspan="4">Choose one of the following numbers to score how well you reached your goals:<br>1 = "I did it!"<br>2 = "I'm not sure I did this right."<br>3 = "I did not do this!"</td><td>Self-reflect and evaluate the strategies used to reach your goals by giving each one a score.<br>1 = NOT helpful<br>2 = OK<br>3 = VERY helpful</td></tr>
<tr><td>I did</td><td colspan="2">Short term</td><td>Score</td><td>Score</td></tr>
<tr><td>1</td><td colspan="2">I did read and comprehend passage A.</td><td></td><td></td></tr>
<tr><td>2</td><td colspan="2">I did read and comprehend passage B.</td><td></td><td></td></tr>
<tr><td>3</td><td colspan="2">I did gather evidence from passage A.</td><td></td><td></td></tr>
<tr><td>4</td><td colspan="2">I did use evidence from passage B.</td><td></td><td></td></tr>
<tr><td colspan="5" align="center">Long term</td></tr>
<tr><td>5</td><td colspan="2">I did write a sentence using evidence from passage A.</td><td></td><td></td></tr>
<tr><td>6</td><td colspan="2">I did write a short paragraph using evidence from passage B.</td><td></td><td></td></tr>
<tr><td>7</td><td colspan="2">I did self-monitor my actions by comparing my work to the goals set for this task.</td><td></td><td></td></tr>
<tr><td colspan="5" align="center">Self-monitoring</td></tr>
<tr><td>8</td><td colspan="2">I did monitor myself by comparing my work to each of the previous goals.</td><td></td><td></td></tr>
<tr><td colspan="5">What can I do better next time? Changes in goals and strategies suggested by peers or teacher.</td></tr>
</table>

- Upon completion of the self-reflection checklist, the teacher will ask students to review Part A of the information map with their self-efficacy ratings for the Forethought, Performance, and Self-Reflection phases. The teacher calls their attention to ways in which their self-efficacy might have changed as they became more familiar with the process and the writing task requirements, or as the task became more challenging. Students should become increasingly aware of how self-efficacy often changes before, during, and after the completion of an academic task.

## Post-Emulation of Reflection

### What Have We Done So Far? How Did We Do It?

Following a thorough review of each of the information maps, both teacher and students discuss their satisfaction with their performance on the writing task.

**Teacher:** Poses questions to students to ascertain if they were satisfied with the process and the outcome of the writing task.

**Students:** With assistance from the teacher, each student selects one area that needs improvement. Each student assesses his ability to move forward towards independently completing a similar writing task. Both the information map (Parts A and B) and the self-reflection checklist can be used as formative assessments of readiness to move to the self-control level that requires more self-directed learning and less scaffolding from the teacher.

## Self-Control Level

### It's Your Turn

### *Sessions 25–36*

**Self-control:** At this level, the teacher gives students more freedom to work independently with less supervision. The teacher observes the students and remains available to them as they set goals, plan, and self-monitor their actions to complete a writing task using evidence only from the informational text. Once again, they will be writing a short paragraph based only on the information obtained from specific informational passages. Students will continue to work in groups and will use the information map with less guidance from the teacher. Students are expected to replicate what they observed and practiced in previous sessions, but with less teacher scaffolding.

## Self-Control of Forethought

### Planning
### My Strategic Approach to Writing From an Informational Text

### *(Sessions 25–28)*

**Forethought:** Students are introduced to two new informational passages and encouraged to work together (as needed) to analyze the task and design an action plan that incorporates the information map. Students at the self-control level will be working more independently than at previous levels, yet are aware that their teacher is available to respond to questions and provide guidance as needed.

## Modeling: Who Is Modeling?

The teacher encourages students to model for each other how to set goals and design an action plan on gathering evidence to use in a paragraph about the two new passages. The teacher remains available to provide support and feedback, and to re-model specific parts of the planning process when needed or to correct misconceptions about the process.

## Self-Efficacy and Task Requirements

The teacher directs students to discuss the requirements of the writing task and to pose questions for clarifications of any areas that are confusing. The teacher's goal is to have students work independently, but he is available to monitor their performance and clear up any misconceptions of the process.

- Students do a close reading of the task requirements and the two new short passages, making annotations where needed to make sure they comprehend the contents before beginning the writing task.
- Students think on and evaluate their self-efficacy to read the passages well enough to complete the writing task (Goals 1 and 2 on the information map).

## Goal Setting and Task Analysis

The teacher directs students to review the information map and pose questions to one another if they need assistance. The teacher also is available to answer questions or provide guidance.

- Students focus their attention on the task requirements and the information map.
- Students discuss their self-efficacy to complete the task successfully.
- Students discuss the importance of using the information map to guide the process towards completion of an article for publication in the school newspaper.
- Students identify the short- and long-term attainable goals in the information map and think about their self-efficacy to attain the remaining goals (Goals 3–7) prior to beginning the writing assignment.

## Strategic Planning

- The students work independently of the teacher, using the information map to guide their actions. They review the strategies for the writing task and discuss with each other how they will use the information map to complete the writing task.
- The teacher reminds the class to discuss in their small groups the purpose of the writing task and the goals, and to first pose questions to one another before they ask the teacher for help.

- Students are also reminded to make notations as they discuss the purpose, review goals, and design their action plan using the information map.

### Self-Monitoring

- The teacher directs students to make notes or add their own tracking reminders to take ownership of the information map and to use it as a personal tracking tool. Part A helps them track their goal progress, and Part B is their guide to writing a paragraph using only information from the text.
- The students work to become more familiar with each component of the information map and discuss where they will get the information to fill in the map during the performance phase.
- Students are reminded to rate Goal 8, which specifically addresses self-monitoring.

## Post Self-Control of Forethought

### Can You Do It?

After working in small groups to prepare for the writing task, students are given time to review the two new reading passages and their information maps and to meet with the teacher to receive feedback.

**Teacher:** The teacher evaluates individual self-efficacy ratings for students, looking for students who remain unsure about the process and the task. Students who feel less confident in their capability to reach the goals will require remodeling and more scaffolding to build self-efficacy ratings.

**Students:** Feedback from the teacher regarding their individual attempts to complete the information map (Parts A and B) helps students become increasingly aware of their abilities to complete the task successfully. Self-efficacy ratings reveal their perceptions of competency and can serve as a formative assessment of how they approach this type of writing task.

## Self-Controlled Performance

### Practicing
### My Strategic Approach to Writing From an Informational Text

#### (Sessions 29–32)

**Performance phase:** Students are closely monitored as they put their plan into action, applying what they have learned to set goals and design an action plan to meet the task requirements. In addition, students are required to complete the writing task by gathering information from two new passages using the information map. Students use Part A to rate their self-efficacy and for goal setting, and Part B for planning, self-monitoring, and completing the writing task.

### Modeling/Peer Modeling

The teacher encourages peer modeling as a method of reinforcement and help-seeking. Peer models demonstrate how to set goals and design (and use) the action plan to gather information from two new passages to write sentences and a paragraph. The teacher remains available to provide support and feedback, and to re-model specific parts of the performance process when needed or to correct misconceptions about the process.

### Self-Efficacy and Goal Attainment

The students perform a close reading of the two informational texts and enter their ratings for self-efficacy for reading and comprehending the passages on the information map (Goals 1 and 2). As students work independently, they think aloud in their groups and discuss any questions they have with each other.

### Goal Progress and Task Performance

Independently, the students discuss each passage and refer to the information map to state the purpose and set goals for the writing assignment. Students follow the sequential steps of the information map (Parts A and B) as a guide and respond to the following questions as they address each of the goals and the purpose of the task:

- *"What is my purpose? To write from sources by setting goals, gathering information, and writing."*
- *"What are my goals? To. . .*
  - Gather evidence from passages (Goals 3 and 4),
  - Use evidence from passages to write a sentence (Goals 5 and 6),
  - Write a short paragraph using evidence from passages (Goal 7)."

The teacher closely monitors the discussions, often contributing guiding questions to move students along in the process. He remains available for questions or assistance if needed. Students begin to evidence increased independence in their learning as they take control over the learning situation.

## Adopting Strategies as Part of an Action Plan

The students gain confidence in their use of the information map and fill in each section as they move through the process of completing the writing task.

- Students state in their own words how they interpret the purpose of the writing assignment. They add their statements to the information map. The purpose statements are similar to those used by the teacher during the observation and emulation levels when he stated, *"Why am I doing this?"* If needed, the teacher assists students to gather information only from the passages to write from sources.
- The students state in their own words how they interpret the goals for the writing assignment and how they would actually gather and use evidence from texts to write a sentence, and then a paragraph.
- Students read and reread the text. They engage in the task of gathering sources and writing as follows:

## Gathering

### Goals 1 and 2: I Can Find Evidence in Passages

**Find the facts:** Students search through the text, thinking aloud as they select facts from the passage. Students do what they have observed and practiced, using the information map to guide their actions. They independently read the passages and gather facts from each one, one at a time. The teacher remains available to assist students in distinguishing what is in the text from creative ideas that might interfere with fulfilling the requirements of the task.

## Writing

### Goals 3 and 4: I Can Use Evidence Only From the Passages

**Evaluate the facts:** Students compare the facts entered into the information map with facts from the passages. They discuss with their peers whether or not all of the information came from the passage and correct any errors they might have made by adding creative ideas to the information map.

### Goals 5 and 6: I Can Write a Sentence Using Evidence From Passages

**Write the sentence:** Students compose a sentence using the facts from each source that could be considered newspaper appropriate.

## Goal 7: I Can Write a Short Paragraph Using Evidence From Passages

**Write a paragraph:** The students use their sentences to write a paragraph on two famous Americans. The students seek help from the teacher only if needed and consult their peers to answer their questions.

### Are You Self-Monitoring During the Writing Task?

Students think aloud, discuss, and rate themselves on Goal 8 regarding self-monitoring. Their discussions are guided by each other and focus on determining if the statements from the sources are in line with the requirements of the writing task.

## Post Self-Control of Performance

### Did I Do It?

Following the completion of gathering evidence for a writing task, students are given time to review their work and ask for feedback from their teacher.

**Teacher:** Meets with each student, calling their attention to whether they met the task requirements and only used facts found in the two passages. Self-efficacy ratings are reviewed along with goal attainment. Based on the completed writing tasks, the teacher begins to evaluate which students are closer to becoming self-regulated in using this one specific approach to an information writing task and which students require more practice under the teacher's supervision.

**Students:** Students meet with the teacher for feedback regarding their performance. Students can use information from the teacher's feedback to evaluate their progress and reflect on the actions that significantly impacted their learning outcomes.

## Self-Controlled Reflection

### Reflecting On

#### My Strategic Approach to Writing From an Informational Text

**Self-reflection:** The teacher encourages students to take a look back and think about what worked and what did not work to help them reach their goals. Which strategies helped them rate their self-efficacy, design a plan, set goals, gather evidence, and write from sources? Students evaluate their writing tasks and describe task-related experiences that would help them improve their performance for future similar tasks across the curriculum.

## Peer Modeling

Individual students re-model the actions in response to the question, "What worked for you?" Students respond by describing specific behaviors that led to better planning, goal setting, gathering of evidence, and writing from sources. Students think aloud as they share the weaknesses and strengths of the planning tools and what they would do to improve their performance on future tasks.

## Partnering Self-Efficacy With Goal Attainment

Students are directed to compare the task requirements with their performance, using the "I Can" statements as a guide, changing the first words to "Did I."

Students complete a self-reflection checklist (see Table 5.7) as they reflect and evaluate which strategies were most (and least) helpful in working on the writing task. They are encouraged to think aloud about the ways in which the information map was helpful and make recommendations of ways performance could be improved on similar tasks in the future by asking, *"What can I do better next time?"* Students list three to five ideas on how to improve their performance.

## Linking Goal Attainment, Planning, and Self-Monitoring

Students are prompted to discuss with the class the sequential processes in their information map, linking their goals, action plan, and completed writing tasks. Students discuss how goal setting and planning increased their ability to self-monitor their progress and reach their goals.

## Evaluating the Plan

Students compare their completed self-reflection checklist with the teacher's model completed during the observation and emulation levels. The teacher has all items related to this lesson readily available to put on the interactive whiteboard or overhead projector for quick review. Students list the specific ways in which the information map was helpful, and make recommendations to improve their performance on similar tasks in the future. Students share and discuss the completed writing tasks specifically to uncover the benefits of using the information map and the benefits of observing and practicing prior to doing the work on their own.

## Post Self-Controlled Reflection

### Are You Satisfied With the Outcome?

Following a thorough review of the three phases of self-regulation using the information map, students and teachers discuss the learning outcomes.

**Teacher:** The teacher evaluates both the student's level of satisfaction and the actual outcome of the writing task. He individually compliments students on their use of the strategies and how focused they remained on a very demanding task, targeting one specific area of improvement.

**Students:** Each student selects one area that needs improvement. The student assesses their readiness towards independently completing a similar writing task based on their past performance. Both the information map and the self-reflection checklists can be used as formative assessments to show their growth and development as self-regulated learners.

## Self-Regulation Level

### On My Own!

#### *Promoting Self-Regulated Learning Experiences*

**Self-regulation:** Students who reach this level readily apply the strategies of goal setting (using the "I Can" statements), planning, task analysis, organization (using the information map), and self-monitoring tools when asked to complete a writing task that requires them to write from sources in other learning environments. This level is marked by independence, and the control of the learning is now in the hands of the students. Students are often assigned new passages for homework. They are expected to independently plan, complete, and reflect on their work. The teacher becomes the facilitator and adviser to students, who may have questions as their writing tasks increase in complexity. Students work both inside and outside of the teacher's supervision, yet know help is available if they need it.

## Self-Regulation of Forethought

### Making My Own Plans to Write From an Informational Text

**Forethought:** Self-regulated students analyze tasks and design action plans that incorporate self-efficacy ratings, goals, and strategies to meet the requirements of similar writing tasks. They ask teachers, the librarian, or peers for assistance and feedback to clear up any questions or confusion they might have regarding the task requirements.

**Modeling**: The teacher consistently models basic planning strategies that include self-efficacy ratings, goal setting, planning, task analysis, and using graphic organizers, such as the information map, for classwork. As students become more familiar with self-regulatory practices and use them in the context of the classroom, they will transfer what they have learned vicariously to other similar academic tasks.

## Partnering Self-Efficacy and Task Requirements

The teacher makes available the completed information map to students for them to reference when working independently (paper, online, and through classroom displays).

- Away from the classroom, self-regulated students think about their ability to complete a task successfully before they begin the task. At the self-regulation level, students incorporate strategies into their study time and use their own judgment to evaluate their usefulness, making adaptations if needed. Text complexity levels offer students the challenge of using information maps to monitor how they gather evidence to write from sources in other subjects.

## Linking Goal Setting and Task Analysis

Students are given opportunities to use the information map as a guide for setting goals in other academic settings or at home. Classroom discussions can be focused on which students are using graphic organizers similar to the information map to state the purpose, set goals, and plan their writing tasks. Hearing their classmates' responses and encouraging students to participate can increase motivation to use the strategies learned when working independently.

## Strategic Planning

The teacher introduces the information map or other types of graphic organizers into ELA third-grade test preparation assignments beginning in the second grade. These homework assignments all include informational texts, information mapping, and self-efficacy ratings. As students complete the assignments, the teacher remains available to provide feedback, clarify misunderstood sections, and build self-efficacy for taking the test in the third grade. Students' familiarity with graphic organizers such as the information map for goal setting and gathering evidence from texts for writing tasks can increase their interest and motivation in applying the strategies to future assignments and test preparation.

## Self-Monitoring

Self-regulated students increase awareness of their actions if they are reminded to look for specific behaviors while they are planning to do a writing task. Part of their planning includes the tools they will use and the availability of help. Teachers who consistently model self-monitoring strategies and discuss the benefits of good planning encourage students to do the same.

# Self-Regulation of Performance

## Working Independently!

**Performance:** Self-regulated students put their plans into action by applying what they have learned about setting goals and following an action plan for writing. The teacher provides opportunities for them to try out their newly acquired strategies, offering guidance and feedback if needed.

## Modeling

The teacher integrates into the curriculum the modeling of strategies that include goal setting (using "I Can" statements), planning, task requirements analyses, the information map, and self-monitoring for new and additional writing assignments. Students may continue to use the teacher's copy of the information map as a model of good writing.

## Partnering Self-Efficacy and Goal Attainment

The teacher makes self-efficacy a familiar term among his second and third graders. Students grow in familiarity with the term and automatically incorporate self-efficacy evaluations into task preparation.

## Goal Progress and Task Performance

The teacher continues to emphasize analyzing tasks and setting goals that are linked to specific task components by making it a teaching strategy. As students observe the teacher consistently link goals with task components, they will eventually do the same.

## Using Task Strategies

The teacher continues to integrate use of the information map or other types of graphic organizers into ELA third-grade test preparation assignments beginning in the second grade. The teacher asks students to discuss some of the strategies they are using at home or in other classes. Students' familiarity with graphic organizers such as the information map for goal setting and gathering evidence from texts for writing tasks increases their interest in applying the strategies to other types of assignments.

**Self-monitoring:** Class discussions focus on how well the teacher self-monitors and the strategies he uses to track his own performance. Students discuss in class how the graphic organizers help them self-monitor their progress towards task completion.

## Self-Regulation of Reflection

### Ongoing Reflection . . .

**Self-reflection:** Self-regulated students at this age respond to guided self-reflection. Feedback from teachers can help begin the process of students independently using reflections on past performances to help them make adjustments to present writing tasks. In addition, feedback on which strategy choices have been noticed to improve their performance on writing tasks helps to reinforce the use of those strategies. Self-regulated students evaluate their writing tasks and describe task-related experiences that they have discovered to be helpful with their peers and their teacher. They consistently look for ways to improve their performance across the curriculum on similar tasks.

### *Modeling*

The teacher integrates into the curriculum the modeling of reflective practices and self-evaluations in his own and his students' work. In addition, the feedback provided for students' writing, and the subsequent revisions, serve as "models" of good writing for each other and students outside of this classroom context.

### *Partnering Self-Efficacy and Goal Attainment*

Students self-evaluate their efforts to use strategies learned from earlier writing tasks with similar requirements. They grow in their realization that goals set too high can have a significant negative impact on self-efficacy. Self-regulated students carefully monitor their progress toward goals and make adjustments if the goals are set beyond their abilities. They will work with their teachers to set realistic and proximal goals.

### *Linking Goal Attainment, Planning, and Self-Monitoring*

Students are given opportunities to reflect on the value of self-monitoring tools when monitoring progress in attaining set goals for short- and long-term assignments completed outside of the classroom. Discussions assist students with evaluating their choice of strategy and the outcome.

Students' self-evaluations reflect familiarity with graphic organizers such as the information map for goal setting and gathering evidence from texts for writing tasks. Improvements in test scores or test preparation assignments should increase their interest in applying the strategies to other types of writing tasks.

## References

Allyn, P. (2013). *Be core ready: Powerful, effective steps to implementing and achieving the Common Core state standards.* Upper Saddle River, NJ: Pearson.

Bandura, A. (1986). *Social foundations of thought and action: A social cognitive theory.* Englewood Cliffs, NJ: Prentice Hall.

Bandura, A. (1988). Self-efficacy conception of anxiety. *Anxiety Research, 1*(2), 77–98.

Bandura, A. (1989). Human agency in social cognitive theory. *American Psychologist, 44*, 1175–1184.

Bandura, A. (1997). *Self-efficacy: The exercise of control.* New York, NY: Freeman.

Calkins, L., Ehrenworth, M., & Lehman, C. (2012). *Pathways to the Common Core: Accelerating achievement.* Portsmouth, NH: Heinemann.

Dermitzaki, I. & Kiosseoglou, G. (2004). Introduction: Individual and social processes in the regulation of learning. *Hellenic Journal of Psychology, 1*(2), 119–127.

Guthrie, J. T., Schafer, W. D., & Huang, C. W. (2001). Benefits of opportunity to read and balanced instruction on the NAEP. *The Journal of Educational Research, 94*(3), 145–162.

Harris, K. R., Graham, S., & Mason, L. H. (2006). Improving the writing, knowledge, and motivation of struggling young writers: Effects of self-regulated strategy development with and without peer support. *American Educational Research Journal, 43*(2), 295–340.

Harris, K. R., Graham, S., & Santangelo, T. (2013). Self-regulated strategies development in writing: Development, implementation, and scaling up. In H. Bembenutty, T. J. Cleary, & A. Kitsantas (Eds.), *Applications of self-regulated learning across diverse disciplines: A tribute to Barry Zimmerman* (pp. 59–88). Charlotte, NC: Information Age Publishing.

Harris, K. R., Schmidt, T., & Graham, S. (1998). Every child can write: Strategies for composition and self-regulation in the writing process. *Advances in Teaching and Learning, 2*, 131–167.

Locke, E. A., & Latham, G. P. (1990). *A theory of goal setting & task performance.* Saddle River, NJ: Prentice-Hall, Inc.

Pintrich, P. R., & Schunk, D. H. (2002). *Motivation in education: Theory, research, and applications.* Upper Saddle River, NJ: Merrill-Prentice Hall.

Schunk, D. H. (1989). Social cognitive theory and self-regulated learning. In B. J. Zimmerman & D. H. Schunk (Eds.), *Self-regulated learning and academic achievement* (pp. 83–110). New York, NY: Springer.

Schunk, D. H. (2001). *Self-regulation through goal setting.* ERIC Digest. Greensboro, NC: ERIC Clearinghouse on Counseling and Student Services. (ERIC Document Reproduction Service No. ED 462 671.)

Zimmerman, B. J., Bonner, S., & Kovach, R. (1996). *Developing self-regulated learners: Beyond achievement to self-efficacy.* Washington, DC: American Psychological Association.

# 6

# BUILDING ACADEMIC LANGUAGE

## Grades 4 and 5

### Inferring Meaning from Context and Morpheme Clues

*Keywords: academic language, vocabulary, self-efficacy, morphemes, context, learning process goals, deliberate practice, self-monitoring, self-evaluation, graphic organizers, Vtrix*

## Reading K–5 Standard for Informational Texts

The focus on text complexity requires that students spend as much time reading informational texts as they spend on more interesting literature. At the fourth-and fifth-grade level of learning, students gain important information by reading domain-specific texts in science and social studies, and they are expected to retain information from what they have read. The vocabulary required to begin reading informational texts is very different from the oral language students are familiar with when they enter school. Often, we can hear a student tell a story using vocabulary that fits the event. However, the Common Core standards require students to share information that is factual using appropriate academic language. There is little doubt that young children cannot describe the scientific attributes of a chick hatched from an incubating chicken egg with as much expertise as they can describe the character Chicken Little from one of their literature books.

Reading informational texts requires a strong and developing academic vocabulary, which is the language that is required to succeed in school. As students transition from primary grades to secondary grades, their academic success is significantly dependent on their abilities to use academic language (Zwiers, 2013). For many of our students in the fourth and fifth grade, acquiring this type of vocabulary can pose significant challenges for both the teachers and learners. Self-regulated learning strategies can assist students with managing and acquiring academic vocabulary and becoming independent readers.

Any delay in academic language acquisition can cause a once-proficient reader to lose ground as a result of poor comprehension and limited life experience.

In the past, even proficient readers entering the fourth and fifth grade would begin to struggle when required to "read to learn" about science, math, technology, social studies, and geography from a textbook. In addition, familiarity with content and grammatical conventions is essential to maintaining strong and sustainable levels of academic vocabulary. For English language learners (ELLs), the Common Core standards that require academic language development to engage in reading more complex texts are an area of concern.

As depicted in Table 6.1, we emphasize the strand of Craft and Structure to call attention to the emphasis placed by the standards for students to not only learn to read and write, but produce evidence of their comprehension of the language used in informational textbooks. Training in self-regulatory strategies that emphasize setting proximal goals, organizing information for memorization and comprehension, self-monitoring, and self-evaluation can provide fourth- and fifth-graders with a systematic approach for growing and sustaining a strong academic vocabulary across the curriculum.

## Do the Crosswalk!

**TABLE 6.1** Linking the Common Core and Self-Regulation

| *College- and career-ready preparation* | *Common Core standards* | *Self-regulated learning target (grades 4 and 5)* |
| --- | --- | --- |
| **Anchor standard for reading**<br>English language arts standards »<br>anchor standards » | **Strand**<br>Reading K–5<br>standards for informational text | **Self-regulation strategy training for academic language acquisition** |
| **College- and career-readiness anchor standards for reading**<br>Interpret words and phrases as they are used in a text, including determining technical, connotative, and figurative meanings, and analyze how specific word choices shape meaning or tone. | **Standard**<br>**Craft and Structure**<br>Determine the meanings of general academic and domain-specific words or phrases in a text relevant to a Grade 4/5 topic or subject area (CCSS.ELA-Literacy. RI.4.4 and CCSS.ELA-Literacy. RI.5.4) | **Strategies**<br>(1) Deliberate practice through setting learning process goals<br>(2) Self-monitoring<br>(3) Self-evaluation<br>(4) Academic vocabulary acquisition using graphic organizers for progress monitoring |
| **College- and career-readiness anchor standards for language vocabulary acquisition and use: CCSS.ELA-Literacy.CCRA.L.4**<br>Determine or clarify the meaning of unknown and multiple-meaning words and phrases by using context clues, analyzing meaningful word parts, and consulting general and specialized reference materials, as appropriate. | **Grades 4 and 5:**<br>Determine or clarify the meaning of unknown and multiple-meaning words and phrases based on Grade 4/5 reading and content, choosing flexibly from a range of strategies.<br>• Use common, grade-appropriate Greek and Latin affixes and roots as clues to the meaning of a word (e.g,. photograph, photosynthesis). | |

# Words Have Parts!

## *Acquiring Academic Language Requires Deliberate Practice*

The Common Core language standards require the student to maintain strong and grade-appropriate levels of academic vocabulary. Fourth- and fifth-grade-level expectations for vocabulary are obtainable when integrating self-regulatory strategy learning with exposure to how a new language is learned. Vocabulary, specifically academic language, should expand and deepen over time, providing college- and career-ready students with a foundation for learning new concepts and processes. *Academic language* can refer to the kind of words that students must know in order to read increasingly demanding text with comprehension (Zwiers, 2005).

Self-regulation for fourth and fifth graders should include *deliberate practice* through instruction in process goal setting and self-evaluation. Deliberate practice demands that the learner be attentive to her errors, weaknesses, and deficiencies and consciously work to remedy them. Research has shown us that the more we utilize specific neural pathways for building skills—such as throwing a ball, multiplying by fives, or recalling all fifty state capitals—the more effectively those patterns become ingrained in our brains and the more likely the correct skills become automatic.

In the classroom, *deliberate practice* engages learners in a focused, planned training activity designed to improve some characteristic of performance. During *deliberate practice*, each learner receives individual and immediate informative feedback on her performance. The learner is then provided with opportunities to repeat the same or similar tasks with full attention towards changing responses that do not meet the standard, thus improving the identified area of weakness and increasing the likelihood of attaining process goals (Duckworth, Kirby, Tsukayama, Berstein, & Ericsson, 2011). Deliberate practice encourages taking risks and learning from errors by listening and taking advantage of self-recordings and/or teacher feedback.

## *Academic Language Complexity*

The Common Core–suggested practice for acquiring academic language is a clear departure from the formal study of words that included creating a large list of disconnected and decontextualized words. Practices that stress conceptual knowledge of words and how words are related show a greater degree of vocabulary growth and, as a result, increase reading comprehension. Research recommends that students learn fewer words accompanied by instruction in how word parts and the English language works so that they can develop a system to infer the meanings of new words. Effective vocabulary instruction is characterized by the deliberate selection of words to be taught in word-rich learning environments where there are frequent opportunities for students to interact with the words in meaningful contexts (Sweeny & Mason, 2011).

## *Academic Language Acquisition Through Self-Regulated Learning*

Developing readers acquire vocabulary primarily through wide independent reading (Nagy & Anderson, 1984), yet those who need to read the most are less likely to read in the absence of supervision. The Common Core recognizes that it generally takes several encounters with a new word to learn it, and students who experience reading difficulties have limited encounters with words and show inadequate vocabulary growth. As a result, they require a consistent and persistent long-term investment in vocabulary development. The Cognitive Academic Language Learning Approach (Chamot, 2009) was designed primarily with ELLs in mind, yet it has been successfully applied to vocabulary acquisition for struggling readers (SRs) and standard English learners (SELs). Metacognitive strategies such as goal setting, self-monitoring, and self-evaluation are noted as especially helpful to ELLs, SRs, and SELs in acquiring standard academic language (Chamot, 2009). Through modeling, teachers can transmit and guide students in acquiring vocabulary knowledge and the techniques needed to increase their academic language, along with providing practice and opportunities to become expert performers.

## *Goal Setting and Academic Language Acquisition*

Self-regulation of vocabulary acquisition includes setting goals that incorporate all of the goal properties outlined in Chapter 5 (Grades 2/3). This chapter focuses specifically on how to set learning process goals. Goals can be distinguished and individualized by identifying what students ultimately are trying to accomplish. A process or learning goal focuses the student on what knowledge, behavior, skill, or strategy needs to be acquired in order to complete a specific task. An outcome or performance goal is focused on the task students are trying to complete. While working on a vocabulary task, a student may have a goal of learning how to use context clues to find the meaning of a challenging word (process) or a goal of getting a good grade on an academic vocabulary quiz (outcome).

Both types of goals motivate behavior; however, they can have different effects on learners' beliefs and cognitive processes. Additional studies have shown (Kitsantas, Reiser, & Doster, 2004; Zimmerman & Kitsantas, 2002) process goals focus the learner's attention on the skills needed to learn. Students often evaluate their progress in learning, and the belief that one *is* learning can raise self-efficacy and enhance motivation. In contrast, outcome goals focus attention on completing tasks. When the task is as complex as acquiring academic vocabulary, goals that focus the learner's attention on strategy execution also provide more opportunities for teacher feedback.

## *Self-Monitoring and Self-Evaluation During Academic Language Acquisition*

Self-regulation of vocabulary acquisition includes linking learning process goals and encouraging self-recording of individual progress (Zimmerman & Kitsantas,

2002). Students set learning process goals in the forethought phase and gauge their progress towards meeting those goals in the performance phase, using self-monitoring tools. Specific to self-monitoring academic vocabulary acquisition, the results of students' progress monitoring is an individualized and realistic self-evaluation in the reflection phase of the three self-regulatory phases. Self-efficacy is an important variable for both students and teachers to monitor because it focuses attention on beliefs about the effectiveness of selected learning methods. Teachers who provide students with an objective way to monitor self-efficacy for attaining learning outcomes help them become more accurate in predicting their performance (Zimmerman, Bonner, & Kovach, 1996).

## Shifting to Be College Ready

### Shifting Slowly: Fourth and Fifth Graders to Acquire Academic Language

The Common Core for K–5 invites students to confront challenging words or phrases by making several attempts to arrive at a viable approximation of the meaning, rather than skipping over them or making one attempt and moving on (Calkins, Ehrenworth, & Lehman, 2012). It is suggested that texts with spiraling-like content in increasing complexity can be an effective means for both students and teachers to become engaged in constantly building a transferable vocabulary.

**TABLE 6.2** Academic Vocabulary Standards and Self-Regulation Instruction

**Academic vocabulary:** Students constantly build the transferable vocabulary they need to access grade-level complex texts. This can be done effectively by spiraling similar content in increasingly complex texts. Academic vocabulary increases reading comprehension and builds students' background knowledge, which means they will be able to read increasingly complex texts. Teachers will strive to consciously use academic vocabulary in context during class discussions.

| *Common Core Targets* | *Self-regulation* |
|---|---|
| **Language Skills** **Fourth Grade** "I can use context clues to figure out word meanings!" "I can determine the meaning of a word by using the affix or root!" | Set **learning process goals** using "I Can" statements  **Self-monitor** by rating self-efficacy and tracking progress using Progress Monitoring Chart |
| **Fifth Grade** "I can use common Greek and Latin affixes and roots to figure out word meanings!" | **Self-evaluation**—Reflection/evaluation of learning outcomes with learning process goals comparisons |
| **Literacy Skills** "I can determine the meaning of words or phrases in a grade-level text!" "I can use strategies to understand unknown words" | **Self-efficacy**—Students' beliefs about their capability to determine the meanings **Strategy use**—Students effectively use strategies to learn |

## The Complex World of Academic Language

Academic language is the language needed to succeed in school, and it is often cited as one of the key factors affecting the achievement gap that exists between high- and low-performing groups of students in our schools.

- Academic language is defined as the language used by teachers and students for the purpose of acquiring new knowledge and skills, imparting new information, describing abstract ideas, and developing students' conceptual understanding (Chamot, 2009).
- Students who cannot handle the linguistic demands of different disciplines will most likely perform poorly as they transition from the primary grades into upper elementary and secondary classes (Wong-Fillmore & Snow, 2000).
- Teachers who are called upon to make the hours spent in their classrooms as language rich as possible encounter the challenges of developing the language needed for success in different content classes, especially when working with a diverse population of individual learners (Zwiers, 2013).

### *Words Have Tiers!*

Beck, McKeown, and Kucan (2002) categorized words into three tiers to help teachers target academic vocabulary words for lesson planning and instruction:

- Tier 1 includes the most basic words that rarely require instruction in school (clock, baby, happy).
- Tier 2 words are high-frequency words for mature language users (coincidence, absurd, industrious, instruction), and these words can add productively to an individual's language ability.
  - Words such as *analyze, effect,* and *indicate* are examples of Tier 2 words encountered in expository texts across the content area of science and social studies, but are only rarely placed in narrative texts or used in everyday conversation. They are also found in the language of standardized testing.
- Tier 3 consists of words whose frequency of use is very limited to specific domains (isotope, lathe, peninsula) and are not likely to affect reading comprehension over a wide range of texts but are still critical to the domain in which they are used.

### *Words Have Parts!*

A working knowledge of academic language is the foundation for learning concepts and processes taught at the middle and high school levels. Without a working knowledge of an academic vocabulary, readers and writers most likely will struggle in classes across the curriculum.

- Teachers cannot possibly teach all of the words students need to know directly; however, they can provide students with tools and strategies for learning words on their own, one such strategy being morphology (Kieffer & Lesaux, 2010).
- Students from Grades 1–6 have shown success in word reading and reading comprehension through training in some aspects of morphology (Bowers, Kirby, & Deacon, 2010).
- Morphology provides a key to developing both word knowledge and high-quality mental representations. This knowledge contributes to word reading and to reading comprehension (Nagy, Berninger, & Abbot, 2006; Nunes & Bryant, 2006).

## *Words Parts Have Meaning!*

- *Morphology* is the study of the structure of words as combinations of smaller units of meaning within words (morphemes).
- *Raising morphological awareness* promotes word consciousness and heightens one's sensitivity to morphological structure and one's ability to manipulate that structure (Bowers, Kirby & Deacon, 2010).
- *Using morphology* to manipulate words is a cognitive strategy, not rules to be memorized (Kieffer & Lesaux, 2007).
- *Promoting word consciousness* creates an interest in words and an awareness of word formations.

## *Words Have Context!*

- *Knowing a word well* involves a combination of several different types of knowledge (Kieffer & Lesaux, 2010). More important than the literal definition is its relationship to other words, its connotations in different contexts, and its ability to be transformed into various other forms (Stahl, 1999).
- *Vocabulary is learned in context.* Contextual analysis involves inferring the meaning of an unfamiliar word by closely examining the text surrounding it. Instruction in contextual analysis involves teaching students to draw on prior knowledge and exposure to the word, and to employ both generic and specific types of context clues (Diamond & Gutlohn, 2006).
- *Building declarative knowledge* about types of context is a well-developed part of word study; however, adding procedural knowledge enhances students' ability to understand the word and its context in a process-oriented manner (Blachowicz, Fisher, & Watts-Taffe, 2005).

## Inferring Meaning From Context and Morpheme Clues

### *Monitoring Academic Vocabulary Acquisition Is an* Outside-Inside *Process!*

- When context clues fail, children can rely on morphology to assist in deciphering the meaning of new words that share the bases and affixes of words previously taught and easily referenced.
- Evidence that students learn words from context (Nagy et al., 2006; Elley, 1998) and equipping students with skills to interpret word meanings when context is insufficient provide them even more access to learning words incidentally (Bauman, Edwards, Boland, Olejnik, & Kame'enui, 2003).
- Researchers found that children who received instruction in using morphemic contextual analysis outperformed their peers who received textbook instruction in vocabulary on a test measuring morphology and contextual analysis skills (Baumann et al., 2003).

### Instructional Components for Self-Regulated Learning

**Self-efficacy:** Self-efficacy ratings are aligned with goal attainment for each phase of the process (see Tables 6.3 and 6.4). They reveal students' self-awareness when using a specific strategy to increase academic vocabulary and serve as a formative and summative assessment. Both teacher and students monitor progress during deliberate practice sessions by rating performance and efficacy of applying the strategy to reading complex texts and using morphemes to identify challenging word meanings. Students who misjudge their self-efficacy can receive feedback from the teacher to correct the error and adjust their ratings.

**Learning process goal setting**: Incorporating "I Can" statements into learning process goals (see Table 6.3) is an excellent way for fourth and fifth graders to personalize how they will learn the strategies to acquire a working academic vocabulary. The "I Can" statements, although aligned with the Common Core, focus on a specific learning strategy, rather than target words or types of morphemes that need to be learned. For example, "*I can increase my word knowledge using context clues and the morpheme chart!*" will guide learners toward using the chart rather than skipping over an unknown word. The checklist, Self-Efficacy for Learning Process Goals: Student (With "I Can" Statements), (see Tables 6.3 and 6.4) lists process goals (Column D) for each phase of self-regulation with accompanying self-efficacy ratings (Columns A, B, and C). The teacher at the observation level introduces Table 6.3 as she thinks aloud, demonstrating how she would use the checklist to monitor self-efficacy ratings for each learning process goal. Students use a similar checklist themselves (see Table 6.4) at the emulation and self-control levels.

**Self-monitoring:** Systematic and deliberate observation of applying the strategy to reading complex texts and using morphemes to identify challenging word meanings is done by comparing one's performance with learning process goals. Self-monitoring and self-evaluation require students to track their progress

Building Academic Language  115

**TABLE 6.3** Self-Efficacy for Learning Process Goals: Teacher's Model (With "I Can" Statements)

| | Teacher Self-Efficacy Ratings ||||
|---|---|---|---|---|
| | The teacher uses the first two words associated with each phase to begin the statement, rating her self-efficacy for attaining each goal one phase at a time as she moves through each phase of self-regulation (0–5, 0 is the weakest).<br><br>Forethought = "I can"<br>Performance = "I did"<br>Reflection = "How did I do?"<br><br>For example:<br><br>A. I can identify words for which I do not know the meaning.<br>B. I did identify words for which I do not know the meaning.<br>C. How well did I identify words for which I do not know the meaning? ||||
| Goal # | A | B | C | D |
| | Forethought "I can" | Performance "I did" | Reflection "How well did I do?" | Learning process goals |
| 1 | | | | Identify words for which I do not know the meanings. |
| 2 | | | | Use context clues to define a word for which I do not know the meanings. |
| 3 | | | | Use morpheme clues to define words for which I do not know the meanings. |
| 4 | | | | Use context and morpheme clues to define words for which I do not know the meanings. |
| 5 | | | | Monitor my progress by identifying, tracking, and categorizing words for which I do not know the meanings. |
| 6 | | | | Evaluate my progress by identifying, tracking, and categorizing words for which I do not know the meanings. |
| 7 | | | | Self-monitor my actions by comparing my progress with the goals set for a specific reading task that requires me to read and comprehend a short informational text. |

and reflect on their learning outcomes to ascertain what worked and what did not work in attaining their goals.

**Self-evaluation:** The cyclical processes of self-regulation provide both learner and teachers with valuable information obtained during the self-reflection phase

**TABLE 6.4** Self-Efficacy for Learning Process Goals: Student's Model (With "I Can") Statements)

|  | Self Efficacy Ratings ||||
| --- | --- | --- | --- | --- |
|  | Use the first two words associated with each phase to begin the statement. Then rate your self-efficacy for attaining each goal as you move through each phase of self-regulation (0–5, 0 is the weakest).<br><br>Forethought = "I can"<br>Performance = "I did"<br>Reflection = "How did I do?"<br><br>For example:<br><br>A. I can identify words for which I do not know the meaning.<br>B. I did identify words for which I do not know the meaning.<br>C. How well did I identify words for which I do not know the meaning? ||||
| Goal # | A | B | C | D |
|  | Forethought "I can" | Performance "I did" | Reflection "How well did I do?" | Learning Process Goals |
| 1 |  |  |  | Identify words for which I do not know the meanings. |
| 2 |  |  |  | Use context clues to define a word for which I do not know the meanings. |
| 3 |  |  |  | Use morpheme clues to define words for which I do not know the meanings. |
| 4 |  |  |  | Use context and morpheme clues to define words for which I do not know the meanings. |
| 5 |  |  |  | Monitor my progress by identifying, tracking, and categorizing words for which I do not know the meanings. |
| 6 |  |  |  | Evaluate my progress by identifying, tracking, and categorizing words for which I do not know the meanings. |
| 7 |  |  |  | Self-monitor my actions by comparing my progress with the goals set for a specific reading task that requires me to read and comprehend a short informational text. |
| 8 |  |  |  | Increase my word knowledge using context clues and morpheme chart. |

to inform future forethought and planning. Proactive learners self-evaluate by comparing their self-monitored outcomes to the goals set in the forethought phase. When learning how to use specific learning strategies, students should be encouraged to self-evaluate their progress using teacher feedback and their self-recorded progress over a short period. Students are asked to reflect on their progress at the emulation and self-control levels (see Table 6.5) by checking their progress and stating what they would do differently to improve goal attainment if the task was assigned again. Some responses could include spending more time on the task, paying closer attention to the strategies, or focusing on their progress.

**TABLE 6.5** Self-Evaluation/Reflection Ratings

| Rate your progress towards attaining each goal using 0/weakest, 5/strongest. Then reflect on your progress and make a statement regarding anything you could do differently the next time a similar task is assigned that would improve your goal attainment. |||
|---|---|---|
| *Learning process goals* | *Self-evaluation rating (0–5)* | *What would I do differently?* |
| Did I identify words for which I do not know the meanings? | | |
| Did I use context clues to define a word for which I do not know the meaning? | | |
| Did I use morpheme clues to define a word for which I do not know the meaning? | | |
| Did I use context and morpheme clues to define a word for which I do not know the meaning? | | |
| Did I monitor my progress by identifying, tracking, and categorizing words for which I do not know the meaning? | | |
| Did I evaluate my progress while identifying, tracking, and categorizing words for which I did not know the meaning? | | |
| Did I self-monitor my actions by comparing my progress with the goals set for a specific reading task that requires me to read and comprehend a short informational text? | | |

## Instructional Components for Academic Language Acquisition

**Modeling:** Self-regulating vocabulary development allows the teacher to set goals for the class, and through deliberate practice, the teacher can work with each student towards attaining individualized and specific goals. The class can be divided into groups at the observation and emulation levels until the Outside/Inside strategy is learned. SRs, SELs, and ELLs will spend a longer time at the observation level and practice the strategy with the teacher or a competent peer model at the emulation level than their peers who will reach the self-regulated competency level faster.

**Graphic organizer:** The *Progress Monitoring Chart (PMC)* is a graphic organizer (see Table 6.6) that serves as a self-monitoring tool and assists students

**TABLE 6.6** Progress Monitoring Chart (PMC)

| \multicolumn{7}{c}{Progress Monitoring Chart} |
|---|---|---|---|---|---|---|
| Name _____ <br> Text Title _____ Text Type _____ ||||||||
| Strangers | Did I use context? | Did I use morphemes? | Did I use both? | Do I now have a guess? | Did I learn the meaning? | Does it help me understand the text? |
| Word 1 | | | | | | |
| Word 2 | | | | | | |
| Word 3 | | | | | | |
| Word 4 | | | | | | |
| Word 5 | | | | | | |
| Acquaintances | Did I use context? | Did I use morphemes? | Did I use both? | I think the word means ... | Did I learn the meaning? | Does it help me understand the text? |
| Word 1 | | | | | | |
| Word 2 | | | | | | |
| Word 3 | | | | | | |
| Word 4 | | | | | | |
| Word 5 | | | | | | |
| Friends | Did I use context? | Did I use morphemes? | Did I use both? | Can I use the word in a sentence? | Did I learn the meaning? | Does it help me understand the text? |
| Word 1 | | | | | | |
| Word 2 | | | | | | |
| Word 3 | | | | | | |
| Word 4 | | | | | | |
| Word 5 | | | | | | |

individually with categorizing their familiarity with a particular group of words assigned by the teacher. Unfamiliar word meanings are categorized as strangers, less familiar are acquaintances, and known words are friends. The chart enables students to track their progress as they use the *Outside/Inside* strategy to move the strangers to the friends' category.

**Strategic word analysis:** White's Outside-Inside strategy was derived from Baumann and his colleagues' *The Vocabulary Rule* (2003) and Ebbers and Denton's revision with renaming, the *Outside-In* strategy (2008). Adaptations were made by White in 2014 to include specific self-regulatory vocabulary learning strategy instruction using the Vtrix worksheet. The Outside-Inside strategy and other types of vocabulary instruction integrated into the lesson plan were chosen because they easily merged with using a Vtrix (see Table 6.7).

**TABLE 6.7** Vtrix

Instructions: As you read the text, remember to follow the Outside/Inside approach to figure out word meanings.
First: Look outside the word (context clues).
Second: Look inside the word for morphemes that can help you figure out the word meanings.

| *Outside: Context clues* | | *Which word?* | | |
|---|---|---|---|---|
| *Type* | *Does the author . . .* | *1* | *2* | *3* |
| Definition | Does the author give you the definition for a word in the sentence? | | | |
| Synonym | Does the author use another word that means about the same thing as the word you don't understand? | | | |
| Antonym | Does the author use a word that is the opposite or nearly the opposite of the word you are trying to understand? | | | |
| Example | Does the author give you several words or ideas that are examples of the word you are trying to understand? | | | |
| General | Does the author give you some general clues to the meaning of the word, often spread over several sentences? | | | |

| *Inside: Morpheme clues* | *Morphemes* | *Meanings* | *Word in text* |
|---|---|---|---|
| **What Actually Is Science?** | caus | a reason | *caus*al |
| Our natural world is a fascinating collection of observable phenomena and causal relationships that we humans have been watching and trying to explain since even before we began recording our history. This drive to understand led to the collection of knowledge we now think of as "science." The word "science" comes from the Latin word for knowledge: *scientia*. | col | to filter | *col*lection |
| | | | |
| | | | |
| | | | |

(*Continued*)

## TABLE 6.7 (Continued)

| Inside: Morpheme clues | Morphemes | Meanings | Word in text |
|---|---|---|---|
| But what actually is science? When you hear that question, you probably get many images in your head of lab coats, microscopes, equations, or the stars. The truth is that science is a tremendously large topic that involves many different human endeavors. While the topic itself is so large that it can be difficult to define, we can begin to understand it a little better by looking at some of its key characteristics. Science focuses on and attempts to explain the natural world through testable ideas. Science relies heavily on evidence. It involves the scientific community and leads to ongoing research. Science also benefits from scientific behavior and the use of what is known as the "Scientific Method," which is an accepted body of techniques for investigation that seeks to gain empirical and measurable evidence. Ultimately, science is the search for the truths about the way our world and universe work in a rational and ongoing, yet reliable, way. We will begin this year by developing an understanding of what science and scientific thinking is, and then carry that through our studies for the rest of the year. | commun | public | *commun*ity |
| | em- | in | *em*pirical |
| | e | from the outside | *e*vidence |
| | equ | even | *equ*al |
| | -vid | to see | e*vid*ence |
| | ex- | plain | *ex*plain |
| | fac- | to do | *fac*ilitate |
| | foc- | central point | *foc*uses |
| | histor | story | *histor*y |
| | image | copy, likeness | *image*s |
| | know- | to know | *know*ledge |
| | lect | gather | col*lect*ion |
| | men- | to project | pheno*men*on |
| | meth | associated with | *meth*od |
| | micro- | small | *micro*scope |
| | od | journey, path | meth*od* |
| | rat | reason | *rat*ional |
| | phen- | to appear | *phen*omenon |
| | pir | trial, to attempt | em*pir*ical |
| | sci | to understand | *sci*ence |
| | scop- | view | *scop*e |
| | techn | art, craft, skill | *techn*ical |
| | tempt | try | at*tempt* |
| | ultim | farthest beyond | *ultim*ately |
| | uni | one | *uni*verse |
| | velop | to wrap | de*velop*ing |
| | vers | to turn (revolution) | uni*vers*e |
| | vestig- | footprint, trace | in*vestig*ate |
| | vid | to see | e*vid*ence |
| | volv- | also | in*volv*es |

**Vtrix:** The Vtrix worksheet includes morpheme definitions (affixes, roots) aligned with target words and a specific informational text, all in the same handout. Students receive the handout to use as a reference when they encounter a word in the text for which the meaning is unknown to them. Using the list of morpheme meanings aligned with the text will raise students' word consciousness and as a result help them incorporate the meaning of challenging words into reading texts. The informational text included on the Vtrix worksheet is a fifth-grade text from a science teacher's wiki acquainting his class with the reasons we study science (5-1 The Scientific Method).

## Prior Knowledge and Lesson Requirements:

- Text selected is appropriate to students' reading levels with a minimum of five challenging, low-frequency Tier 2 words.
- Students have experience in reading informational texts and using context clues to devise the meaning of unknown words.
- Instruction in identifying word parts using morphemes (basic).
- Instruction in context clues from text.
- Students have experience in reading explanatory texts and using context clues to devise the meaning of unknown words.
- Students have been exposed to and become familiar with morphemes such as root words and affixes and identified word parts.

## Materials Master List (see Table 6.8 for detailed distribution of materials):

- Pencils (students)/markers (teacher)
- Writing surfaces (blank)
- Text—informational text (required reading for upcoming unit)
- Begin with shorter texts and increase in length as students become familiar with the strategy
- Text written on large (3 x 3 surface)
- Worksheets/rating sheets/checklists (see Table 6.8)

## The Plan: Monitoring Academic Vocabulary Acquisition: Inferring Meaning From Morphemes and Context Clues

**Objective:** Students will independently monitor their academic vocabulary acquisition using the self-regulatory strategies of setting process goals, self-monitoring, and self-evaluation.

**Sessions:** Vocabulary learning requires teachers and administrators to be flexible regarding how many words individual students can be required to learn over a specific period and often can best be accomplished interactively and in groups. Research supports dividing a word list associated with a specific unit of study into sections and introducing three to five words over time, perhaps targeting three to five words per week (for the class in general), making adjustments for individual learners.

**122** Elementary School

**TABLE 6.8** Worksheets/Rating Sheets/Checklists

| Artifacts | When used | By whom | Purpose | Table |
|---|---|---|---|---|
| **Task related** | | | | |
| *Progress Monitoring Chart* | All levels—Reading informational text | Students Teacher | Vocabulary Self-monitoring tool | 6.6 |
| *Vtrix (worksheet)* Morphemes and target words list with informational text Outside/Inside strategy | Vocabulary task— All phases and levels | Teacher Student | Demonstration To monitor progress | 6.7 |
| **Self-regulation related** | | | | |
| *Self-Efficacy for Learning Process goals:* Teacher's Model (With "I Can" Statements, three phases) | Observation level | Teacher | Demonstration | 6.3 |
| *Self-efficacy for learning process goals:* Student's Model (With "I Can" Statements, three phases) | Emulation and self-control levels | Students Teacher | Rating self-efficacy and learning progress | 6.4 |
| *Reflection/Evaluation Rating* | All phases— Emulation and self-control levels | Students Teacher | Guided questions for reflection of progress, self-evaluation. Students complete one self-evaluation, all three phases, at emulation and self-control levels. | 6.5 |
| *Teacher Performance Rating* | Observation—All Phases | Teacher | Students predict teacher's effectiveness in using the Vtrix and Progress Monitoring Chart during the forethought phase and then evaluate the outcome at the end of the performance phase. During the reflection phase, students evaluate the teacher's progress towards attaining learning process goals. | 6.10 |

## Observation Level

### Watch It!

#### Sessions 1–9

**Observation:** The teacher uses think-alouds (verbal modeling) and visual aids to make her thought processes transparent as she sets learning process goals, chooses a strategy, self-monitors, and self-evaluates by comparing her progress with the learning process goals. As a coping model, the teacher demonstrates the challenges of using both morphemes and context clues to figure out words encountered for the first time in a reading of an informational text. Students observe the teacher and follow along as directed. Students are actively engaged in learning as they complete all of the same handouts as the teacher, using the teacher's scores as the teacher models all aspects of learning new and challenging vocabulary words.

At this level, the task materials are displayed and the teacher refers to them as she models. Students are engaged by completing some of the same handouts as the teacher if it does not divert their attention from the task.

### Observation of Forethought

#### Planning

##### *A Strategic Approach to Reading Informational Texts*

##### Sessions 1–3

**Forethought:** Students observe as the teacher prepares to read from an informational text. The teacher introduces the aligned Common Core standards from which the "I Can" statements are generated. These statements are helpful in ensuring that learning process goals are aligned with the standards and the upcoming reading task from an informational text. Students have copies of all worksheets that the teacher is using and are instructed to copy exactly what the teacher enters in the handouts as they proceed through the lessons for the forethought phase.

#### *Modeling: What Is the Teacher Doing?*

The teacher thinks aloud as she reads aloud and analyzes the reading task requirements, emphasizing specific parts. *"I will need to read every word in the text using word parts and context clues to fully understand what the author intends for me to know based on my reading of the text. When I come to a word for which I don't know the meaning, I will figure it out rather than skip it, using clues from the context and word parts."*

- The teacher continues thinking aloud that she is pretty good at context clues but will review them to make sure the process is understood.
- The teacher refers to Vtrix context clues (see Table 6.7)—specifically, the section with instructions for finding context clues in a text.
- The teacher continues as a coping model who does not have a working knowledge of word parts.
- The teacher refers to Vtrix morpheme meanings (see Table 6.7), calling each student's attention to how useful both morphemes and context clues can be to figure out word meanings.
- Thinking aloud, the teacher demonstrates how using the chart might help to read a text with words she does not know the meaning of and help comprehend the text.
- The teacher reads through the text, underlining the words for which she does not know the meanings, and calls students' attention to the displayed Progress Monitoring Chart (see Table 6.6). Students are instructed to refer to their copies of the text and Progress Monitoring Chart (PMC) as they pay close attention to what the teacher is doing.
  - Thinking aloud, the teacher enters five words classified as strangers into the PMC, stating how this will help keep track of learning their meanings to better comprehend the reading text. Students are instructed to replicate exactly what the teacher did on their copies of the chart.

## What Is Self-Efficacy?

The teacher models how to conduct a task analysis. She assesses her self-efficacy to not skip words and use word parts and context clues to figure out word meanings she does not know.

- Thinking aloud, the teacher assesses the text complexity, stating that there are words in the text (strangers) for which she does not know the meaning, and skipping them will get the "reading" done, but she will not understand what she has read.
  - The coping model thinks aloud while making the decision to skip the words for which she does not know the meaning and stating this practice is a waste of time since she needs to know the words to understand the text.
  - Slowly rereading the text, the teacher underlines five words that she will need to learn the meanings of to understand the text. Students are instructed to underline the same five words in their copies of the text.
  - Thinking aloud, the teacher refers to the large visual aid of the "I Can" statements (see Table 6.9) that reflect the task requirements and serve as

**TABLE 6.9** Sample "I Can" Statements

I Can identify words for which I do not know the meanings.

I Can use context clues to define a word for which I do not know the meanings.

I Can use morpheme clues to define words for which I do not know the meanings.

I Can use context and morpheme clues to define words for which I do not know the meanings.

I Can monitor my progress by identifying, tracking, and categorizing words for which I do not know the meanings.

I Can evaluate my progress by identifying, tracking, and categorizing words for which I do not know the meanings.

I Can self-monitor my actions by comparing my progress with the goals set for a specific reading task that requires me to read and comprehend a short informational text.

---

short-term learning process goals to guide her actions to read and comprehend the text.
- The "I Can" statements can be used to identify strengths and weaknesses associated with her ability to read and comprehend a selected informational text.
- Thinking aloud, the teacher emphasizes what she can do (strengths) and cannot do (weaknesses) based on her present skill assessment. Referring to the displayed Self-Efficacy for Learning Process Goals: Teacher's Model (With "I Can" statements) (see Table 6.3), the teacher rates her self-efficacy for each learning process goal in Column A and instructs students to copy the teacher's scores onto their worksheets.

### What Are Learning Process Goals?

Teacher thinks aloud, using the "I Can" statements (see Table 6.9) to demonstrate how to evaluate and set individual learning process goals. All of the "I Can" statements cannot be accomplished at once; therefore, the teacher prioritizes which learning process goals can be monitored and how to use the PMC (Table 6.6) to track performance.

### What Is Self-Monitoring?

Teacher thinks aloud, demonstrating how she plans to use the PMC and the accompanying Vtrix (with context and morpheme clues) to track her performance, emphasizing the need to maintain systematic and deliberate self-observations of progress.

### What Is Self-Evaluation?

Teacher thinks aloud, demonstrating how she plans to self-evaluate the use of the learning process goals and the PMC to evaluate progress towards using context clues and morpheme clues (Vtrix) to figure out challenging words in a reading text.

## Post-Observation of Forethought

### Evaluate!

### *Will the Teacher Be Able to Reach Each Learning Process Goal Based on Your Observations?*

**Teacher:** Introduces a Teacher Performance Rating checklist (see Table 6.10) to each student and poses questions to students asking them to predict if the teacher will be able to meet the set goals using the PMC and Vtrix.

**Students:** Choosing a number from 0–5 (0 = low, 5 = high), students predict the teacher's performance based on the observed actions and think-alouds that accompanied her introduction of the PMC with Vtrix. They enter their predictions in Column A. Later on in the process, the outcome evaluation will be entered in Column C of the Teacher Performance Rating checklist.

**TABLE 6.10** Teacher Performance Rating

| | Teacher Performance Rating | |
|---|---|---|
| | Now: In Column A use the words "Teacher can" to begin the statement to predict your teacher's performance for attaining each goal (0–5, 0 is the lowest). | |
| | Later: In Column C use the words "Teacher did" to begin the statement to evaluate your teacher's performance (outcome) of attaining each goal (0–5, 0 is the weakest). | |
| | *A* | *B* | *C* |
| | *Rating* | *Learning process goals* | *Rating* |
| | Predict "Teacher can" | | Outcome "Teacher did" |
| 1 | | Identify words for which I do not know the meanings. | |
| 2 | | Use context clues to define a word for which I do not know the meanings. | |
| 3 | | Use morpheme clues to define words for which I do not know the meanings. | |
| 4 | | Use context and morpheme clues to define words for which I do not know the meanings. | |
| 5 | | Monitor my progress by identifying, tracking, and categorizing words for which I do not know the meanings. | |
| 6 | | Evaluate my progress by identifying, tracking, and categorizing words for which I do not know the meanings. | |

|   | *A* | *B* | *C* |
|---|---|---|---|
|   | Rating | Learning process goals | Rating |
|   | Predict "Teacher can" |   | Outcome "Teacher did" |
| 7 |   | Self-monitor my actions by comparing my progress with the goals set for a specific reading task that requires me to read and comprehend a short informational text. |   |

## Observation of Performance

## Doing

## *A Strategic Approach to Reading Informational Texts*

## *Sessions 4–6*

**Performance:** The teacher emphasizes that all learners, even teachers, need to pay close attention to actions and behaviors and monitor progress in order to know what to do and how to do it. Thinking aloud, the teacher calls attention to the displayed Vtrix and the Outside/Inside strategy instructions that will serve as resources to define word parts and use context clues. In addition, the teacher calls attention to the PMC as a tool that will help the teacher self-monitor and self-evaluate her own performance. Students observe as the teacher reminds them that planning to use specific tools is very different than actually using them to complete a reading task. The teacher explains that learning how to use these tools will help with future readings of complex texts. The teacher demonstrates the Outside/Inside strategy of looking both outside (context) and inside (word parts) words to determine their meaning.

### *Modeling: How Am I Doing?*

The teacher models how learning process goals in the Self-Efficacy for Learning Process Goals: Teacher's Model checklist and the PMC with stranger words will both guide and help monitor the teacher's actions when attempting to read a text with difficult words. The teacher comments about how difficult it is to keep track of the academic vocabulary she needs to learn and how challenging it is to use certain strategies. The teacher demonstrates the Outside/Inside strategy by looking first outside a word for context clues, and then inside a word for morpheme clues using Vtrix. Thinking aloud, the teacher demonstrates for the students the actions taken, such as not skipping words, but rather finding their meaning to better comprehend the texts.

## Aligning Self-Efficacy with Setting Learning Process Goals

- The teacher reads aloud one text (displayed on large sheet of paper, interactive whiteboard, or overhead projector), thinking aloud and identifying the words for which the meanings are not known as the students follow along.
- The teacher thinks aloud, modeling how to read the "I Can" learning process goals (see Table 6.9), one at a time, and sets up the reading task by emphasizing the order of actions required to complete the task successfully.
- The teacher thinks aloud, modeling how to determine the accuracy of the self-efficacy rating (from the forethought phase). Now that the teacher is actually performing the task, the teacher confirms that she has the skills to actually figure out the word meanings using the selected tools and strategy.
- The teacher enters her self-efficacy rating for the performance phase in Column B of the Self-Efficacy for Learning Process Goals: Teacher's Model (Table 6.3), explaining why the self-efficacy rating should be higher in the performance phase than the forethought phase now that the teacher has tools and a strategy to use for defining words and checking her progress. The students are instructed to copy the scores entered by the teacher when rating her self-efficacy on their copies of the rating sheet.
- The teacher emphasizes that sometimes self-efficacy for performance might be lower than previously thought. If this happens, students should meet with the teacher to discuss adjusting goals to meet individual skill sets. Students are reminded of the importance of realistically rating one's self-efficacy and that it is ok when ratings differ among individual students and tasks.

## Self-Monitoring and Self-Evaluation

Thinking aloud, the teacher focuses students' attention to the PMC and the goals section of the Self-Efficacy for Learning Process Goals checklist (1–5), and begins the task by lining up her actions with the process goals as depicted in the following sequence (Table 6.11).

## Post-Observation of Performance

### Evaluate!

### Did the Teacher Reach Each Learning Process Goal Based on Your Observations?

**Student:** Each student has a Teacher Performance Rating checklist (see Table 6.10), having completed the predicted performance section (Column A) at the end of the forethought phase. Now, at the end of the performance phase, students assess their teacher's performance based on the progress made towards attaining

**TABLE 6.11** Teacher Actions and Student Engagement Aligned With Learning Process Goals

| Learning process goals | Teacher action | Students' engagement |
|---|---|---|
| 1 Identify words for which I do not know the meanings. | Teacher identifies and writes the words that she does not know onto the PMC as acquaintances (I think I know) or strangers (I don't have a clue). | Students are engaged in observing how the teacher selects and categorizes words as strangers and acquaintances while entering them into the PMC. |
| 2 Use context clues to define a word for which I do not know the meaning. | Teacher uses context (outside) clues to define the word, referring to Vtrix as a guide and entering responses. | Students are engaged in observing how the teacher uses the Vtrix handout with context clues to define the word. |
| | | Students are engaged in observing the teacher enter responses into the PMC, and they copy exactly what the teacher has done. |
| 3 Use morpheme clues to define a word for which I do not know the meaning. | Teacher thinks aloud and uses morpheme (inside) clues to define the word, referring to the Vtrix handout with prefixes, suffixes, and root meanings to define the word. | a. Students are engaged in observing how the teacher uses the Vtrix and morpheme clues to define the word. |
| | | b. Students are engaged in observing the teacher enter responses onto the PMC and enter the same exact responses that the teacher entered. |
| 4 Use context and morpheme clues to define a word for which I do not know the meanings. | Teacher uses both context and morpheme clues to figure out word meanings. | a. Students are engaged in observing how the teacher uses Vtrix with context and morpheme clues to define the word. |
| | | b. Students are engaged in observing the teacher enter responses into the PMC and continue to copy the teacher's model. |
| 5 Monitor my progress by identifying, tracking, and categorizing words for which I do not know the meaning. | Teacher evaluates her progress as tracked using the PMC, asking: (1) Did any "strangers" become "acquaintances"? "Friends"? (2) Can I write a sentence using the word as it is used in the context of the text? | a. Students are engaged in observing how the teacher determines the responses to the questions regarding any improvement in defining words for which she does not know the meaning. |
| | | b. Students are engaged in observing the teacher enter her responses onto the PMC and enter the same responses on their copies of the PMC (Table 6.4). |

the learning process goals. They enter their outcome evaluations choosing a number from 0–5 (0 = weak and 5 = strong) in Column C of the Teacher Performance Rating checklist (see Table 6.10).

**Teacher:** Monitors as students enter outcome evaluation into each component of the reading task as listed on the Teacher Performance Rating checklist, reminding them to base their ratings on observations of her performance/progress towards attaining each learning process goal (Column C).

## Observation of Self-Reflection

### Reflecting On

### *A Strategic Approach to Reading Informational Texts*

### *Sessions 7–9*

**Self-reflection:** Students observe the teacher as the teacher evaluates her performance, indicating whether or not the Outside/Inside strategy with the Vtrix were effective tools when used to determining word meaning, and if the PMC was effective for self-monitoring and self evaluation of her progress. One of the goals of the self-reflection phase is to evaluate one's performance and determine whether or not one is satisfied with the results. It provides the learner with the opportunity to think about what went well (or not) and to make recommendations for improvements for the next time.

### *Modeling: How Did the Teacher Do?*

The teacher models how she uses the information entered into the PMC (self-monitoring tool) to track and evaluate progress. Thinking aloud, the teacher links the learning outcomes to the strategies and tools used to figure out word meaning, self-monitor progress, and self-evaluate. The teacher emphasizes how using the PMC and the learning process goals (from "I Can" statements) provided information for the reflection phase, linking learning outcomes to the strategic processes to determine effectiveness.

### *Linking Self-Efficacy With Learning Process Goal Attainment*

The teacher thinks aloud as she reviews the learning process goals that guided actions. What began as "I Can" statements transformed into learning process goals are now "Did I" questions posed by the teacher to herself to direct a clear and focused reflection of the performance phase. As the teacher responds to each "Did I" question (see Table 6.5), she evaluates the learning outcomes using a scale of 0–5 (5 being the highest rating) and enters reflective notes attributing specific actions that led to accomplishing (or not accomplishing) each learning process goal. Students are directed to copy exactly what the teacher records.

## Evaluating Self-Efficacy

The teacher thinks aloud, reflecting on each learning process goal and discussing strengths and weaknesses encountered during the forethought and performance phases. The teacher enters a self-efficacy rating for the reflection phase into Self-Efficacy for Learning Process Goals: Teacher's Model checklist (Table 6.3, Column C) showing evidence of higher self-efficacy in some learning goals and not in others due to areas that still require skill development. Students copy the teacher's ratings on their forms.

## Linking Learning Process Goals, Self-Monitoring and Self-Evaluation

The teacher thinks aloud, describing how she met or came close to meeting the learning process goals using the Outside/Inside strategy, the PMC, and the Vtrix handout. The teacher specifically links actions to learning outcomes, explaining the effects of using the strategy and self-monitoring tools to define a word for which she did not know the meaning, and as a result, now has better reading comprehension of an informational text.

- Thinking aloud, the teacher looks for evidence of progress by displaying her PMC and the Vtrix handout.
- The teacher calls students' attention to the completed PMC and describes the actions that led to some or all of the words becoming "friends" by the end of the process, attributing the success to the self-monitoring tool.
- Thinking aloud, the teacher reflects on the use of the Outside/Inside strategy and the Vtrix handout and whether or not they were effective as an attempt to figure out meanings of words that she did not know.
- Thinking aloud, the teacher uses information gained from the self-regulatory cycle to consider what to do differently the next time she reads a text with words that have unfamiliar meanings. Will she skip the word or figure out the meaning using the strategy and tools just practiced?

*Note: The completed PMC is displayed in a grouping with the self-efficacy ratings for each phase of the cycle, the Vtrix handout, and the "I Can" learning process goals for students to evaluate their teacher's performance.*

## Post-Observation of Self-Reflection

### Evaluate!

#### *Do You Think the Teacher Reached the Learning Process Goals?*

**Students:** Each student has her Teacher Performance Rating checklist with forethought phase predictions and performance phase outcomes. Students reflect on their teacher's learning outcomes (Column C) and how effectively she used the strategic approach to acquire academic vocabulary by comparing the target learning process goals (Column B) and the expected outcomes (Column A) with the overall results.

A post-observation evaluation can help determine which of the students is ready to move on to the emulation level, where they will be asked to imitate the behaviors they observed with some assistance from the teacher. The teacher asks students to individually rate their self-efficacy and will use those ratings to help decide which students would benefit from observing the process again and which students are ready to move on to the emulation level.

## Emulation Level

### Work Together!

#### *Sessions 10–18*

**Emulation:** The teacher instructs the students to work in small groups to imitate what they observed the teacher do during the observation level. The teacher scaffolds students through the process of setting learning process goals, selecting strategies, self-monitoring their actions, and self-evaluating their progress. The teacher encourages students to identify their own strengths and weaknesses as they attempt to use both morphemes and context clues to figure out words encountered for the first time in an informational text. Students work alongside the teacher using individual PMCs (see Table 6.4) and the Self-Efficacy for Learning Process Goals: Student's Model checklist (see Table 6.3) to keep track of their performance and are now rating themselves under the close supervision of the teacher. The teacher maintains control of the learning environment and paces the students according to their learning needs. The students should begin to demonstrate signs of self-directed learning as they work through the three phases of self-regulated learning.

**Materials (see Table 6.8)**

## Emulation of Forethought

### Planning

#### *A Strategic Approach to Reading Informational Text*

#### *Sessions 10–12*

**Forethought:** Students attempt to recall their teacher's thought patterns and behaviors as she prepared to read a text from an informational text at the previous level. Initially, the teacher works with students to locate and use Common Core–aligned "I Can" statements to set learning process goals and rate their self-efficacy to complete the reading task using Vtrix and by monitoring their performance as they work towards attaining set goals. The teacher and students read the learning process goals together while reviewing the Self-Efficacy for Learning Process Goals: Student's Model checklist. Students become engaged by identifying the sections of the PMC and discuss which sections are linked to the outcomes of the learning process goals.

### *Modeling. What Can We Do Together?*

The teacher focuses students on the informational text, asking them to participate in designing a plan to learn from the text what the author wants them to know. Students should be looking for words that they would prefer to skip over rather than figure out. The teacher states, *"Together, we will read every word in the text, stopping to identify words for which we do not know the meaning. Instead of skipping the words, you will use Vtrix to figure out the meaning, and track your progress using the Progress Monitoring Chart."*

### *Thinking About Setting Learning Process Goals for the Reading Task Requirements*

The teacher asks students to share their prior knowledge of using context clues and word parts to figure out word meanings.

### *Setting Learning Process Goals*

- Teacher and students read Common Core–aligned "I Can" statements, turning them into learning process goals and discussing the expected outcomes for goal attainment.
- The teacher refers to the Vtrix worksheet—specifically, the section with instructions for finding context clues in a text.

- The teacher refers to the Vtrix worksheet, calling each student's attention to how useful the chart can be to figure out word meanings.
- Thinking aloud, the teacher asks students to explain how using the Vtrix might help them read a text with words for which they do not know the meaning of and help them understand the text as the author intended.

## Thinking About Self-Efficacy

The teacher and students prepare to read the text, underlining the words for which they do not know the meaning. They discuss how to self-monitor using individual PMCs.

- Together, the teacher and students read the text and select five words in the text they will need to learn the meaning of to comprehend the author's intent.
- **Individualize:** The teacher reminds the students that they are able to choose five words independent of the teacher's modeling since it is likely that some students are at different levels of vocabulary skills development. Allowing students to choose words will provide them with motivation to participate and, as a result, students who are comfortable doing this will be demonstrating more self-directed learning.
- **Rating self-efficacy**: The teacher focuses students' attention on the "I Can" statements listed on the Self-Efficacy for Learning Process Goals: Student's Model for the forethought phase (Column A).
  - **Discussion:** Both the teacher and students share what they perceive to be personal or general strengths and weaknesses associated with their ability to read and comprehend the selected informational text using the learning process goals to guide the discussion. Students are reminded to consider their strengths and weaknesses associated with their ability to read and comprehend informational text using the strategy and tools provided for them.
    - **Rating:** The teacher and students individually rate their self-efficacy for each learning process goal using a blank copy of the Self-Efficacy for Learning Process Goals: Student's Model (Table 6.4) introduced at the observation level (0 = being the weakest and 5 = strongest) to rate the teacher.

## Thinking About Self-Monitoring and Self-Evaluation

The teacher and students review the components of the PMC:

- Teachers provide students with an opportunity to study the completed model of a PMC along with their blank individual charts before discussing how to use the chart.

- Students discuss why using a graphic organizer (PMC) will help them track their performance when reading a text and figuring out the meanings of words for which they do not know the meanings.

## Post-Emulation of Forethought

### Evaluate!

### *Will You Be Able to Reach Each Learning Process Goal Based on Your Planning and Strategy Use?*

Fourth and fifth graders require time to debrief and evaluate the complexities of the process of preparing for a reading task using self-regulatory strategies. Individualized teacher feedback is necessary to review self-efficacy ratings and determine which students are ready to move ahead to the performance phase and which require additional time and support at the emulation level.

**Teacher:** Individually reviews with students their self-efficacy ratings and learning process goals (Self-Efficacy for Learning Process Goals: Student's Model) to determine which students are ready to move ahead to the performance phase and which students require re-modeling of specific sections of the lesson, less complex texts, and the support provided at the emulation level.

**Students:** With the teacher's assistance, each student works to obtain an accurate self-efficacy rating for each learning process goal and their ability to figure out word meanings rather than skip words for which they do not know the meaning. The self-efficacy ratings and their understanding of the PMC should provide evidence of each student's level of competency to actually use the learning process goals to self-monitor and self-evaluate during a reading task that requires a working knowledge of academic language.

## Emulation of Performance

### Practicing

### *A Strategic Approach to Reading Informational Text*

### Sessions 13–15

**Performance:** Students attempt to become better acquainted with the strategy and tools by imitating the behaviors they observed their teacher perform when she set and evaluated learning process goals and used the PMC for self-monitoring and self-evaluation. The teacher checks to be sure each student has a Vtrix handout to use as a resource to define words using morphemes and to use context clues. In addition, each student is prepared to self-monitor and self-evaluate her performance using their learning process goals and the PMC. Students and the teacher become more familiar with using the Outside/Inside strategy of looking both outside and inside words to determine their meaning.

### Modeling/Peer Modeling: Doing It Together

The teacher and the students read a portion of the informational text together. The teacher encourages students to discuss what they recall about the Outside/Inside strategy and Vtrix. The teacher assists students who volunteer to model how they use Vtrix to help them figure out the words for which they do not know the meanings. Further peer modeling of identifying unknown words and using the PMC are part of the short instructional segment for the performance phase.

### Aligning Self-Efficacy With Setting Learning Process Goals

Together, the teacher and students read closely through the text (individual copies match those displayed on a large sheet of paper, interactive whiteboard, or overhead projector). The teacher and students review "I Can" statements, turning them into learning process goals and discussing the expected outcomes for goal attainment. The teacher and students discuss the order of implementing actions to attain the learning process goals. Students recite back to the teacher the learning process goals and the actions required to attain them.

- The first step is choosing five words for which they do not know the meanings and to categorize them as "strangers," entering them into the PMC (with the goal that they will move up to acquaintances and friends).
- Next, the students use context clues to define the words, using hints from the Vtrix handout.
- Third, the students use morpheme clues to define the word, pulling hints from the Vtrix handout.
- In the next step, students use both context and morpheme clues to figure out or hypothesize the word meanings.
- In the final step, students state how to track progress on the PMC.

Students rate their self-efficacy as accurately as possible for the performance phase using the Self-Efficacy for Learning Process Goals: Student's Model (With "I Can" Statements) checklist. The teacher oversees how students rate their self-efficacy. The teacher provides feedback individually to be sure the self-efficacy ratings are accurate and aligned with learning process goals.

## Self-Monitoring and Self-Evaluation

The teacher directs students to study their own PMCs and to choose one word that they previously identified as a word for which they did not know the meaning. This word should be a "stranger" word on their PMC. The following steps should be used to help students understand how to find a word's meaning to improve comprehension:

- After choosing a word, students read the text, stopping to use context and morpheme clues, tracking their progress on the PMC as they observed their teacher do at the observation level. The teacher remains close by to help students enter tracking information into the chart correctly.
- The teacher directs students to use context clues (outside) to define the word, using Vtrix as a resource. Students and the teacher discuss specific words and how the context clues are helping them figure out the meaning of words for which they do not know the meaning.
- The teacher directs students to use morpheme clues (inside) to define the word, using Vtrix as a resource.
- The students and the teacher discuss specific words and how the morpheme clues are helping them figure out words for which they do not know the meaning.
- The students are then instructed to enter a hypothesis for the word meaning.
- The teacher directs students to evaluate their progress as noted on the PMC individually, and to discuss the outcome of their use of the Outside/Inside strategy.
- Students and the teacher then respond to questions based on what has been recorded on the PMC: (1) Did any strangers become acquaintances? Friends? (2) Bonus: Can the word be used in a sentence in the same way.

## Post-Emulation of Performance

### Evaluate!

### How Close Did We Come to Attaining Our Learning Process Goals?

Fourth- and fifth-grade students require time to realistically assess their progress on assignments that include reading informational texts and learning new vocabulary simultaneously. They need to discuss their experiences with strategy choices, such as the Outside/Inside strategy and Vtrix. Under close supervision, each student works to add information to the Self-Efficacy for Learning Process Goals: Student's Model for the performance phase (Column B). The teacher remains readily available and watching carefully as students begin to work with less supervision.

**Teacher:** Poses questions to students to guide them to assess individually if they were able to accomplish the learning process goals using the Outside/Inside strategy and Vtrix.

**Students:** Respond to questions from the teacher, noting specific areas of their performance that require improvement. Students use teacher feedback to assess whether or not they were able to attain the learning process goals using the Outside/Inside strategy and Vtrix.

## Emulation of Self-Reflection

### Reflecting On

### *Strategic Approach to Reading Informational Texts*

### *Sessions 16–18*

**Self-reflection:** The teacher and students work together to evaluate individual performances, indicating whether or not the Outside/Inside strategy with the Vtrix handout was effective for determining word meanings and if the PMC was an effective self-monitoring and evaluation tool.

### *Modeling*

The teacher encourages students to think aloud along with her as they reflect on outcomes of the processes used to determine word meaning, self-monitor, and self-evaluate. *"What worked?"* is a question that can be discussed among the students attributing specific actions that led to learning outcomes. Peer models can be led to discuss how the use of the PMC and the entries recorded on the Self-Efficacy for Learning Process Goals: Student's Model (With "I Can" Statements) checklist provided them with important information for future similar tasks, linking learning outcomes to strategic processes.

### *Linking Self-Efficacy with Learning Process Goal Attainment*

Together, the teacher and students complete the Self-Evaluation/Reflection Ratings checklist (see Table 6.5). The teacher guides students to rate which goals were fully attained, partially attained, or not met at all. Students enter reflective thoughts into the column *"What would I do differently?"* for future assignments with similar requirements.

## Evaluating Self-Efficacy

Together, teacher and students reflect on each learning process goal, discussing strengths and weaknesses encountered during the forethought and performance phases. Now that they have accumulated some experiences using the strategy and the self-monitoring and self-evaluation tools, students are asked to rate their self-efficacy in Column C of the Self-Efficacy for Learning Process Goals: Student's Model (With "I Can" Statements) checklist to not skip words and to figure out meanings. The teacher looks for evidence that self-efficacy has increased and provides feedback to students for future word-meaning challenges.

## Linking Learning Process Goals, Self-Monitoring, and Self-Evaluation

Together, teacher and students discuss how they met or came close to meeting the learning process goals by using the Outside/Inside strategy, the PMC, and Vtrix. The students are scaffolded to specifically link behaviors to learning outcomes, explaining the effects of using the strategy and self-monitoring tools to define words.

- Students look for evidence of progress in their PMCs and describe the actions that led to some or all of the words becoming "friends" by the end of the process.
- The teacher guides students to reflect on how they used the Vtrix handout and whether or not the clues helped them figure out meanings of words they did not know.
- Students are asked to use information gathered from the entire self-regulatory cycle to consider what they would do differently the next time they read a text with words that have unfamiliar meanings. Will they skip the word or figure out the meaning using the strategy and tools made available to them for increasing their reading comprehension?

## Post-Emulation of Reflection

### Evaluate!

There are many challenges to this task that require fourth and fifth graders to have individual conferences with the teachers to review all of the artifacts gathered from the emulation level. They need to talk about their progress and gather support from their teacher to continue on with their efforts and maintain self-efficacy for the task. The PMC, Self-Efficacy for Learning Process Goals: Student's Model (With "I Can" Statements) checklist, and the Self-Evaluation/

Reflection checklist, along with the Vtrix, can provide both teachers and students with significant information to assess satisfaction with their performance thus far.

**Teacher:** Poses questions to students to ascertain if they were satisfied with the learning process and outcome of the reading comprehension task.

**Students:** With assistance from the teacher, each student evaluates her PMC and the Self-Efficacy for Learning Process Goals: Student's Model (With "I Can" Statements) checklist. These self-evaluations can be used as formative assessments, indicating readiness to move to the self-control level, or a need to work more directly with the teacher by repeating the emulation level.

## Self-Control

### It's Your Turn!

### *Sessions 19–27*

**Self-control:** This level is marked by an increase in independence as students work with less oversight outside of the teacher's constant supervision. The teacher's dominant role shifts to that of an available assistant, allowing students to take charge of their own learning. The teacher remains available to help students upon request. Following a clear introduction to the reading comprehension task, a new text is given to the students along with the Vtrix, self-monitoring, and self-evaluation tools. Students are assigned to small groups with access to the teacher, but are encouraged to work together and use the self-regulatory strategy of help-seeking if they are stuck. Students with similar academic vocabulary development levels should be grouped together. At the self-control level, students are expected to gain independence in reading an informational text without skipping over words for which they do not know the meaning. They are expected to figure out their meanings using context and morpheme clues to better comprehend the author's intent.

### *Materials Readily Available to Students*

1. Informational text(s)
2. "I Can" checklist and handouts for learning goals
3. Vtrix and Outside/Inside handouts
4. Self-Efficacy for Learning Process Goals: Student's Model (With "I Can" Statements) checklist
5. Progress Monitoring Chart
6. Evaluation/Reflection Ratings checklist

# Self-Controlled Forethought

## Planning
## My Strategic Approach to Reading an Informational Text

### Sessions 19–21

**Forethought:** The teacher introduces a new text and assigns students to cooperative learning group work as they prepare to read an informational text without skipping over words they can decode, but for which they might know the meaning. During this phase, students are planning how to deal with words that are important to comprehending the reading task. Students will examine their self-efficacy, goals, strategy use, and self-monitoring skills as they work independently of the teacher. The teacher introduces self-regulatory learning activities with specific instructions requiring students to work with group members to complete the forethought phase within a specific time frame. The teacher remains available to students who may have questions or require clarification.

- Students begin by taking turns reading Common Core–aligned "I Can" statements provided by their teacher to set learning process goals in the Self-Efficacy for Learning Process Goals (With "I Can" Statements) checklist.
- Students discuss their goals with peers and how they will incorporate what they have learned from their observations and practice sessions.
- Students are reminded to refer to the PMC and how they will use it to monitor their actions and evaluate their learning outcomes.

### Modeling/Peer Modeling

The teacher encourages students to model how learning process goals can guide their actions when they come across an unfamiliar word and need to know the meaning to gain from the text the author's intent. Students take turns in their small groups by stating, *"When I come to a word I do not know, I plan to ... ."* Describing their intended behaviors reinforces the student's plan of action and encourages their classmates who might not have high self-efficacy for this specific skill. Their likeness to the peer model can increase their motivation.

### Thinking About Setting Learning Process Goals

With some prompting from the teacher, but mostly on their own, students:

- Share their prior knowledge and experiences using context clues and word parts to figure out word meanings.

- Read the "I Can" statements and discuss the learning process goals and their expected outcomes.
- Identify the Vtrix handout and explain its use to their small group.
- Identify the Self-Efficacy for Learning Process Goals (With "I Can" Statements) checklist and explain how to fill it out to the small group.
- Identify the PMC and explain how to enter words to their small group.
- Identify the Self-Evaluation/Reflection Ratings checklist and explain the importance of feedback from realistic self-evaluations.

### Thinking About Self-Efficacy

Students prepare to read the text and make a plan to not skip over words they do not know. They should be underlining these words in preparation for how they will self-monitor using individual PMCs.
- Students choose five words, independent of their peers, since it is probable that some of the students will have stronger vocabulary skills than others. This will provide students with the opportunity to learn and review more than just the five words they selected. Students are reminded of what an effective tool the Outside/Inside strategy is to figure out word meanings.
- **Rating self-efficacy:** Students rate their self-efficacy to carry out the plan using the learning process goals and expected outcomes to guide them. Students are reminded to consider their strengths and weaknesses associated with their ability to read and comprehend informational text using the strategy and tools provided for them.
  - Students individually enter their ratings into the Self-Efficacy for Learning Process Goals (With "I Can" Statements) checklist for the forethought phase (Column A).

### Thinking About Self-Monitoring and Self-Evaluation

- Students review the components of the PMC.
  - The teacher observes to make sure students notice the links between each learning process goal and self-monitoring questions.
  - The students discuss why using a graphic organizer (PMC) will help them track their performance when reading a text and to figure out word meanings.

## Post Self-Control of Forethought

### Evaluate!

### *Will You Be Able to Reach Each Learning Process Goal Based on Your Planning and Strategy Choice?*

Fourth and fifth graders require time to individually review their Self-Efficacy for Learning Process Goals: Student's Model (With I Can Statements) checklist and the PMC before submitting them to the teacher for feedback. Teacher feedback is critical to students remaining motivated to stay in this challenging a task. The teacher determines which students' evidence readiness to move on to the performance phase.

**Teacher:** Individually reviews self-efficacy ratings and learning process goals to determine which students are ready to move to the performance phase and which students require more practice. The teacher also might determine that for some students, the informational text includes too many unfamiliar word meanings and changes in texts need to be made in order for the student to practice the self-regulated learning strategies effectively.

**Students:** The students describe how they arrived at their self-efficacy rating for each learning process goal. The teacher responds with feedback regarding their perceived ability to figure out word meanings rather than skip words and to the accuracy of their rating. Students' self-efficacy ratings and their understanding of the self-regulatory learning strategies should provide the teacher with evidence of each student's level of competence to actually self-regulate their understanding of challenging words.

## Self-Controlled Performance

### Practicing
### My Strategic Approach to Reading an Informational Text

### *Sessions 22–24*

**Performance:** Students are closely observed as they put their plans into action. In addition to using the Outside/Inside strategy, students are expected to self-monitor and self-evaluate their performance during the reading of an informational text. Students are reminded to work with each other, pose questions to the teacher or peers, and use feedback to improve their performance.

### *Modeling/Peer Modeling*

The students read a portion of the informational text in their small groups. When they come to an unfamiliar word, peer models demonstrate how to use the Outside/Inside strategy. Students think aloud as they work in groups, and this provides a source of cognitive modeling.

## Aligning Self-Efficacy With Setting Learning Process Goals

The students review their logged information from the Self-Efficacy for Learning Process Goals (With "I Can" Statements) checklist, now using the statements and learning process goals to realistically evaluate their progress.

- Students read closely through the text, taking turns thinking aloud as they identify a word for which they do not know the meaning. Each student underlines five words.
- Students rate their self-efficacy as accurately as possible now that they are actually carrying out the plan in the performance phase.
  - **Teacher Response**: Deliberate practice requires teachers to oversee how accurately students rate their self-efficacy and to provide feedback individually to help students through the process of aligning their skills with learning process goals.

## Self-Monitoring and Self-Evaluation

The teacher remains close to help students move through the following steps sequenced in Table 6.12. The students monitor their progress and self-evaluate as they use their learning process goals to guide their actions.

**TABLE 6.12** Learning Progress Goals Guide Student Actions

| | *Learning progress goals* | *Student actions* |
|---|---|---|
| 1 | **Students** work with their individual PMCs, replicating independently what they practiced in previous sessions and using the PMC to self-monitor. | **Choose** five stranger words.<br>**Enter** all five words into the PMC.<br>**Reread** text using Outside/Inside strategy.<br>**Begin to track** behaviors and progress on PMC. |
| 2 | **Students** use context clues to define the word. | **Look** outside the word.<br>**Consult** Vtrix.<br>**Enter** progress on PMC. |
| 3 | **Students** use morpheme clues to define the word. | **Look** inside the word.<br>**Consult** Vtrix.<br>**Enter** progress on PMC. |
| 4 | **Students** use both context and morpheme clues to define the word. | **Combine** information obtained from context and morphemes.<br>**Apply** to word.<br>**Enter** progress on PMC. |
| 5 | **Evaluate** progress in small groups using PMC. | **Review** information entered on PMC.<br>**Discuss** outcomes and satisfaction with performance. |

## Post Self-Controlled Performance

### Evaluate!

#### *Were You Able to Come Close to Meeting Your Learning Process Goals?*

Fourth and fifth graders enjoy sharing their learning experiences. Discussing what they think about their experiences with setting learning process goals and using those goals to monitor and evaluate progress can serve as a catalyst for future use of the strategies. Students review their self-efficacy ratings for the forethought and performance phases of self-regulation and are encouraged to assess their strengths and weaknesses when challenged with reading informational texts and learning new vocabulary simultaneously.

**Teacher:** Poses questions to encourage students to assess individually if they were able to come close to attaining any of their learning process goals.

**Students:** Respond to the teacher, noting areas that require improvement. Students use teacher feedback to assess whether or not they were able to attain the learning process goals using the Outside/Inside strategy and Vtrix, rather than relying on individual perceptions. Individually, students complete Columns A and B of the Self-Efficacy Learning Process Goals: Student's Model (With "I Can" Statements) before reflecting on their progress.

## Self-Control of Reflection

### Reflecting On

#### *My Strategic Approach to Reading an Informational Text*

#### *Sessions 25–27*

**Self-reflection:** Students are encouraged to use teacher feedback to reflect on the effectiveness of the strategies and monitoring tools used. Students use these sessions as an opportunity to explore what they might do differently in the future by evaluating their outcomes. Analysis of their Self-Evaluation/Reflection Ratings checklist can help to shape their reflections, specifically calling their attention to what they would do differently to improve their performance in the future.

## Peer Modeling

Students think aloud, reflecting on their learning outcomes and the processes they used. Posing and responding to questions such as *"Did I find the strategy effective?"* and *"Did I benefit from having a plan?"* as well as *"What worked?"* and *"What did not work?"* can guide students to reflect on specific parts of the self-regulation and attribute performance to specific actions.

## Linking Self-Efficacy With Learning Process Goal Attainment

Students compare all three columns (A/B/C) of the Self-Efficacy for Learning Process Goals (With "I Can" Statements) checklist, looking at the outcomes of individual performances. Students then turn their attention to the Self-Evaluation/Reflection Ratings checklist (Table 6.5) and self-evaluate and rate which goals were fully attained, partially attained, or not met at all. Students enter reflective thoughts into the column *"What would I do differently?"* for future assignments with similar requirements.

## Evaluating Self-Efficacy

The teacher provides the venue for students to reflect on each learning process goal. Students use the time to rate their self-efficacy to not skip words and figure out their meanings and the author's intent. Students are encouraged to look for evidence that self-efficacy has increased or decreased during the self-regulatory cycles. The teacher's feedback includes how to strengthen the skills they have learned for future word-meaning challenges.

## Linking Learning Process Goals, Self-Monitoring, and Self-Evaluation

The students link their behaviors to the learning outcomes by finding evidence of progress in their PMCs. They analyze the actions that led to some or all of the words becoming friends by the end of the process, attributing success to the self-monitoring tools, increased self-efficacy, and self-evaluation.

- The teacher guides students to reflect on the effectiveness of strategies used.
- Students are asked to use information from the entire self-regulatory cycle to consider what they would do differently the next time they read a text with words that have unfamiliar meanings. Will they skip the word or figure out the meaning using the strategy and tools made available to them for increasing their reading comprehension?

## Post Self-Controlled Reflection

### Evaluate!

#### *Are You Satisfied With the Outcome When You Compare Your Progress to Your Learning Process Goals?*

Fourth- and fifth-grade students need time to review their Self-Efficacy for Learning Process Goals: Student's Model (With "I Can" Statements) checklist and their PMCs individually before submitting them to the teacher for feedback. They need to attribute outcomes to specific actions. Students are encouraged to take the lead, seeking out teacher feedback and sharing satisfaction or dissatisfaction with their learning outcomes.

**Teacher:** Poses questions to get students to think about their level of satisfaction with the learning process and outcome of the reading comprehension task. The teacher asks students to brainstorm about improvements that can be made in future tasks.

**Students:** With assistance from the teacher, each student selects one area that needs improvement. Each student assesses her ability to move forward towards independently completing a reading assignment without teacher supervision based on their past performance, which is what they will be doing in the self-regulation level. Both the PMC and Self-Efficacy for Learning Process Goals: Student's Model (With "I Can" Statements) checklist can be used as formative assessments, indicating readiness to attempt tasks at the self-regulation level where students are working outside of the classroom context and must be able to make unanticipated adaptations.

## Self-Regulation

### On My Own!

#### *Promoting Self-Regulated Learning Experiences*

**Self-regulation:** Students work independently within the context of completing academic tasks, knowing help is available if needed. They apply the strategies learned and practiced in previous sessions to comprehend text with difficult vocabulary words. When challenged with a difficult reading assignment, they set learning process goals for determining word meanings, use the Outside/Inside strategy with Vtrix, and self-monitor using the PMC chart independent of teacher supervision as they pace their own learning. The teacher's role is more of a facilitator at this level, providing opportunities for students to use learned strategies outside of the classroom setting. Students' self-regulated experiences can last for days or weeks, as they independently activate their newly acquired skills.

*Materials* are readily available in the classroom, online, and upon request.

## Self-Regulated Forethought

## Making My Own Plans to Read Informational Texts

### *Flexible Time Frame*

**Forethought:** Students are assigned informational texts from different text types for homework. Students work independently in planning how they will learn new vocabulary words by applying the Outside/Inside strategy. They choose individual learning process goals from teacher-provided Common Core "I Can" checklists and incorporate them into a blank Self-Efficacy for Learning Process Goals: Student's Model (With "I Can" Statements) checklist to rate self-efficacy and track progress. To assess academic vocabulary acquisition and self-monitor, students use the PMC. Teachers provide a Vtrix with expanded morphemes with their meanings and target word lists as a resource to be used across the curriculum.

### *Modeling*

Teachers across the curriculum consistently model forethought strategies that include setting learning process goals and using the strategies to define words for which the meaning is not known or unfamiliar. Students, acting as peer models, share the strategy and inform others how to find and use "I Can" statements to set learning process goals. They discuss their learning outcomes as a result of self-monitoring and self-evaluation tools with students who skip words rather than figure out their meanings. Now that they are working outside of the classroom context, others such as parents, older siblings, or the librarian may serve as models from which students can obtain assistance.

### *Learning Process Goals*

- Students consistently access and incorporate the "I Can" statements/goals checklist to set learning process goals for all reading assignments.
- In class, students discuss their reading of the first text and the use of the "I Can" statements. Students also discuss similar tasks and how they can apply the learned strategies to other types of texts.
- The teacher and peers provide feedback during these class discussions.

## Rating Self-Efficacy

- Students consistently align their self-efficacy ratings with "I Can" statements by using Self-Efficacy for Learning Process Goals (With "I Can" Statements) checklists.
- Students become increasingly comfortable adding self-efficacy ratings as they prepare for similar assignments and adjust learning process goals after obtaining feedback from teachers, peers, or others such as a parent, older sibling, or librarian.

## Self-Monitoring and Self-Evaluation

- Generic Outside/Inside strategy handouts, "I Can" checklists, Self-Efficacy for Learning Process Goals: Student's Model (With "I Can" Statements) checklists, PMCs, Vtrix handouts, and Self-Evaluation/Reflection Ratings checklists (used during the self-reflection phase) are made available to students (paper or online) for use across the curriculum to monitor their actions and evaluate learning outcomes.
- Students are encouraged to discuss in class how and when they are using the PMC relative to reading any text with words they find difficult.
- Students are rewarded when they voluntarily discuss the strategic approaches they use for completing their homework.
- Teachers periodically check students' self-monitoring and self-evaluation methods, providing positive feedback regarding areas of significant improvement.

## Ongoing Evaluations

The teacher consistently evaluates how students apply learned self-regulated planning strategies to other assignments. By inviting students to share their Self-Efficacy for Learning Process Goals (With "I Can" Statements) checklists and outcome attributions for other assignments, the teacher encourages use of the tools beyond the classroom setting.

## Self-Regulated Performance

### Independence!

**Performance:** Students independently engage in identifying challenging academic vocabulary words during this phase. They consistently use the strategies, worksheets, checklists, and self-monitoring tools when working independently at home. When homework or other assignments include similar tasks, students often opt to help each other, pose questions to the teacher or peers, and use feedback to improve their performance.

## *Modeling/Peer Modeling: How Are We Doing?*

Teachers and peers consistently model self-regulatory strategies for reading tasks. During class discussions, students are asked to model for peers how they apply self-regulatory learning strategies such as aligning their actions with learning process goals and using self-monitoring information to evaluate learning outcomes for homework, test preparation, and independent reading assignments.

## *Aligning Self-Efficacy With Setting Learning Process Goals*

For homework, students access the "I Can" statements aligned with the Common Core. They choose to read closely through assigned texts independently, identifying words for which they do not know the meaning and rate their self-efficacy for the reading task.

- Students increasingly apply the following strategies to reading tasks:
  - Identifying words
  - Entering strangers into PMC
  - Using context clues
  - Using morpheme clues
  - Using both context and morpheme clues
  - Stating how progress is being tracked
- Students independently rate their self-efficacy in the performance phase column while engaged in the task as accurately as possible and share their findings in class.

## *Self-Monitoring and Self-Evaluation*

Students independently move through the steps practiced during prior classroom experience as they work towards attaining learning process goals. Independently, students carefully enter the information that will help them track their performance on the PMC, using context clues and morpheme clues to define unknown words. They evaluate their progress by comparing their self-efficacy when planning (forethought phase) and performing (performance phase) tasks that include reading informational texts over a set period.

## **Ongoing Reflection**

Proactively seeking teacher feedback for specific areas of their performance that require improvement is a key characteristic of a self-regulated learner. Students requesting teacher feedback for unassigned work or homework done outside of the classroom is critical to taking charge of learning. In some cases, students need to learn how to apply feedback from adults and peers to assess the effectiveness of their use of self-regulatory strategies for assigned reading tasks completed independently. Over time, they become increasingly aware of their self-efficacy by assessing themselves and taking notice if they need assistance or teacher feedback to complete the task successfully. The teacher takes advantage of opportunities to provide feedback regarding improvements in performance when self-regulatory learning strategies are applied to reading tasks.

## Self-Regulated Reflection

### The Reflective Learner

**Self-reflection:** Students incorporate feedback received from others into their reflections regarding the effectiveness of the self-regulatory strategies used to determine word meanings. They analyze the effectiveness of applying self-monitoring and self-evaluation tools (PMC) across the curriculum, making adjustments to the process for future reading. Students evaluate whether the self-efficacy statements, goal setting, strategy use, and self-monitoring processes would help in other academic contexts. Students also discuss unanticipated situations (such as text complexity) and their reactions to them.

### *Peer Modeling*

Students share with peers their reflections on learning outcomes resulting from using the processes selected to determine word meanings, self-monitor, and self-evaluate. Posing and responding to questions such as *"Did I find the strategy effective?"* and *"Did I benefit from having a plan?"* as well as *"What worked?"* and *"What did not work?"* help students evaluate specific behavior and attribute success or failure to specific actions.

### *Linking Self-Efficacy With Learning Process Goal Attainment*

Students consistently reflect on and evaluate their performance; even in the absence of checklists, they use their self-evaluations and reflective "What can I do better?" statements to make adjustments when planning future assignments with similar requirements.

### *Evaluating Self-Efficacy*

Students consistently reflect on learning process goals and become increasingly aware of the role self-assessment plays in learning. They independently evaluate their strengths and weaknesses and learn how to attribute noticeable changes in their self–efficacy ratings to specific actions and behaviors.

## Linking Learning Process Goals, Self-Monitoring, and Self-Evaluation

Students link their behavior to the learning outcomes. They share with their teachers and peers in other learning environments the effects of using the strategy and self-monitoring tools to define unfamiliar words. Teachers consistently provide opportunities for students to obtain feedback regarding their performance and encourage their use of self-regulatory strategies. Students find evidence of progress in their PMC and can attribute their success or failures to use of the self-monitoring tools that led to some or all of the words becoming friends. Students discuss whether each time they completed a homework assignment, the self-monitoring helped and whether they would use these tools in other similar situations.

## Fostering Self-Regulation

Students are given opportunities to share with each other adaptations made to the PMC, how to set better learning process goals, and better ways to reflect and evaluate their performances. The classroom becomes an open forum where both teacher and students discuss their satisfaction with their performance on future reading tasks in light of the effectiveness of using self-regulated learning strategies.

The teacher takes every opportunity to affirm students by commenting on their persistence in reaching goals and remains available to students. The teacher also seeks feedback from other instructors to determine if students are using the tools taught and if their reading of informational texts has improved. She encourages all students to practice using self-regulatory strategies until they become automatic. As previously mentioned, self-efficacy increases as students have positive experiences. Providing students with the tools they need to learn challenging material builds their self-efficacy that will ultimately lead to greater effort and persistence when met with academic content with which they are unfamiliar.

## References

Baumann, J. F., Edwards, E. D., Boland, E. M., Olejnik, S., & Kame'enui, E. (2003). Vocabulary tricks: Effects of instruction in morphology and context on fifth-grade students' ability to derive and infer word meanings. *American Educational Research Journal, 40*(2), 447–494.

Beck, I. L., McKeown, M. G., & Kucan, L. (2002). *Bringing words to life.* New York, NY: The Guilford Press.

Blachowicz, C. L. Z., Fisher, P. J., & Watts-Taffe, S. (2005). *Integrated vocabulary instruction: Meeting the needs of diverse learners in grades K–5.* Naperville, IL: Learning Point Associates.

Bowers, P. N., Kirby, J. R., & Deacon, S. H. (2010). The effects of morphological instruction on literacy skills: A systematic review of the literature. *Review of Educational Research, 80*(2), 144–179.

Calkins, L., Ehrenworth, M., & Lehman, C. (2012). *Pathways to the common core: Accelerating achievement*. Portsmouth, NH: Heinemann.

Chamot, A. U. (2009). *The CALLA handbook: Implementing the cognitive academic language learning approach* (2nd ed.). White Plains, NY: Pearson Education/Longman.

Diamond, L., & Gutlohn, L. (2006). *Vocabulary handbook*. Berkley, CA: Consortium of Reading Excellence.

Duckworth, A. L., Kirby, T. A., Tsukayama, E., Berstein, H., & Ericsson, K. A. (2011). Deliberate practice spells success: Why grittier competitors triumph at the national spelling bee. *Social Psychological and Personality Science, 2*(2), 174–181.

Ebbers, S. M., & Denton, C. A. (2008). A root awakening: Vocabulary instruction for older students with reading difficulties. *Learning Disabilities Research & Practice, 23*(2), 90–102.

Elley, W. B. (1998). An insider's view of the IEA reading literacy study. *Studies in Educational Evaluation, 24*(2), 127–136.

5-1 The Scientific Method. (n.d.). Retrieved August 10, 2014 from the LREI Wiki: https://sites.google.com/a/lrei.org/jdwiki/5th-grade/5-1-the-scientific-method

Kieffer, M. J., & Lesaux, N. K. (2007). Breaking down words to build meaning: Morphology, vocabulary, and reading comprehension in the urban classroom. *The Reading Teacher, 61*(2), 134–144.

Kieffer, M. J., & Lesaux, N. K. (2010). Morphing into adolescents: Active word learning for English-language learners and their classmates in middle school. *Journal of Adolescent & Adult Literacy, 54*(1), 47–56.

Kitsantas, A., Reiser, R. A., & Doster, J. (2004). Developing self-regulated learners: Goal setting, self-evaluation, and organizational signals during acquisition of procedural skills. *Journal of Experimental Education, 72*, 268–287.

Nagy, W. E., & Anderson, R. C. (1984). How many words are there in printed school English? *Reading Research Quarterly, 19*, 304–330.

Nagy, W., Berninger, V. W., & Abbott, R. D. (2006). Contributions of morphology beyond phonology to literacy outcomes of upper elementary and middle-school students. *Journal of Educational Psychology, 98*(1), 134–147.

Nunes, T., & Bryant, P. (2006). *Improving literacy by teaching morphemes*. London: Routledge.

Stahl, S. A. (1999). Different strokes for different folks? A critique of learning styles. *American Educator, 23*(3), 27–31.

Sweeny, S., & Mason, P. (2011). *Research-based practices in vocabulary instruction: An analysis of what works in grades PreK–12*. Report for Studies & Research Committee of the Massachusetts Reading Association.

White, M. (2015, January 22). Why morphemes? (Blog post). Retrieved from http://mariewhiteblog.com/2015/01/22/why-morphemes/

Wong-Fillmore, L., & Snow, C. (2000). *What teachers need to know about language*. (Contract No. ED-99-CO-0008.) U.S. Department of Education's Office of Educational Research and Improvement, Center for Applied Linguistics.

Zimmerman, B. J., Bonner, S., & Kovach, R. (1996). *Developing self-regulated learners: Beyond achievement to self-efficacy*. Washington, DC: American Psychological Association.

Zimmerman, B. J., & Kitsantas, A. (1999). Acquiring writing revision skill: Shifting from process to outcome self-regulatory goals. *Journal of Educational Psychology, 91*(2), 241.

Zimmerman, B. J., & Kitsantas, A. (2002). Acquiring writing revision and self-regulatory skill through observation and emulation. *Journal of Educational Psychology, 94*, 660–668.

Zwiers, J. (2005). The third language of academic English. *Educational Leadership, 62*(4), 60–63.

Zwiers, J. (2013). *Building academic language: Essential practices for content classrooms, grades 5–12*. Edison, NJ: John Wiley & Sons.

# PART III
# Middle School

# 7
# THE SELF-REGULATED WRITER READS LIKE A WRITER

Grades 6, 7, and 8

*Keywords: Self-regulation, mentor texts, self-efficacy, help seeking, text craft and structure, self-management, self-evaluation, self-regulatory strategies of self-instruction*

Transitioning into the middle grades is a major educational concern for teachers and parents of young adolescents. Often, this period is accompanied by a general deterioration in academic performance, motivation, self-perceptions of ability, and relationships with peers and teachers (Dembo & Eaton, 2000). The Common Core standards require writing at the middle school stage of academic development to be fully integrated with reading across different content areas with a range of writing applications to specific subjects. This is not only a challenge for students, but also for the teachers who are asked to teach them these skills. What actions can both teachers and students take to reach the goals set by the Common Core standards for literacy in history/social studies?

Students are required to become comfortable with writing tasks that require them to devote varying segments of time to reflecting on and revising their work. The Common Core standards require writing routinely over an extended time frame to ensure students will be able to research a topic thoroughly, to reflect on feedback or self-evaluations, and to devote their efforts to revise written work until the standard is met. The types of writing assignments include essays and reports that reflect the ability to write in a range of styles (e.g., argumentative, informative/explanatory, narrative) and for a range of audiences, tasks, and purposes. Writing assignments are shorter in length and considered preparation for research papers at the high school level.

Expert writers use specific self-regulatory processes to achieve their goals. Goal setting, effective planning, and self-monitoring can serve as a means for students to detect mismatches between what was intended and what was actually written. Research supports strategy instruction as the most effective intervention for building reading and writing skills (Palinscar & Brown, 1984). The teacher can emphasize the importance of using self-instruction statements to guide strategic planning and goal setting. In addition, the strategies of self-evaluation and help seeking are tools that can help middle schoolers become engaged in the writing process and evaluate their performance.

Self-regulated students are inclined to seek out and use resources to help them attain their goals. As depicted in Table 7.1 for this area of writing and the Common Core, we have selected to focus on the production and distribution of writing and the craft and structure of reading, recognizing the significant impact they have on each other. Training students to self-monitor and self-evaluate using self-instruction statements in regards to planning can increase the motivation to revise an assignment when goals have not been met. As a result of attributing errors in writing outcomes to poor planning or time management rather than low ability, students will be more likely to adapt and revise their work to show continuous growth and development as writers preparing to be college and career ready.

## Do the Crosswalk!

**TABLE 7.1** Linking the Common Core and Self-Regulation

| *College- and career-ready preparation* | *Common Core Standards* | *Self-regulated learning target (Grades 6/7/8)* |
|---|---|---|
| **Anchor** | **Strand and standard** | **Strategy training** |
| **Reading: Craft and structure** (CCSS.ELA-Literacy.CCRA.R.4) Interpret words and phrases as they are used in a text, including determining technical, connotative, and figurative meanings, and analyze how specific word choices shape meaning or tone. | (CCSS.ELA-Literacy.RL.6.4) Determine the meaning of words and phrases as they are used in a text, including figurative and connotative meanings; analyze the impact of a specific word choice on meaning and tone. | Strategies for: Self-questioning Self-monitoring Self-evaluation Text craft and structure monitoring |
| (CCSS.ELA-Literacy.CCRA.R.5) Analyze the structure of texts, including how specific sentences, paragraphs, and larger portions of the text (e.g., a section, chapter, scene, or stanza) relate to each other and the whole. | (CCSS.ELA-Literacy.RL.6.5) Analyze how a particular sentence, chapter, scene, or stanza fits into the overall structure of a text and contributes to the development of the theme, setting, or plot. | |
| (CCSS.ELA-Literacy.CCRA.R.6) Assess how point of view or purpose shapes the content and style of a text. | (CCSS.ELA-Literacy.RL.6.6) Explain how an author develops the point of view of the narrator or speaker in a text. | |

| College- and career-ready preparation | Common Core Standards | Self-regulated learning target (Grades 6/7/8) |
|---|---|---|
| **Middle school writing standards** | | |
| Grade 6 | Grade 7 | Grade 8 |
| **Production and distribution of writing**<br>Produce clear and coherent writing in which the development, organization, and style are appropriate to task, purpose, and audience.<br>CCSS.ELA-Literacy.CCRA.W.4<br>(Standard covers 6–10) | | |
| **Range of writing**<br>Write routinely over extended time frames (time for research, reflection, and revision) and shorter time frames (a single sitting or a day or two) for a range of tasks, purposes, and audiences.<br>CCSS.ELA-Literacy.CCRA.W.10<br>(Standard covers 6–10) | | |

## Becoming Writers

### Writing Requires Accessible Models

The Common Core emphasizes strategic reading and writing, requiring students to acquire knowledge of both the conventions and craft of good writing. The writing standards delineate the expectations for middle schoolers to be able to gain expertise when writing opinions and arguments, informational essays, and narratives in many forms and genres, as described in Table 7.2.

Standard 4 (CCSS.ELA-Literacy.CCRA.R.4) expects students to become writers who can produce clear and coherent writing in which the development, organization, and style are appropriate to the task, purpose, and audience (see Table 7.2).

**TABLE 7.2** Craft and Structure of Writing Requirements for the Common Core

| Types of writing | Examples |
|---|---|
| Narrative | Personal narrative, fiction, historical fiction, fantasy, narrative memoir, biography, narrative nonfiction |
| Persuasive/opinion/argument | Persuasive letter, review, personal essay, persuasive essay, literary essay, historical essay, petition, editorial, op-ed column |
| Informational/functional/procedural | Fact sheet, news article, feature article, blog, website, report, analytic memo, research report, nonfiction book, directions, recipe, lab report |

In this chapter we emphasize the significant role of self-efficacy beliefs as a factor determining student engagement in writing tasks. In addition, we focus on the self-regulatory strategies of self-instruction, self-evaluation and help seeking as examples of self-monitoring techniques educators can introduce to middle schoolers. One of the literacy methods we stress is the importance of learning how to use mentor texts as models of good writing to teach a particular skill or craft (Orttenburger, 2013). The definition of *mentor text* that best fits the purpose of the chapter is a published (or unpublished) professional piece of writing whose ideas, structure, or written craft can be used to inspire a student to write something original. It is a piece of quality literature text that students can use as an exemplar text to model their own attempts for writing (Kane, 2012).

## *Shared Responsibility for Literacy Development*

A quick review of the types of writing and examples displayed in Table 7.2 should alert educators to the challenges faced in training students to write across the disciplines. The Common Core move towards "shared responsibility" is not new. It has been ten years since the National Commission on Writing for America's Families, Schools, and Colleges (2003) identified writing as the "Neglected R." These findings served as a catalyst for the Common Core to make writing more central in schools (National Governors Association Center for Best Practices & Council of Chief State School Officers, 2010) and have increased the challenges teachers face as they design writing instruction for schools that value high-stakes testing and mandated curriculum (McCarthey, 2008; McCarthey, Woodard, & Kang, 2011; Stillman & Anderson, 2011).

Research has shown that integrating reading, talking (speaking and listening), and writing strategies into content areas engaged middle school students who were reading below grade level to read the text, gather and interpret information, and write about their interpretations (Holloway, 2002). For many years, critics of the prepackaged workbooks and skill sheets advocated sweeping reform to include addressing teachers' understanding of the psychological nature of reading and writing processes (Nolen, McCutchen, & Berninger, 1990). The distribution of writing between types of texts puts writing instruction in the hands of teachers at the middle school level who might not have experience or training in literacy integration. Both teachers and students could benefit from adding mentor texts to their classroom resources (Ray, 2004; Griffith, 2010; Orttenburger, 2013).

Before we can ask middle schoolers to write routinely over extended time frames (time for research, reflection, and revision) and shorter time frames (a single sitting or a day or two) for a range of tasks, purposes, and audiences, we must show them what good writing looks like. The present emphasis on writing requires collaboration and gives teachers the opportunity to work closely with school librarians, who now have an enhanced role as critical partners in designing instruction to meet the Common Core. They are the best supporters for teachers who need to make texts available to their students that represent the specific writing style required for individual discipline. Collective efforts in embracing reading and literacy instruction can lead both students and teachers to a better understanding of the elements of good writing. Educators play a critical role in the process, and promoting the availability of mentor texts alone is not enough. Students require a competent model to engage them in observing the behaviors required to read like writers, so they can write like writers. They need models that will teach them how to make the shift from looking for *what* is in the text to noticing *how* a text is written (Zimmerman & Kitsantas, 2002; Gallagher, 2014).

## *The Craft of Writing*

In order to write like a writer, students first must learn what the writer does on the page and between the lines. To read like a writer, students require exposure to a wide variety of texts and training to become sensitive readers of their own and others' work. We could cite multiple authors and practitioners who have used the phrase "read like a writer"; however, the concept originates from the work of Frank Smith who is credited with the phrase "reading like a writer." In *Joining the Literacy Club: Further Essays into Education* (Smith, 1992), Smith raises educator awareness to the role of the classroom teacher to ensure that their classrooms are learning environments filled with meaningful and useful reading and writing.

Reading like a writer is not reading for comprehension of the text, although at some point examining the craft will increase understanding (Griffith, 2010). Reading like writers requires the tools to analyze a text for *how* it is written, not *what* it says (Ray, 2004, 2012). We also need students to revise their work as many times as it takes to meet the standard—editing and proofreading are not enough to shape college- and career-ready writers. In other words, before we can ask our students to write in discourses that are new to them, we need to show them what writing in that discourse looks like. It is common sense that in order to do something well, it is beneficial to see someone doing it well, whether it is making a pizza, learning to dance, or writing. When we read something in a way that reveals to us how it is fitted together, we can then break it down into meaningful parts and attempt to mimic the author.

## Mentor Texts: Reading Like a Writer

A mentor text can be one or more sentences, a paragraph, a section of newspaper, a magazine article, or any work written by a professional writer, including the teacher. It is a piece of quality literature text that students can use as an exemplar

**TABLE 7.3** Uses of Mentor Texts

**Mentor texts are:**
- To be read, analyzed, and then imitated.
- To show students what good writing looks like.
- Models from which students identify and attempt new strategies.
- Literary pieces that students can read independently or with some support.
- To be used to self-evaluate.

**Purposes of mentor text in writing instruction include:**
- Imitating style or learning a new target skill from a model text (grammar/conventions/punctuation).
- Noticing the techniques writers use to get their point across.
- Identifying ideas.
- Identifying voice.
- Identify and understand a genre.
- Identifying structure and organization.
- Word choices that identify the writer's purpose.
- A standard for self-evaluation of writing progress.

text to model their own attempts for writing, and can be reread for many different purposes. The uses of mentor texts for writing instruction are included in Table 7.3.

## Self-Regulation and Middle School Writing

### Self-Efficacy: A Significant Factor in Middle School Writing Performance

Researchers suggest students' beliefs about their own writing competence are instrumental to their ultimate success as writers (Pajares, Johnson, & Usher, 2007). Over time, middle schoolers have had a significant amount of experiences that have given them an accumulated set of beliefs regarding their writing competence. Phrases such as "Why do we need to write another paper?" "I hate writing!" I'm a terrible writer!" are not isolated to a small group of students, but are often heard by teachers from students whose past failures have diminished their self-efficacy. Past experiences are the most influential source when students assess their capabilities to perform a specific task. However, there are ways teachers can design learning environments to help students increase their self-efficacy and decrease uncertainty about doing a specific task.

Observing models do a task can have a significant influence on students who are uncertain about their own abilities. Teachers can serve as writing models, using mentor texts to show students that even the best writers require strong models to emulate when creating new text (Smith, 1992; Griffith, 2010; Gallagher, 2014). In classrooms where writing is a cooperative effort, students also have opportunities to observe peers as they write. These vicarious experiences help create self-efficacy beliefs when they are uncertain about their own abilities (Pajares, Johnson, & Usher, 2007).

Positive encouragement cultivates students' beliefs in their capabilities to do a specific task while providing assurance that success is possible. Negative influences such as focusing on errors, rather than providing constructive feedback, weaken self-efficacy beliefs more than a teacher's positive comments. Teachers can remove some of the anxiety and stress that come from past failures if they allow their students to self-evaluate their writing using a mentor text for comparison.

## *From Help-Seeking to Help-Avoidance*

In transitioning from elementary to middle school, the Common Core increases the complexity of writing requirements at a time when students are most hesitant to ask for help. Help-seeking has been described as an uncomfortable and embarrassing act that requires a degree of courage. Yet, help-seeking is a self-regulatory strategy that encourages the learner to choose specific models, teachers, books, the Internet, or other available resources when a task becomes too difficult to do independently (Karabenick & Newman, 2006). Seeking help for students of all ages is always accompanied by weighing the costs and benefits, and for adolescents, the decision to not seek help is often influenced by the stigma associated with needing assistance. The context of the classroom reportedly influences adolescents' help-seeking avoidance, especially if autonomy is rewarded more than cooperative learning. When teachers provide a socioemotional nurturing context, students have been able to improve their help-seeking behaviors.

## Self-Management Strategies

### *Self-Instruction*

Self-instruction in the form of self-statements can be an effective strategy to monitor performance, encourage persistence, and raise self-efficacy. Self-directed reminders regarding specific task instructions can increase task control. Students can be taught to make lists that will help them strategically talk themselves through tasks, using self-statements that are personal and customized to the writing task. Teachers who have adopted the Self-Regulated Strategy Development (SRSD) model include self-statements while modeling the strategy to demonstrate how they focus attention, monitor performance, cope with anxiety, and reinforce effort (Harris, Graham, & Santangelo, 2013).

We have embedded examples of self-instruction statements aligned with the lesson planning into the three cyclical phases of self-regulation specific to the forethought, performance, and reflection phases. Teachers who regularly incorporate self-instruction statements into modeling help their students set and monitor specific goals as they progress through the phases of self-regulatory learning. Example self-statements that can be helpful during the self-regulatory learning phases can be similar to those found in Table 7.4.

**TABLE 7.4** Self-Instruction During Three Phases of Self-Regulation

| Self-regulation phase | Self-instruction statement | Purpose |
|---|---|---|
| Forethought | "What do I need to do to read like a writer?" | Define the problem/purpose |
|  | "How do I choose a mentor text?" | Define an action |
| Performance | "How do I use a mentor text as a model?" | Explain a process |
|  | "How do I analyze a mentor text?" | Explain a process |
|  | "Is this helping me be a better writer? How?" | Self-instruction |
| Reflection | "This really helped me!" | Self-evaluation |
|  | "I did it (accomplished my goals) by using the strategy!" | Self-reinforcement |
|  | "I will make some adjustments to the strategy by . . . for the next time I have an assignment like this one." | Attribute outcomes |

Teachers have generated "I Can" statements for each Common Core standard, providing students with a method to personalize the standards and turn them into goals. These statements can be converted into "How can I . . ." and used as self-statements to guide students through specific types of writing tasks. Each statement can be broken down into proximal learning goals to help students monitor their progress towards meeting the standard. For example, "I Can" self-statements might include similar wording to those in Table 7.5, forcing students to take a stronger look at their skills and the complexity of the assignment before they begin.

**TABLE 7.5** How Can I . . . ?

| Grade-level standard reference | How can I . . . self-statements |
|---|---|
| 6th grade—Reading literature | How can I analyze the impact of specific word choice on the meaning and tone of the passage? |
| 6th grade—Writing | How can I write an argument with clear reasons and relevant evidence? |
|  | How can I use words, phrases, and clauses to clarify relationships among claims and reasons, and establish and maintain a formal style? |
| 6th grade—Writing | How can I write an informative piece that examines a topic and conveys ideas? |
| 6th Grade—Writing | How can I write a real or imagined narrative with descriptive details? |

## Self-Evaluation

Self-evaluation requires ongoing observations and assessments of students' thoughts, feelings, and actions as they pursue goals. The best way to ascertain if a strategy is leading towards the accomplishment of the goal is to encourage students to ask themselves, "How am I doing?" "Did I set the goal too high?" Students who keep track of their performance know when they have set their goals too high, need assistance, or are making progress. Training students to self-evaluate during task performance is one way to shift the responsibility from the teacher to the learner to adjust their learning activities as they investigate the quality of their work (Zimmerman & Kitsantas, 2005).

Students can help teachers meet the Common Core requirements of formative assessments by frequently comparing their writing progress to the standard or criterion set for the task. Revisions are a key component of the standards for writing, and the lack of time is an area of concern among middle school teachers and students. Editing the draft for grammatical and stylistic errors is most often the only feedback students receive on their writing assignments. Peer and self-evaluations of writing tasks using mentor texts that reflect the expected outcomes can provide both teachers and students with an important revision tool.

## The Evolving Writer

The Common Core significantly increases the outcome expectations for writing tasks as students move up the staircase of reading complexity from the sixth to twelfth grades. Taking their lead from the 2011 National Assessment of Educational Progress writing framework (National Center for Education Statistics, 2012), the Common Core standards direct teachers to spend more time on writing to persuade and to explain and less time on writing about real or imagined experience. The shift does not eliminate the narrative entirely, but rather encourages educators to incorporate narrative writing with arguments and informative/explanatory texts. In other words, prompts are no longer just about what we did on our summer vacation; they must include real and tangible references to the geography or historical value of visiting the seashore.

The standards were revised in 2012 to emphasize student writing assignments should be carefully designed to focus on the elements or characteristics of good writing, including drawing sufficient evidence from texts, writing coherently with well-developed ideas, and writing clearly with sufficient command of standard English (Coleman & Pimentel, 2012).

Instructional implications include the use of mentor texts to teach text features and structures and to apply them to writing. In addition, teachers are asked to model expectations for writing and use rubrics and student work to help students learn how to self-evaluate. Time should be set aside for collaboration to discuss feedback and begin the process of revision before editing and proofreading.

## Shifting Focus: Self-Regulated Writing Workshop

**TABLE 7.6** Shifting to Be College Ready

| *CCSS reading and writing shifts* | *Common Core Targets "I Can" (Wulber, 2010)* | *Self-regulation* |
|---|---|---|
| **Writing: Text types, responding to reading, and research**<br>The standards acknowledge the fact that whereas some writing skills, such as the ability to plan, revise, edit, and publish, are applicable to many types of writing, other skills are more properly defined in terms of specific writing types: arguments, informative/explanatory texts, and narratives throughout the document. | **Writing**<br>• "I can use guidance from my peers and adults to plan, revise, and edit my writing."<br>• "I can try new approaches and focus on addressing my purpose and audience in my writing." | Self-instruction—self statements<br><br>Self-evaluation—writing performance<br><br>Self-efficacy for writing tasks<br><br>Help-seeking |
| **Reading, writing, and speaking** grounded in evidence from the texts, both literary and informational. Although the standards still expect narrative writing throughout the grades, they also expect a command of sequence and detail that are essential for effective argumentative and informative writing. | **Writing**<br>• "I can write an argument with clear reasons and relevant evidence."<br>• "I can write an informative piece that examines a topic and conveys ideas."<br>• "I can write a real or imagined narrative with descriptive details and effective technique." | |
| **Building knowledge through content-rich nonfiction**<br>In Grades 6–12, the standards for literacy in history/social studies, science, and technical subjects ensure that students can independently build knowledge in these disciplines through reading and writing. Reading, writing, speaking, and listening should span the school day from K–12 as integral parts of every subject. | **Language**<br>• "I can use resources to gather word knowledge when needing a word important for comprehension and/or expression."<br>**Reading informational text**<br>• "I can trace and evaluate the argument and claims in a text."<br>**Reading informational text**<br>• "I can assess whether an author's reasoning is sound and whether he has enough evidence to support the claims he makes." | |

## Standardized Test Relevance

Today's standardized tests require middle schoolers to analyze and glean information from professional literary pieces and write an essay. Narrative tasks measure students' ability to produce clear and coherent writing in which the development, organization, and style are appropriate for the task, purpose, and audience. In the writing assessment for grades 6, 7, and 8, students can be asked to write a story, detail a scientific process, write a historical account of important figures, or describe an account of events, scenes or objects. Students are expected to demonstrate that they can apply the knowledge of language and conventions in their writing while tracing and evaluating an argument and specific claims from a text.

## Transforming Writers' Workshop with Self-Regulated Learning

Many teachers who incorporated writers' workshops into their curriculum can trace their initial exposure to Nanci Atwell's *In the Middle: Writing, Reading, and Learning with Adolescents* (1987). Initially, the writing workshops extended writing time for multiple revisions, gave students ownership of their work, and provided a venue where they were able to connect their personal lives to writing tasks. In all, the success stories were plentiful, but in reality, many teachers' experiences led them to think they were doing something wrong when the "miracles" described by writing workshop advocates such as Atwell (1987) and Donald Graves (1983) did not occur (Lensmire, 1994).

Atwell revisited the original writing workshop model and acknowledged that not all students are motivated to become engaged even in the best student-centered learning environments. Rather than returning to the prescriptive format of teaching writing with the teacher as the controller, Atwell describes a balanced approach that promotes the teacher as facilitator, then writing mentor, mediator, and model in a more structured writing environment. Included in the role of the teacher is finding ways to reveal to students what experienced writers do and to allow young writers to observe their teachers' writing emerge into publishable works along with their own.

The integrated model provides clear direction on how writing workshops within the context of attaining self-regulatory competency can increase students' use of self-regulatory skills using the basic tenets teachers are familiar with from writers' workshops. Table 7.7 describes what both teachers and students can be doing at each level while writing within a framework of the Common Core requirements and self-regulated learning.

**TABLE 7.7** Self-Regulated Writing Workshop

**Strategic teaching method:**
Modeling Teachers model the strategy, thinking aloud and demonstrating sequential steps aligned with goals and learning outcomes. Teachers who act as coping models make errors and then promptly correct them, helping students to identify and eliminate errors (Zimmerman & Kitsantas, 2002).

| *Levels of self-regulatory development* | *Teacher actions* |
|---|---|
| **Lesson** **Observe** | At the observation level, teachers think aloud, setting goals and demonstrating a writing strategy, carefully monitoring students' engagement. The observation can be repeated multiple times until students have gained the necessary skills to imitate the behaviors that have been observed. |
| **Emulate** | At the emulation level, the teacher selects specific behaviors for students to imitate under close supervision. As the students begin to imitate what they saw their teacher do, the teacher is visible and actively engaged in re-modeling or working with individual students who require further demonstration. The teacher checks for students' self-efficacy, reminding them of their strengths and how well they have done on tasks similar to the present activity. In addition, self-monitoring of goals set during the observation phase is checked. |
| **Writing** **Self-control** | At the self-control level, the teacher remains available to students while they are actively engaged in the observed writing task. The teacher circulates around the room, monitoring students' performance and providing assistance as needed to complete the task independently. As students begin to work independently in small groups or with peers, they check progress towards goal attainment and levels of self-efficacy. Students access assistance and use feedback from both peers and teacher to move the task forward. |
| **Collaboration** **Self-control** | At the self-control level, students work with peer models or others, self-monitoring and self-evaluating their progress. During this time, the teacher withdraws support slowly, having students complete the task with as much autonomy as possible. |
| **Independent application** **Self-regulation** | At the self-regulation level, students independently apply the learned strategy to similar tasks outside of the supervision of the teacher. |

## Instructional Component for Self-Regulated Learning

## Middle Schoolers (Grades 6, 7, and 8)

**Self-efficacy:** Teachers engage in practices and create interventions aimed at reinforcing positive self-conceptions and diminishing negative ones throughout the writing task (Pajares, Johnson, & Usher, 2007). Learning to read like a writer is a challenging skill, and some middle schoolers have past experiences that lead them to believe they do not have the skills to use mentor texts as models of good writing. Evaluating self-efficacy at the four sequential levels of observation, emulation, self-control, and self-regulation during the entire activity is a form of self-monitoring. As the demands of the writing task increase or require more independence, students are encouraged by teachers to identify parts of the task that are particularly challenging and parts of the task that are easily accommodated. Students will use self-instruction statements from their checklist as criteria for assessing self-efficacy.

**Self-instruction:** Customized, specific self-statements or self-directed reminders regarding the specific task help students focus on their goals and monitor their progress. For each phase of the self-regulatory cycle, students' self-statements serve to guide their progress monitoring and goal attainment. Lists of self-instruction statements are made during the forethought phase, checked during the performance phase, and evaluated during the reflection phase, as depicted in Table 7.8.

**Goal setting and Self-evaluation:** The cyclical processes of self-regulation provide both learner and teacher with valuable information gathered before, during, and after the task. Students can evaluate their progress by rereading their work and comparing it to the mentor text. Goals are set during the forethought phase; however, students conduct ongoing self-evaluations through self-observations to ascertain if a strategy is leading towards goal attainment. Guided by self-instruction statements and teacher feedback, students record their progress for the duration of an essay-writing task using the self-instruction and self-efficacy ratings checklists (see Table 7.8).

For each cyclical phase of self-regulation, at the observation, emulation, and self-control levels, students are expected to evaluate the usefulness of the strategies in accomplishing the goals.

- For use only at the observation level, Table 7.9 focuses students' attention on the details of what they are observing in order to evaluate the planning and strategies used by their teacher to complete the writing task.
- For use at the emulation and self-control levels, Table 7.10 guides students in evaluating the usefulness of the strategies for themselves by making judgments at the end of each phase. Part A asks students to predict the effectiveness of the planning strategies at the end of the forethought phase. Part B asks students to evaluate the outcomes following the performance phase. Part C asks students to reflect on the usefulness of the strategies after they were applied to a specific writing task.

**TABLE 7.8** Self-Instruction and Self-Efficacy Ratings: All Phases

**Think about it: Read each self-instruction statement, goal, and strategy choice.** Based on your observations and what you know about the writing task, do you think you will be able to carry out this action plan?
Rate your self-efficacy for being able to reach the "I Can" goals one phase at a time:
0 = Very difficult; 5 = Very easy

| A | B | C | D | E | F |
|---|---|---|---|---|---|
| Self-Instructional Questions | "I Can" Statements | Strategy Choice | Fore-thought | Perfor-mance | Reflection |
| How can I analyze the impact of specific word choice on the meaning and tone of the passage? (Reading Like a Writer) | "I can analyze the impact of specific word choice on the meaning and tone of the passage in a mentor text by reading like a writer." | Read Like A Writer | | | |
| How can I write an argumentative/persuasive essay? (Resources) | "I can do a craft analysis using five elements of good writing and identify loaded words and phrases." | Help/Resources | | | |
| What do I need to do to read like a writer? (Resources) | "I can write an argumentative/persuasive essay using the mentor text as a model." | Follow Teacher's Model/Resources | | | |
| Who will help me choose a mentor text? (Resources) | "I can ask the librarian or use other sources to help me choose a mentor text and answer questions I might have about the writing task." | Teacher/Librarian/Peer | | | |
| How will I know that I am on the right track? (Self-Evaluation and Feedback) | "I can track my progress towards my goal of writing an argumentative essay using a mentor text as a model using the RLW and WLW charts." | Self-Evaluation/Feedback | | | |
| How difficult will it be to do this writing task? (Self-Efficacy) | "I can analyze the impact of specific word choice on the meaning and tone of the passage in a mentor text by reading like a writer." | Track Self-Efficacy/Get Help | | | |

**TABLE 7.9** Evaluate! All Three Phases of Self-Regulation: Observation Level

| | **Part A—Forethought prediction rating: Will the plan work?**<br>Instructions: Rate how useful the strategy choices will be based on your observation of your teacher's planning. (1 = not useful; 10 = useful) | |
|---|---|---|
| Goals | *The plan will help the teacher. . . .* | *Forethought predictions* |
| 1 | Analyze the impact of specific word choice on the meaning and tone of the passage in a mentor text by reading like a writer. | |
| 2 | Do a craft analysis using the five elements and identify loaded words and phrases. | |
| 3 | Write an argumentative/persuasive essay using the mentor text as a model. | |
| 4 | Ask the librarian or my teacher to help me choose a mentor text and answer questions I might have about the writing task. | |
| 5 | Use a self-evaluation chart to track my progress towards my goal of writing an argumentative essay using a mentor text as a model. | |
| | **Part B—Outcome rating: Did the plan work?**<br>Instructions: Rate how useful the strategy choices were based on your observations of your teacher's performance. (1 = not useful; 10 = Very useful) | |
| Goals | *The strategies and planning helped the teacher:* | *Performance outcome evaluation* |
| 1 | Analyze the impact of specific word choice on the meaning and tone of the passage in a mentor text by reading like a writer. | |
| 2 | Do a craft analysis using five elements and identify loaded words and phrases. | |
| 3 | Write an argumentative/persuasive essay using the mentor text as a model. | |
| 4 | Ask the librarian or my teacher to help me choose a mentor text and answer questions I might have about the writing task. | |
| 5 | Use a self-evaluation chart to track my progress towards my goal of writing an argumentative essay, using a mentor text as a model. | |
| | **Part C—Refection rating: Is this a plan you can use?**<br>Instructions: Rate how useful the strategy choices would be for future similar tasks based on your observations of your teacher's performance. (1 = not useful; 10 = very useful) | |
| Goals | *The strategies and planning were useful to:* | *Reflection outcome evaluation* |
| 1 | Analyze the impact of specific word choice on the meaning and tone of the passage in a mentor text by reading like a writer. | |
| 2 | Do a craft analysis using five elements and identify loaded words and phrases. | |

*(Continued)*

**TABLE 7.9** (Continued)

| Goals | The strategies and planning were useful to: | Reflection outcome evaluation |
|---|---|---|
| 3 | Write an argumentative/persuasive essay using the mentor text as a model. | |
| 4 | Ask the librarian or my teacher to help me choose a mentor text and answer questions I might have about the writing task. | |
| 5 | Use a self-evaluation chart to track my progress towards my goal of writing an argumentative essay using a mentor text as a model. | |

**TABLE 7.10** Evaluate! All Three Phases of Self-Regulation

### (1) Forethought (2) Performance (3) Self-Reflection

**Part A—Forethought predictions rating: Circle one! Emulation/self-control level**
Instructions: Rate how useful the strategy choices will be in meeting your goals (1 = not useful; 10 = very useful)

| Goals | The plan will help me. . . . | Forethought predictions |
|---|---|---|
| 1 | Analyze the impact of specific word choice on the meaning and tone of the passage in a mentor text by reading like a writer. | |
| 2 | Do a craft analysis using the five elements and identifying loaded words and phrases. | |
| 3 | Write an argumentative/persuasive essay using the mentor text as a model. | |
| 4 | Ask the librarian or my teacher to help me choose a mentor text and answer questions I might have about the writing task. | |
| 5 | Use a self-evaluation chart to track my progress towards my goal of writing an argumentative essay using a mentor text as a model. | |

**Part B—Performance outcome rating: Circle one! Emulation/self-control level**
Instructions: Rate how useful the strategy choices were based on your performance. (1 = not useful; 10 = very useful)

| Goals | The strategies and planning helped me: | Performance outcome evaluation |
|---|---|---|
| 1 | Analyze the impact of specific word choice on the meaning and tone of the passage in a mentor text by reading like a writer. | |
| 2 | Do a craft analysis using five elements and identifying loaded words and phrases. | |
| 3 | Write an argumentative/persuasive essay using the mentor text as a model. | |

| Goals | The strategies and planning helped me: | Performance outcome evaluation |
|---|---|---|
| 4 | Ask the librarian or my teacher to help me choose a mentor text and answer questions I might have about the writing task. | |
| 5 | Use a self-evaluation chart to track my progress towards my goal of writing an argumentative essay using a mentor text as a model. | |

**Part C—Reflection outcome rating: Circle one! Emulation/self-control level**
Instructions: Rate how useful the strategy choices would be for future similar tasks based on your observations of your performance. (1 = not useful; 10 = very useful)

| Goals | The strategies and planning were useful to: | Reflection outcome evaluation |
|---|---|---|
| 1 | Analyze the impact of specific word choice on the meaning and tone of the passage in a mentor text by reading like a writer. | |
| 2 | Do a craft analysis using five elements and identifying loaded words and phrases. | |
| 3 | Write an argumentative/persuasive essay using the mentor text as a model. | |
| 4 | Ask the librarian or my teacher to help me choose a mentor text and answer questions I might have about the writing task. | |
| 5 | Use a self-evaluation chart to track my progress towards my goal of writing an argumentative essay using a mentor text as a model. | |

**Help-seeking:** Teachers can create learning environments that train students in adaptive help-seeking, which is what successful learners do when they become "stuck." What identifies help-seeking as a self-regulatory strategy is that the learner asks for only enough information to complete the task independently. One way to encourage this behavior is by removing the stigma that is associated with needing help, especially for middle schoolers, who devote a significant amount of time to building a strong image for their peers. Another way is for teachers to model help-seeking behaviors and share with their students the struggles they have with writing tasks. In addition, teachers can share personal resources, such as mentor texts, with their students, with instructions of how they use these models of good writing when faced with a challenging writing task.

## Instructional Components for Using Mentor Texts
### To Read and Write Like a Writer

**Modeling:** Students can acquire new writing skills using the four sequential levels of observation, emulation, self-control, and self-regulation when the instructor provides a clear image of how the specific skill should be performed (Schunk & Zimmerman, 1997; García-Sánchez & Fidalgo-Redondo, 2006).

- The instructor models how to use a mentor text and the self-regulatory strategies needed to attain writing goals. The mentor texts are works from professional authors, teachers, or peers that model the specific writing skill being taught.
- Teachers who write themselves write with their students' model while thinking aloud about generating an idea, struggling through a draft and revisions, searching for vocabulary, and refining the sentence fluency.
- Modeling the writing process as a series of routine behaviors increases vicarious learning and provides a map for students to follow when their self-efficacy is low and motivation is gone. Conversations that include "Did you see the argumentative essay online yesterday about sugary drinks?" send a message to your students that the teacher is not only a writer but also a reader.
- Piquing their interest, making a real-life connection, and providing a mentor text are all modeling techniques that indicate the teacher is writing alongside students (Kittle, 2008).

**Read like a writer:** Reading aloud and studying a mentor text as a whole class can clear away misconceptions about what it means to read with a "writer's eye."

- While the teacher is thinking aloud, analyzing the craft and structure of the piece, students become increasingly aware of well-crafted writing and develop an ear to recognize what it sounds like (Griffith, 2010).
- Students can practice how to find five elements of good writing in a mentor text before using those elements in their own essays. To increase their understanding about how words become argumentative, persuasive, descriptive, and informational in essays, students can use this method of text analysis to identify ideas, organization, voice, conventions, sentence fluency, loaded words (appeal to senses), and word connotations that convey the author's tone. Teachers have had significant success using the 6 + 1 framework (Culham, 2005) as a method to assess their students' writing; we designed a model to include only five of the elements of good writing and included additional criteria to analyze mentor texts.
- Analyzing mentor texts helps students learn how to convey their own thoughts and information and to write effectively. It is a form of craft analysis that teachers can use and adapt to learning situations where students are given short mentor texts and trained to identify the elements of good writing, "loaded" language and words, and word connotations. "Loaded" language and words refer to words that have the potential to generate emotions or feelings.
- Students can be instructed to track their progress using a Read Like a Writer Worksheet (see Table 7.11) that contains a mentor text and columns to record evidence of the five elements of good writing and persuasive techniques (loaded words and language, and word connotations).

**Write like a writer:** Professional writers compare their work to more proficient writers to track their progress and assess the strength of their writings.

**TABLE 7.11** Read Like a Writer Worksheet

Instructions: Read the mentor text like a writer, looking for the elements of good writing and the persuasive techniques. Use the space provided to enter your responses and evidence of good writing.

| Read like a writer | Elements of good writing | Persuasive techniques: Writer's use of words and language | |
|---|---|---|---|
| **Mentor text:** Argumentative (Next lessons can insert Informative, Persuasive, and Descriptive into template). | **Read like a writer:** Look for the five elements of good writing. | **Loaded words/ language:** Look for words or phrases that appeal to senses. | **Word connotations:** Look for words or phrases that convey the author's tone behind the ideas and purpose. |
| The facts are in. The science is definitive. The question is no longer whether climate change is happening, but whether we can afford not to act. In the western United States, changes in our climate are fueling wildfire seasons that are longer and more intense—putting people, communities, and businesses at risk. As we're seeing right now, wildfires unquestionably have devastating impacts on the lives of many Americans. This weekend, California declared a state of emergency as two major wildfires scorched acres of land, threatening towns and forcing many to evacuate. These are just two of the fourteen fires that are currently burning throughout the state. Make no mistake: The cost of inaction on wildfires and climate change is too high a price for Americans to pay, particularly when we have a chance to address this right now. As a new report from the Council of Economic Advisors points out, the consequences of climate change reach beyond our environment. The impacts of climate change threaten our homes, our health, and our economic prosperity. In fact, delaying action for a decade would increase the cost of responding to climate change by 40 percent. | **Ideas:** What is the writer writing about? How is the writer putting forth the purpose? **Organization:** Are the ideas in order? Do they flow from one idea to the next? What are the leads? Are there transitions? Sequencing? Pacing? **Voice:** How does the writer feel about what he is saying? Can you feel the writer's passion for the topic? Does the writer reveal emotion? **Conventions:** How does the writer use conventions to make it easier to read and meaningful? Is anything unusual done with grammar and punctuation? **Sentence fluency:** How does it sound read aloud? Does it have a rhythm? Are the sentences short? Long? Do they vary? | | |

Students can learn to emulate good writing, not copy it, following the "Benjamin Franklin" model, who mastered the art of formal writing through modeling. When Franklin came upon a written passage that was especially well written, he would try to emulate it—he would make brief notes about each sentence and then attempt to rewrite the passage from his notes. Finally, he would compare his version with the original one and revise his writing until it came close to the model (Zimmerman, 1994).

- Students can be instructed to track their progress using a Write Like a Writer Worksheet (Table 7.12) to write their essay alongside the mentor texts, checking for similarities and differences.

**Persuasive techniques (loaded words, language, and connotations):** Loaded words and phrases reflect deliberate and purposeful vocabulary choice by the writer to move the audience in a specific direction.

- Many middle schoolers are just beginning to learn about the power of words on readers' emotions.
- Loaded words and phrases can carry attitude and feeling. Their unique connotations are based on the response the author intended to get from his audience. They also can indicate the author's own perspective on the topic. For example, a child can be described as curious or nosy—one connotation infers the child is annoying, the other that the child is inquisitive.
- Finding words in the mentor text that have positive and negative effects on the reader is an important skill for writers to develop. Using loaded words correctly that invoke a response determines whether an essay is persuasive, argumentative, or informative.
- Students who practice identifying and evaluating specific types of words and sentence structure as positive, negative, or neutral increase their writing vocabulary and construct stronger essays (Rog & Kropp, 2004).
- The Reading Like a Writer Worksheet includes columns for students to identify loaded words in the mentor text and their connotations.
- The Writing Like a Writer Worksheet includes columns for students to identify loaded words in their own writing and their connotations.

### *Prior Knowledge and Lesson Requirements*

- Selected mentor text appropriate to students' reading levels.
- Mentor texts selected for this lesson have been previously read using close reading strategies and are familiar to the students.
- Mentor text selected for genre being taught.
- Students have prior knowledge and practice with the three types of writing: narrative, persuasive/argumentative, and informative.
- Minimum of one hour a day devoted to writing workshop.

**TABLE 7.12** Write Like a Writer Worksheet

| Instructions: Now it is your turn to use the mentor text model to write a short essay about a similar topic of your choice. The mentor text is about climate change. You can choose from a list of topics provided by your teacher. Write your essay and then analyze it by checking for elements of good writing, persuasive techniques, and similarities to the mentor text. |||
|---|---|---|
| *Mentor Text (Excerpt)* | *Write Like a Writer* | *Checking for Elements of Good Writing in My Text* |
| The facts are in. The science is definitive. The question is no longer whether climate change is happening, but whether we can afford not to act. In the western United States, changes in our climate are fueling wildfire seasons that are longer and more intense—putting people, communities, and businesses at risk. As we're seeing right now, wildfires unquestionably have devastating impacts on the lives of many Americans. This weekend, California declared a state of emergency as two major wildfires scorched acres of land, threatening towns and forcing many to evacuate. These are just two of the fourteen fires that are currently burning throughout the state. Make no mistake: The cost of inaction on wildfires and climate change is too high a price for Americans to pay, particularly when we have a chance to address this right now. As a new report from the Council of Economic Advisors points out, the consequences of climate change reach beyond our environment. The impacts of climate change threaten our homes, our health, and our economic prosperity. In fact, delaying action for a decade would increase the cost of responding to climate change by 40 percent. | **My text:** Argumentative | **Ideas:** What is the writer writing about? How is the writer putting forth the purpose? |
| | | **Organization:** Are the ideas in order? Do they flow from one idea to the next? What are the leads? Are there transitions? Sequencing? Pacing? |
| | | **Voice:** How does the writer feel about what he is saying? Can you feel the writer's passion for the topic? Does the writer reveal emotion? |
| | | **Conventions:** How does the writer use conventions to make it easier to read and meaningful? Is anything unusual done with grammar and punctuation? |
| | | **Sentence fluency:** How does it sound read aloud? Does it have a rhythm? Are the sentences short? Long? Do they vary? |
| | | **Persuasive techniques** |
| | | **Loaded words?** |
| | | **Connotations?** |

- Teacher familiarity with reading like a writer practice.
- Teacher familiarity with levels and phases of self-regulation.
- Instruction in loaded words and phrases.
- Exposure to mentor text concept.

### *Materials Master List*

- Pencils
- Writing surfaces (blank)
- Argumentative text (short)
  - Mentor text displayed on 3 x 3 surface
- Read Like a Writer Worksheet (Table 7.11) (display, individual)
- Write Like a Writer Worksheet (Table 7.12) (display, individual)
- Self-instruction and self-efficacy ratings checklist (Table 7.4)
- Evaluate! Predict/Outcome/Reflect
  - Observation level (teacher focus) (Table 7.9)
  - Emulation and self-control levels (student focus) (Table 7.9)

**The Plan: Self-Regulated Writing Begins with Good Reading**

**Grades 6, 7, and 8**

**Objective:** Students will do a craft analysis of a mentor text and write an essay using the self-regulatory strategies of goal setting, self-instruction, self-evaluation, and help-seeking.

**Sessions:** Increased complexity of writing skills is an individual and slow process for many middle school students. Due to past failures, self-efficacy in this academic area is low, which impacts motivation and task engagement. Writing instruction using the integrated framework is time consuming, yet rewarding, when used in conjunction with current methods of writing instruction. A self-regulated writing workshop can become part of current curriculum practices by integrating self-regulatory training into lessons that target specific skills.

## Observation Level

### Watch It!

### *Sessions 1–15*

**Observation:** The teacher uses extensive think-alouds (verbal modeling) and visual aids, making his thought processes transparent as he prepares to do a writing task (argumentative) that requires specific skills and language that might not yet have been mastered. Focusing students' attention on the model's feelings of self-efficacy, the teacher uses self-instruction statements, self-evaluation strategies, and help-seeking to self-monitor his performance while learning to read and write like a writer. Students are observing the teacher at this level and are actively engaged by the teacher to follow every action and verbalization the teacher models.

**Materials:** At this level, the task materials are displayed and the teacher refers to them as he models. Students are engaged in using the Evaluate! checklist for all three phases when they are asked to assess the usefulness of the teacher's strategies and action plan.

## Observation of Forethought

### Planning
### A Strategic Approach to Writing Task

#### Sessions 1–5

**Forethought:** Students observe the teacher prepare to write an argumentative essay. Using a writing prompt similar to those found on state standardized tests, the teacher introduces the Common Core standards aligned with the task. The standards are used for the teacher to generate self-instruction questions to guide his actions. The teacher stresses how low his self-efficacy is for the writing task and the help-seeking behaviors he will use to meet the goals.

### *Modeling: What Is the Teacher Doing?*

Students are engaged in watching the teacher think aloud as he reads aloud and analyzes the writing task, noting it has similar properties to prompts on the latest state exam. The teacher emphasizes a specific prompt often seen on the state exams, asking students to write a text-based response that analyzes the strength of a particular claim.

- The teacher pauses to discuss what it means to analyze the strength of a claim. Thinking aloud, the teacher states that an argument consists of two main components: a claim and reasons for that claim. Therefore, any essay that requires the writer to support the strength of a claim would be either persuasive or argumentative.
    - Students are engaged in the observation by a show of hands to agree or disagree with the teacher's choice of the type of essay (argumentative/persuasive) required to support the strength of a claim.
- The teacher continues thinking aloud, talking about himself as a coping model—someone who has struggled with writing in the past, and someone who has had some successes. While thinking aloud, the teacher attributes these past performances towards specific strategies: *"I am not sure (low self-efficacy)*

*that I remember how to write an essay that persuades or presents an argument. I know I will need help (help-seeking) and to keep track of my progress (self-evaluation) if I am going to do this writing task successfully!"*

- The teacher thinks aloud, brainstorming about what tools will be needed to complete the writing task successfully. The teacher then introduces the concept of using mentor texts as models, thinking aloud: *"What do good writers do when they need help with their writing?"*
    - The students are engaged in the observation by offering suggestions of where good writers get help from when they need to write.
    - The teacher keeps students focused on observing him by listing resources where good writers can get help, including Benjamin Franklin!
    - Thinking aloud, the teacher chooses and displays a mentor text that models a persuasive essay.
    - Thinking aloud, the teacher expresses doubts that reading the mentor text alone will be of any help to write the argumentative/persuasive essay.
        - The teacher states that the mentor text is only a tool and that how the tool is used needs a strategy.
        - Reading like a writer is a strategy that will help him write like a writer. The teacher introduces the read like a writer strategy (see Table 7.7), explaining specific parts of the strategy and focusing students' attention on each section, describing how he plans to use it.

### *Why Is Self-Efficacy Important to Writing Tasks?*

The teacher explains to the students that teachers are writers too who face the challenges of writing tasks every day. Thinking aloud, the teacher shares examples with the students how his own past experiences have shaped his self-efficacy as a writer. As the teacher assesses the complexity of the task, he expresses doubts about writing an argumentative essay without help from a more experienced writer.

### *Why Is Self-Instruction Important to Writing Tasks?*

The teacher begins to design a plan of action to complete the task successfully:

- The teacher lists the many ways in the past that using mentor texts has been helpful to see the expected outcome of the task and serve as a model.
- The teacher emphasizes that reading like a writer is a strategy to show a reader how something was written.
- Thinking aloud, the teacher refreshes his memory of the Common Core requirements, and begins to work on self-instruction statements to guide his actions and raise his self-efficacy.

- The teacher then discusses how the *self-instruction* can be rephrased into goals ("I Can" statements) and used to guide the process of writing the argumentative essay using mentor texts and the strategy of reading like a writer. The teacher thinks aloud about his self-efficacy for reaching the goals, and the students observe exactly what the teacher is saying as they follow along on their copies of the self-instruction and self-efficacy ratings checklist (see Table 7.8).
- Students are focused on the self-instruction and self-efficacy ratings checklist while the teacher adds some strategies to help track his actions once the task is in progress. Then the teacher rates his self-efficacy for the forethought phase.
- Thinking aloud, the teacher refers to the self-instruction statements and emphasizes what can and cannot be based on the teacher's perceptions of his skills.

## Why Is Self-Evaluation Important for Writing Tasks?

The teacher then calls the students' attention to the Read Like a Writer (RLW) and the Write Like a Writer (WLW) worksheets, tools that can help organize their actions for writing tasks. The teacher explains how the worksheets are part of an action plan to use the mentor text as a model to write a persuasive/argumentative paragraph. The teacher thinks aloud, describing how both worksheets (RLW, WLW) are included the action plan to read and write like a writer using a mentor text.

## Why Is Help-Seeking an Important Strategy for Writing Tasks?

The teacher reminds students that seeking help is a known strategy used by successful learners. The teacher models how to move forward with tasks using resources such as mentor texts, peers, instructors, and the librarian. The goal for the teacher is to remove the stigma from asking for help by providing examples of what adaptive help-seeking looks like.

## Post-Observation of Forethought

### Evaluate!

### *Predict: Will Using the Observed Strategies and Action Plan Result in Writing a Strong Argumentative/Persuasive Essay?*

**Students:** After observing the teacher's think-alouds and accompanying actions, each student enters his predictions regarding whether or not the teacher's strategies and plan will lead to successful completion of the writing task (see Evaluate! Part A, Table 7.9).

## Observation of Performance

### Doing

#### A Strategic Approach to a Writing Task

#### Sessions 6–10

**Performance:** The teacher emphasizes that all writers need models of good writing in order to write well. The teacher explains to students that during this phase, the plans made in the forethought phase will be put into action. The teacher reminds students to pay close attention to the teacher's self-instruction and self-efficacy ratings during the forethought phase (Column D) and use the information to closely monitor the teacher's actions and behaviors as he completes the writing task. Students participate by taking notes on what they observe. Thinking aloud, the teacher moves through the writing task, systematically using the self-instruction statements/goals as a guide (see Table 7.8). The teacher thinks aloud, clearly stating when he is self-evaluating help-seeking while keeping track of his self-efficacy.

### *Modeling: Are the Strategies and Action Plan Working?*

Making sure the students' attention is focused on the mentor text section of the displayed RLW worksheet, the teacher reads the mentor text aloud, modeling how to find evidence of five elements of good writing. As the students observe, the teacher indicates how he feels about the task, when he is confident and when he is unsure (self-efficacy). Thinking aloud, the teacher demonstrates what to do when a task becomes too difficult to do independently and the type of resources he can use to get help. The teacher also demonstrates how resources and assistance from others are hints that move him forward towards task completion. The students are engaged by using their self-instruction and self-efficacy ratings (from the forethought phase) to monitor and make notes regarding the effectiveness of the teacher's choices.

### *The Relationship Between Self-Efficacy and Writing Tasks*

The teacher begins the task using the tools and strategies in the action plan. The teacher thinks aloud as he attributes his ability to maintain high levels of self-efficacy to the support available and the strategies and instructional components in the RLW and WLW worksheets. As the teacher reads each self-instruction statement, he takes action to carry out the plan, being transparent about the ups and downs of the process.

- RLW—While reading the mentor text, the teacher thinks aloud regarding what it means to read like a writer. The teacher identifies five elements of good writing and the persuasive techniques, and enters the information into the RLW.
- The teacher discusses the process with the students, noting areas of strengths and weaknesses, gaining confidence in his skills to read like a writer and find evidence of how the paragraph is written. Once the RLW worksheet is completed, the teacher allows some time for discussion about self-efficacy and writing tasks before moving on to writing his own essay.
- WRW—The teacher thinks aloud while writing an argumentative paragraph similar to the mentor text. Some difficulties arise that could hinder progress, and the teacher considers the choices to seek help or persist alone. The teacher calls attention to how in the past, seeking help has increased self-efficacy and struggling alone has lowered it. One resource readily available is the mentor text; another is the librarian or a peer.

## Self-Instruction Statements Shape Performance Goals

The teacher uses the Common Core–aligned "I Can" statements (self-instruction statements) to track his performance and monitor self-efficacy for the task. The teacher thinks aloud as he reviews the self-efficacy ratings from the forethought phase (see self-instruction and self-efficacy ratings, Table 7.8) and consistently monitors current levels of self-efficacy as the task increases in complexity. At this point, the teacher enters his self-efficacy rating for the performance phase in Column E (see Table 7.8).

## Self-Instruction and Self-Evaluation Track Performance

As the teacher works on the elements of the writing task (as sequenced in self-instruction and self-efficacy ratings, Table 7.8), he verbally evaluates progress towards the goals. The teacher consistently self-evaluates his actions, specifically the behaviors that lead towards writing a paragraph that emulates the mentor text.

The teacher focuses students' attention on the RLW and WLW worksheets, making sure students are engaged and working with the teacher (not independently) as he moves through the plan to complete the writing task. As the teacher enters his responses to the guiding questions on the RLW and WLW worksheets, students copy the information onto their worksheets, adding notes if possible. By the end of the performance phase, the teacher will have completed a basic craft analysis of the mentor text, written an argumentative paragraph, and evaluated the paragraph by comparing his writing with the mentor text (using five elements of good writing). The students will then have a model of the entire process for later use.

### Help-Seeking Strategies Are Important to Writing Task Completion

The teacher gives specific examples of how he has been able to move forward with tasks using resources such as mentor texts, peers, instructors, and the librarian. The goal for the teacher is to remove the stigma from asking for help while he provides examples of what adaptive help-seeking looks like.

## Post-Observation of Performance

### Evaluate

### Outcome: Do You Think the Teacher's Strategies and Action Plan Resulted in Writing a Strong Argumentative/Persuasive Essay?

**Students**: After observing the teacher's think-alouds and accompanying actions, each enters his evaluations whether or not there is evidence to conclude that the teacher's strategy and plan led to a successful completion of the writing task (see Evaluate! Table 7.9, Part B).

## Observation of Self-Reflection

### Reflecting On

### A Strategic Approach to a Writing Task

### Sessions 11–15

**Self-reflection:** The teacher thinks aloud, reflecting on the processes used and the completed argumentative essay. The teacher analyzes the self-instruction statements (which became the learning goals) and his ability to stick to the plan. He poses the guiding question, "*Did reading like a writer make a difference in writing like a writer?*" It is important for the teacher to attribute success or failure to specific behaviors, self-efficacy, distractions, help-seeking, and self-tracking (monitoring). One of the objectives of this phase is to also think about how useful the strategies and worksheets have been and whether their uses can transfer to future similar academic tasks.

### Modeling: Did the Strategies and Action Plan Work?

Calling the students' attention to the completed RLW worksheet, the teacher reads aloud his argumentative paragraph and compares it to the mentor text. The teacher thinks aloud, looking for feedback from the students as to whether or not the teacher's writing is similar to the mentor text. The teacher points to evidence of how well he was able to identify and use the information gained from the RLW worksheet to complete the WLW worksheet. As the students observe, the teacher indicates how he feels about the outcome and what can be done differently the next time a similar writing task is assigned. Thinking aloud, the teacher attributes success to seeking help and using resources when stuck to move forward towards task completion.

### Did Self-Efficacy Influence the Outcome of the Writing Task?

The teacher thinks aloud, linking his feelings of self-efficacy with learning outcomes. Referring to the self-instruction and self-efficacy ratings checklist, the teacher assesses his performance and rates his self-efficacy now that the task is completed. Students are engaged by discussing what they think of the teacher's performance based on observations of his reflections and level of confidence. The teacher explains to the students how monitoring his thoughts, feelings, and actions and expressing confidence in his abilities contributed to a positive learning outcome. In addition, the teacher describes how meeting the challenges of this task with strategies helped increase his self-efficacy.

### Were Self-Instruction Statements Useful to Track Performance and Write Learning Goals?

The teacher reflects on how he used the self-instruction statements to monitor performance. Thinking aloud, the teacher rates the effectiveness of the statements in monitoring his progress and guiding his behaviors towards goal attainment.

### Would Self-Instruction and Self-Evaluation Be Helpful Strategies for Future Writing Tasks?

The teacher completes the reflection phase with a summary of the process. While thinking aloud, he gathers evidence from the forethought and performance phases that can help him plan for similar future tasks. The teacher shares with the students how self-efficacy increases with positive self-evaluations of successful task completion.

### How Can the Strategy of Adaptive Help-Seeking Improve Performance on Writing Tasks?

The teacher thinks aloud about the times he would have not completed the tasks, including this one, if he had not asked for help from peers and others. The teacher asks students to share their experiences as help seekers and help avoiders and how both behaviors impacted their learning outcomes. Students are prompted to respond to the following questions:

- "Did you ask for help? Why not?"
- "How did you know you needed help?"
- "When you asked for help, did it make a difference or were you just as stuck as before you asked?"
- "Did you avoid seeking help? Why?"

Students discuss how each type of "help"—mentor texts, peers, instructors, and the librarian—were used as resources. Finally, students identify what they would do to get assistance for a similar future task.

## Post-Observation of Self-Reflection

### Evaluate!

### *Reflect: Do You Think the Teacher's Strategies and Action Plan Will Be Useful to Write a Strong Argumentative/Persuasive Essay?*

**Students:** After observing their teacher make the last entry into the self-instruction and self-efficacy ratings worksheet (see Table 7.8, Column F), the teacher focuses their attention on the final evaluation. Now that students have observed three phases of self-regulation, ending with the successful completion of a writing task, each student evaluates whether or not the teacher's plan and strategy would be useful for similar tasks in the future (see Evaluate! Table 7.9, Part C).

## Emulation Level

### Work Together!

### *Sessions 16–30*

**Emulation:** The teacher guides students through the preparation process for a writing task that requires skills they might not yet have mastered: reading and writing like a writer. Now that they have observed a full cycle of the self-regulatory phases and the strategies have been modeled, they are instructed to prepare to do their own piece of writing. The teacher focuses students' attention on feelings of self-efficacy, the benefits to using self-instruction statements, the use of self-evaluation strategies, and the importance of seeking help as they prepare to write a persuasive/argumentative short essay (two paragraphs). The teacher instructs students to keep what they observed in mind as they work through each of the three phases. The teacher scaffolds and monitors students' performance as he continues to control the pacing of the learning environment.

### Individual Materials Can Be Given to Students at Teacher Discretion:

1. Passages from mentor text in a genre for specific type of writing (argumentative/persuasive, informational, narrative)
2. Read Like a Writer worksheet
3. Write Like a Writer worksheet
4. Evaluate! (A) Predict (B) Outcome, (C) Reflection
5. Self-instruction and self-efficacy ratings checklist

## Emulation of Forethought

### Planning

*A Strategic Approach to a Writing Task*

#### Sessions 16–20

**Forethought:** Students imitate the behaviors seen at the observation level by activating images of the teacher's actions stored in their memories. Under the teacher's close supervision, students plan how to complete the writing task using the self-regulatory processes previously modeled. The teacher works with the students; however, they are now focusing on their own feelings and goals as they design an action plan. At this level, students are expected to practice using a mentor text to increase writing proficiency with close teacher supervision. At the observation level, students copied what the teacher had written onto the worksheets and took notes of their own; at this level, students will enter their own information.

### *Modeling: What Can We Do Together?*

The teacher reads aloud the requirements of the writing task, checking that students understand the skills needed to complete the task successfully. The teacher and students refer to the self-instruction statements that guided the model's performance at the observation level. They agree to use the same statements to guide their performance because they are aligned with the Common Core. The teacher will refer students to the strategies and tools used by the model (see RLW, WLW, self-instruction and self-efficacy ratings, Evaluate!) and as a group they discuss the usefulness of each one.

## Why Self-Efficacy Is Important to Planning Writing Tasks

The teacher focuses students' attention on the RLW worksheet with the mentor text, five elements of good writing, and persuasive techniques. Together, they read/recite the displayed self-instruction statements with goals and self-efficacy ratings (see self-instruction and self-efficacy ratings, Table 7.8). Following a discussion of the task demands, students are led to focus on their self-efficacy for the writing task and asked to make realistic assessments of their skills to complete the writing task successfully. Students are led in a discussion about how one's self-efficacy impacts plans of action as well as present performance.

## Why Self-Instruction Statements Are Important to Writing Tasks

Students' reread the mentor text aloud, following along with the teacher as they work together to read like writers. Referring to the self-instruction statements (see Table 7.8, Column A), both teacher and students discuss how self-instruction statements can be reminders of what needs to be done to complete a writing task. Thinking aloud, the students respond to each question, activating prior knowledge from what they observed their teacher do, and rate their self-efficacy for the forethought phase (see Table 7.8, Column D) at the emulation level.

The teacher and students discuss how to use self-instruction statements to (1) set goals to guide the process using mentor texts and (2) focus on the strategy of reading like a writer to write an argumentative essay. Students are encouraged to think aloud as they discuss what can and cannot be accomplished based on their perceptions of their skills. The students then review and discuss as a class how they rated their self-efficacy for reaching the goals.

## Why Self-Evaluation Is Important to Writing Tasks

The teacher focuses students' attention on their individual RLW and WLW worksheets. The teacher relies on students to peer model how they will use the information from the worksheets (in sequence) to organize and monitor their actions to complete the writing task. For example, *"How will the worksheets help you remain on track and evaluate your work?"* Students' responses should center on how to use the mentor text as a model of what good writing looks like, and how to follow the teacher's modeling of how to evaluate the mentor text.

## Why Help-Seeking Is an Important Strategy for Writing Tasks

The teacher guides students through a discussion about help-seeking in general and the implications of needing help. The teacher provides students with a list of resources available to them to complete the writing task successfully. The teacher elicits feedback from students about the benefits of seeking help, asking them to give examples of how the teacher, a peer, or an individual helped them move forward with a task rather than persist alone. Students are encouraged to talk among themselves and to identify at least one source of help they would use to complete this task and to share that with each other.

## Post-Emulation of Forethought

### Evaluate!

### *Do You Think the Strategies You Identified and Your Action Plan Will Result in Writing a Strong Argumentative/Persuasive Essay?*

**Students:** Each student is given an Evaluate! checklist to predict the usefulness of the strategies and planning. The predictions link the goals to self-evaluations of whether or not the student believes using the plan will lead to the successful completion of an argumentative essay. (see Evaluate! Table 7.9, Part A)

## Emulation of Performance

### Practicing

### *A Strategic Approach to a Writing Task*

### Sessions 21–25

**Performance:** The performance phase gives students the opportunity to try out the observed strategies while still under the close supervision of the teacher. The teacher reminds the students that they will be working on the writing task as a class, supporting each other's efforts. Students with stronger writing proficiency are expected to be available to help peers who require more individualized instruction. The teacher continues to scaffold and provide feedback.

### *Modeling: Are the Strategies and Action Plan Working?*

The teacher emphasizes that all writers need models of good writing in order to write well. Mentor texts can be their teacher's writings or passages from professional writers. The teacher moves through the writing task, systematically using the self-instruction statements/goals as a guide.

- Making sure the students' attention is focused on the RLW worksheet, the teacher and students read aloud the mentor text, modeling for each other

how to find evidence of persuasive techniques and five elements of good writing. The teacher remains attentive as peer models demonstrate what they do when a task becomes too difficult to do independently and the type of resources they use to move forward.
- While students are engaged in the writing part of the task (WLW), the teacher closely monitors what they are doing, asking them to think aloud and make statements that indicate self-evaluation, help seeking, and self-efficacy. For example, students think aloud as they apply the information gathered from the mentor text when writing their own short essay describing what they are doing and how they are doing it.

### *How Important Is Self-Efficacy to Writing Tasks?*

Together, teachers and students discuss challenges they have faced when asked to do writing tasks in the past. The discussion is focused on how past experiences shape present performance and how poor strategy choices can lower performance. The students are reminded to use self-instruction and self-efficacy ratings checklists to monitor their performance and rate their self-efficacy as they apply each observed strategy to the writing task. The teacher calls attention to the changes in the way the class now approaches tasks that were once challenging, as they have increased their skills and use of strategies, and as a result, their self-efficacy.

### *How Important Are Self-Instruction and Self-Evaluation to Writing Tasks?*

Together, teacher and students make the connections between the self-instruction statements, goals, self-efficacy ratings, and self-evaluations. During the performance phase, students are entering valuable snapshots of information into the writing worksheets, self-instruction and self efficacy ratings checklist, and their evaluations. Teachers closely monitor how each student is using these self-regulatory strategies as they complete a challenging writing task. Left to themselves, the students will not make the connections; the emulation level provides an opportunity for the teacher to guide students' thinking about self-regulation during their performance: "What are we doing now?" "Is it working," "Write it down!"

### *How Important Is Adaptive Help-Seeking for Completing Writing Tasks?*

While students are working on segments of the writing task, the teacher asks them how they are seeking help. Students are consistently reminded that resources and assistance from others are hints (not answers) that can help them move forward towards task completion. Students monitor who and when they ask for help and the outcome in order to share with their peers which help-seeking strategies led to independent problem solving.

## Post-Emulation of Performance

### Evaluate!

### *Outcome: Do You Think the Strategies and Action Plan Resulted in Writing a Strong Argumentative/Persuasive Essay?*

**Students:** After completing the writing process tasks alongside the teacher and peers, each student evaluates whether or not the planning and strategies used led to a successful completion of the writing task using the Evaluate! checklist (see Table 7.9, Part C).

## Emulation of Self-Reflection

### Reflecting On

### *A Strategic Approach to a Writing Task*

### *Sessions 26–30*

**Self-reflection:** Together, teachers and students discuss the process used to write an argumentative/persuasive essay in conjunction with individual learning outcomes.

The following questions guide the discussion as students are asked to analyze the self-instruction statements that became his learning goals and his ability to stick to the plan.

- How did reading like a writer make a difference in writing like a writer?
- Can you attribute success or failure to specific behaviors? Low self-efficacy?
- What were the distractions from focusing on goals?
- Did you experience help avoidance? What did you do?
- What are your self-evaluation strengths?
- What would you do differently next time you have a similar task?

### *Modeling: Did the Strategies and Action Plan Work?*

Calling the students' attention to the following artifacts, the teacher asks students for their feedback regarding the entire process that led to a completed writing task (argumentative essay).

1. Evaluate! checklist (emulation)
2. RLW worksheet

3. WLW worksheet
4. Self-instruction and self-efficacy ratings checklist

Students are asked to model for each other how they used specific strategies to increase their likelihood of successfully completing the writing task. They are required to provide evidence of how they used the RLW and WLW worksheets to write their own essay and evaluate the outcome of the writing task.

### How Did Self-Efficacy Impact Performance on Writing Tasks?

Students think aloud, linking self-efficacy ratings with learning outcomes. Teachers and students discuss how self-efficacy increases with positive experiences and cite specific examples from the writing task. In addition, the students describe how they met the challenges of the writing task, describing the strategy choices that helped them overcome low self-efficacy.

### Were the Self-Instruction Statements Helpful to the Writing Task Process?

The teacher directs students to demonstrate for their peers how they used the self-instruction statements to monitor performance. Thinking aloud, students rate the effectiveness of the statements in monitoring their progress and guiding their behaviors towards goal attainment.

### Were Ongoing Self-Evaluations Helpful to the Writing Task Process?

The teacher directs students to demonstrate how they checked performance by ongoing self-observations and assessments. Students respond to questions about their use of the mentor text to make revisions. The teacher asks, *"Was the mentor text a model of good writing that could be used for comparison and to make revisions following individual conferencing with the teacher?"*

### How Can Self-Instruction and Self-Evaluation Help Future Writing Tasks?

The teacher and students complete the reflection with a summary of the process. Students cite evidence from the forethought and performance phases that will be helpful when assigned similar future tasks. Demonstrating how they changed self-instruction statements into goal directed, outcome-monitoring checklists, the students think aloud as they assesses their progress and verbalize confidence in their skills. The teacher demonstrates for the students how monitoring his thoughts, feelings, and actions and expressing confidence in his abilities contributes to a positive learning outcome.

## What Effect Did Adaptive Help-Seeking Have on Goal Attainment?

The teacher guides students as they discuss help-seeking, help avoidance, and the social implications of needing help. Students fill in their responses to prompts such as:

- I asked for help when . . .
- I knew I needed help because . . .
- When I asked for help, did it make a difference? (Students should respond how the assistance moved them along with completing the task successfully.)
- I was just as stuck as before I asked for help because . . . (Students should respond with who or what they attribute the strategy not being effective to: choosing a less knowledgeable person to ask, wrong resource, etc.)
- I avoid asking for help because . . . (Students should respond with not wanting to feel dumb, no idea what to do or who to ask.)

Students share with each other resources that helped to complete the writing task successfully. The teacher remains involved, eliciting feedback from students about the benefits of seeking help, asking them to give examples of how a teacher, a peer, or an individual helped them move forward with a task rather than persist alone

## Post-Emulation of Self-Reflection

### Evaluate!

### *Reflect: Do You Think the Strategies and Action Plan Will Be Useful to Write a Strong Argumentative/Persuasive Essay?*

**Students:** After reflecting on the writing process tasks (alongside the teacher and peers), each student evaluates whether or not the plan and strategy used led to a successful completion of the writing task using the rating sheet (see Evaluate! Table 7.9, Part C). Each student evaluates whether or not the planning and strategy choices would be useful for similar tasks in the future.

## Self-Control Level

### It's Your Turn!

### *Sessions 30–45*

**Self-control:** The teacher remains available to assist students as they take on more responsibility for their learning. Following a clear introduction to the writing task, similar mentor text passages are introduced using the RLW worksheet. Students are assigned to small groups with access to the teacher, but are encouraged to work together and use the self-regulatory strategy of help-seeking if they are stuck. At the self-control level, students are expected to analyze a mentor text and construct an argumentative/persuasive short essay with limited assistance from the teacher. In this form of guided practice, the teacher assists learners in choosing the self-instruction statements (using the Common Core) and making realistic self-evaluations, but slowly withdraws support, giving students the opportunity to work independently or with each other.

**Materials:**

1. RLW worksheet
2. WLW worksheet
3. Self-instruction and self-efficacy ratings checklist
4. Evaluate! checklist (self-control)

## Self-Controlled Forethought

### Planning My Strategic Approach to a Writing Task

#### Sessions 31–35

**Forethought:** Students begin the preparation process for a writing task that requires skills they have observed and practiced but might not yet have mastered. Now that they have practiced a full cycle of the self-regulatory behaviors and strategies with their teacher, they are instructed to apply these strategies as they prepare to do a writing task (argumentative) using those skills on their own and in their small groups.

*Modeling/Peer Modeling*

The teacher encourages students to model for each other, thinking aloud as they make their plans to work on the writing task. Think-alouds will serve as a form of peer modeling, and the mentor text will serve as a model of good writing. The teacher distributes the handouts and observes as students think aloud while prioritizing the task requirements, including the self-regulation strategies. Students are instructed to work in small groups and model the following components of the writing task:

- Read aloud the RLW/WLW, sharing with each other how they will complete the writing task.

- Students review goals and rate their feelings of self-efficacy for the ability to complete the writing task successfully based on current skills.
- Students think aloud as they plan the sequence and gather the materials they will need for the task. The teacher monitors the interactions to correct misconceptions and provides only enough help to complete the planning process when requested. A sequence is suggested, but not required, for students who might need further assistance with organizing their plan.

### Linking Self-Efficacy to Writing Tasks

Students lead the discussion about how one's self-efficacy impacts plans of action as well as performance and the strategies that may help improve self-efficacy. The teacher observes the students and provides reinforcement and encouragement to use the strategies and resources to maintain a level of self-efficacy to successfully complete the writing task.

### Linking Self-Instruction, Self-Evaluation, and Self-Efficacy to Writing Tasks

The teacher observes to see which students will follow the practiced protocols independently and in their groups. Students take turns reading the mentor aloud as they work together to read like writers. Gathering information from the self-instruction and self-efficacy ratings checklist (see Table 7.8), students discuss how self-instruction statements can be reminders of what needs to be done to complete a writing task.

Students respond to the following questions associated with the three phases of self-regulation and strategies, activating prior knowledge from what they observed and practiced. The teacher guides small group discussions and checks for understanding and misconceptions as students gather information before beginning to work on a writing task.

- How can I analyze the impact of specific word choice on the meaning and tone of the passage? (RLW worksheet)
- How can I write an argumentative/persuasive essay? (WLW worksheet)
- What do I need to do to read like a writer? (resources, mentor text, graphic organizer)
- Who will help me choose a mentor text? (resources, teacher, librarian, peer)
- How will I know that I am on the right track? (self-instruction, self-evaluation, feedback)
- How difficult will this task be for me to complete? (self-instruction and self-evaluation ratings checklist)

## Linking Help-Seeking to Writing Tasks

Students discuss the availability of resources to complete the writing task successfully and how they plan to access them. For example, they will need to know in advance where the best resources can be found for this particular type of writing task. Students should be sharing the resources they have found helpful in the past and help others by making suggestions in their groups.

# Post Self-Controlled Forethought

## Evaluate

### Predict: Do You Think the Strategies and Action Plan Will Result in Writing a Strong Argumentative/Persuasive Essay?

**Students:** Following a closer examination of the task from their perspective as writers, students rate how useful the planning and strategies will be when they begin applying them (see Evaluate! Table 7.9, Part A).

**Teacher:** Observes students to see if they are making predictions about meeting their goals.

# Self-Controlled Performance

## Applying My Strategic Approach to a Writing Task

### Sessions 36–40

**Performance:** The performance phase gives middle schoolers an opportunity to work with peers and show the teacher what they can do as independent learners. Students are challenged to try out the plan designed in the forethought phase without the constant supervision of the teacher. The teacher reminds the students that they will be working on an individual writing task in small groups and that each member of the group must complete the task. By now, students should be familiar with the handouts that have been used for writing tasks. Groups should be arranged so that students with stronger writing proficiency can help peers who might require further modeling or individualized instruction. The teacher remains close by as students apply what they have learned during the observation and emulation levels. The writing task requirements are clear; however, students are reminded to help each other follow the same strategic approach as they have been doing over the last few weeks.

### Modeling/Peer Modeling: How Are We Doing?

Students take turns reading aloud the mentor text in their small groups so that each member can see and hear the author's writing craft. Upon request or when a need arises, peers may model what they are doing if a group member is finding the reading challenging. The teacher remains available if students become stuck or need help. As students begin the writing task, they are expected to demonstrate for each other how to analyze the mentor text using five elements of good writing and persuasive techniques. In addition, they are to write an argumentative essay and compare their writing with the mentor text, making revisions until they are satisfied with the results. Simultaneously, students assist each other with monitoring self-instruction and self-efficacy throughout the process.

### Monitoring Self-Efficacy During Writing Tasks

Students discuss with their peers the challenges they have faced when asked to do writing tasks in the past. Choosing the self-instruction and self-efficacy ratings checklist, students rate their self-efficacy to complete the writing task successfully for each goal (self-instruction statement).

### Self-Instruction and Goals During Writing Tasks

Students use goals to monitor performance and share with each other when they have accomplished a specific goal or when they are struggling. Students are reminded to refer to the self-instruction statements (goals) to monitor their performance. Students remind each other to measure the usefulness of each strategy during the performance. If they are not satisfied with their performance, they should tell the teacher and decisions can be made to adjust the goals or get help.

### Self-Instruction Statements and Self-Evaluation During Writing Tasks

Students are prompted to make connections between the self-instruction statements, goals, self-efficacy ratings, and self-evaluation. During the performance phase, students enter valuable snapshots of information into the self-instruction and self-efficacy checklist, the RLW, and WLW worksheets. Left on their own, the students will not make the connections—the performance phase provides an opportunity for the teacher to prompt students to write down what is happening during their performance that keeps them focused on their goals. They can use the following questions to check each other's progress and evaluate their own performance:

a. "What am I doing right now?" "What are you doing right now?"
b. "What strategy am I using right now?" "What strategy are you using right now?"
c. "Is it working?"

*Linking Help-Seeking to Writing Tasks*

While students are working on segments of the writing task, the teacher evaluates their use of resources and assistance from others. Students enter the identity of whom they ask for help, and the outcome, in order to identify help-seeking strategies that lead to independent problem solving.

## Post Self-Controlled Performance

### Evaluate!

### *Outcome: Do You Think the Strategies and Action Plan Resulted in Writing a Strong Argumentative/Persuasive Essay?*

**Outcome:** After completing the writing process tasks with some supervision from the teacher and peer assistance, each student evaluates whether or not the plan and strategy used led to a successful completion of the writing task using the rating sheet (see Evaluate! Table 7.9, Part B).

At the end of the performance phase, each student should be ready to have individual conferences with the teacher for feedback and the following items completed:

1. Evaluate! checklist
2. RLW worksheet
3. WLW worksheet
4. Self-instruction and self-efficacy ratings checklist

## Self-Controlled Reflection

### Reflecting On

### *My Strategic Approach to a Writing Task*

### Sessions 41–45

**Self-reflection:** Students are encouraged to incorporate feedback from their teacher and peers to attribute their performance to their use of specific strategies. The teacher circulates among the groups, listening for insights and reflections, calling the class's attention to specific comments that would benefit the whole group. Using self-evaluations and learning outcomes, students make judgments about how much effort they gave to using the self-regulatory strategies. The following questions guide the discussion as students remain in small groups to analyze the self-instruction statements that became their learning goals and their ability to stick to the plan.

- Did reading like a writer make a difference in writing like a writer?
- Can you attribute success or failure to specific behaviors? Low self-efficacy?
- What did you do about any distractions that kept you from focusing on goals?
- What did you do when you experienced help avoidance?
- What are some self-evaluations that helped you better monitor your performance?
- What would you do differently next time you have a similar task?

### Modeling: Did the Strategies and Action Plan Work?

Students are asked to model for each other how they used specific strategies to increase their likelihood of successfully completing the writing task. They are required to provide evidence of how they used their RLW worksheets to complete the WLW worksheets. In addition, students model for each other how they incorporated information from the self-instruction and self-efficacy ratings checklist into their planning and performance. As the students observe their peers, the teacher monitors only to check for miscomprehensions of the process.

### Did Self-Efficacy Influence Writing Performance and Goal Attainment?

Students are encouraged to link self-efficacy ratings with learning outcome by reviewing their self-instruction and self-efficacy ratings checklist for the emulation and self-control level. The students describe how they met the challenges of the writing task, citing strategies that helped them increase self-efficacy. The teacher observes students as they demonstrate for their peers how they used the self-instruction statements to reach their goals. Thinking aloud, students rate the effectiveness of the statements in monitoring their progress and guiding their behaviors towards goal attainment.

### Were Self-Instruction Statements Helpful?

Students describe how monitoring thoughts, feelings, and actions and expressing confidence in abilities contributed to a positive learning outcome. The teacher asks, "*Can you give examples of what thoughts, feelings, or actions increased or decreased your confidence in your abilities to complete the writing task specifically?*"

- Students share what they recorded on all their worksheets, checklists, and evaluations to identify the processes that were easier to do and others that were more difficult to do.

- Students cite evidence from the forethought and performance phases that will be helpful when assigned similar future tasks. Students are asked to center their discussion around the following prompts as they discuss how it felt to use self-instruction techniques and the likelihood of using them in the future.
  - Can you demonstrate how to transform self-instruction statements into goals?
  - What is the connection between them?
  - Do self-instruction statements provide evidence to be used in assessments?
  - Can you cite evidence that specific behaviors led to goal attainment?

### Were Self-Evaluations Helpful?

Students demonstrate how they checked their performance by making ongoing self-observations and assessments. Students respond to questions about using the mentor text as a model for comparison. The teacher asks: *"Was the mentor text a model of good writing that could be used for comparison and for revisions?"*

### What Effect Did Help-Seeking Have on Goal Attainment?

Students discuss help-seeking and help avoidance and the social implications of needing help. Students fill in their responses to prompts such as:

- When I asked for help . . . (Students should respond how the assistance moved them along with completing the task successfully.)
- I was just as stuck as before I asked for help because . . . (Students should respond with who or what they attribute to the strategy not being effective: choosing a less knowledgeable person to ask, wrong resource, etc.)
- I avoid asking for help because . . . (Students should respond with not wanting to feel dumb, no idea what to do or who to ask.)

Students share with each other resources that helped to complete the writing task successfully. The teacher becomes involved, eliciting feedback from students about the benefits of seeking help, asking them to give examples of how a teacher, a peer, or an individual helped them move forward with a task rather than persist alone.

## Post Self-Controlled Self-Reflection

### Evaluate!

### Reflect: Do You Think the Strategies and Action Plan Will Be Useful to Write a Strong Argumentative/Persuasive Essay When Working on Your Own?

**Students:** After reflecting on the process for writing the essay, each student evaluates whether or not the plan and strategy used led to a successful completion of the writing task (see Evaluate! Table 7.9, Part C). Each student evaluates whether or not the planning and strategy choices would be useful for similar tasks in the future without teacher supervision.

## Move Forward . . . Slowly

Post-observation assessment of students' artifacts can help determine which of the students are ready to work independently as self-directed learners. Middle schoolers will transition to this level in some tasks and not in others. A considerable amount of time should be spent at the self-control level, accompanied by opportunities to self-regulate as students decrease their dependency on the teacher and take on more responsibility for their learning.

## Self-Regulation Level

### On My Own!

**Self-regulation:** Students are considered self-regulated when they are able to make changes or adapt their behavior based on the challenges they encounter as they work towards reaching their goals and when they feel self-efficacious enough to modify their strategies and plans accordingly. At this level, the responsibility of the work is shifting entirely from the teacher to the student. Students readily apply the "reading like a writer" strategies to other types of writing tasks. Students independently seek out mentor texts to serve as models of assigned writing tasks because they recognize the benefits that accompany craft analysis. They carefully prepare for writing tasks that require skills they have observed, practiced, and now mastered.

## Self-Regulated Forethought

### Flexible Time Frame

**Forethought:** Students begin the preparation process for a writing task that requires skills they have observed and practiced and now mastered. Their success with using mentor texts as models of good writing automatically become part of their writing preparation. Teachers make all materials, including samples of completed RLW and WLW worksheets, available online and in the classroom settings. Students begin each writing task with self-instruction statements, and then change them into goals. Students review goals and rate their feelings of self-efficacy for the ability to complete the writing task successfully and on their own.

## Modeling

Teachers across the curriculum stress the importance of mentor texts as models of how writers write. They consistently model forethought strategies that include self-instruction statements, self-efficacy evaluations, and self-evaluation charts and worksheets. Students, acting as peer models, demonstrate their "reading like a writer" strategies and mentor texts craft analysis with fellow students as a form of reinforcement and increased mastery of the skills.

## Self-Efficacy Should Be Evaluated Before Each Writing Task

Self-regulated students consistently think about their self-efficacy in terms of the task and recognize the risk of failure if they begin a writing task for which they do not believe they have the skills. They make realistic assessments of their skills to complete the writing task and share them with their teacher prior to beginning the task to incorporate teacher feedback into the process.

## Self-Instruction Statements Lead to Goal Setting

Students habitually include self-instruction statements when they begin a new writing task. They respond to each question, activating prior knowledge from prior learning experiences, and gather the appropriate materials.

- How can I analyze the impact of specific word choice on the meaning and tone of the passage? (RLW worksheet)
- How can I write an argumentative/persuasive essay? (RLW/WLW worksheets/resources)
- What do I need to do to read like a writer? (RLW worksheet)
- Who will help me choose a mentor text? (Resources/help-seeking)
- How will I know that I am on the right track? (Self-evaluation, teacher and peer feedback)
- How difficult will this task be for me to complete? (Self-efficacy ratings)

## Self-Evaluation Increases Goal Attainment

Self-regulated students regularly conduct several close readings of a mentor text before they begin a craft analysis. When students prepare to do a writing task, they carefully assess what is involved in the task, the availability of help, and how realistic and proximal goals can guide the process. Students become more flexible in their thinking as they evaluate their goals and the processes previously used, often making adjustments to both.

## Help-Seeking Can Increase Writing Proficiency

Self-regulated students keep track of their resources. When planning writing tasks, students will include a list of peers, teachers, and resources that have been evaluated as helpful and available. Students maintain a portfolio of the completed worksheets to refer to when faced with similar writing tasks in the future. These students often return to the teacher for strategy worksheets and additional modeling if their memory fades or for help when they begin to organize and monitor their actions to write an essay.

## Self-Regulated Performance

### Independence!

**Performance:** Students independently follow the plans they have made during the forethought phase. They use the new strategic approach to a writing task without the close supervision of the teacher. Self-regulated students use every opportunity to apply the learned strategies to writing assignments in other subjects and genres. Mentor texts and identifying elements of good writing strategies are used consistently and eventually become an automatic response for writing task completion. Self-regulated students review their self-instruction statements regularly to guide them through each writing task. They consistently monitor and evaluate their thoughts, feelings, and actions as they follow a plan that will get the writing task accomplished successfully. If the plan is not working in any way, the self-regulated student changes strategies, resets goals, or asks for help.

## Modeling

Teachers across the curriculum use the "read like a writer" strategic approach to writing and vicariously reinforce the skills learned at the observation, emulation, and self-control levels. Mentor texts continue to serve as models of good writing, and students will often see their teachers' writing as good writing models.

## Self-Efficacy

Self-regulated students have a heightened level of awareness when it comes to self-efficacy. They consistently monitor and evaluate levels of self-efficacy during task performance. When self-efficacy begins to lower, self-regulated students will reexamine goal and strategy choices, seek help, and do whatever is needed to make the outcome of their efforts successful.

## Self-Instruction Statements

Students consistently monitor what they are doing by using self-instruction statements to set goals. They do not depend on their memory of how they reach their goals—they write down performance indicators and check them against their progress towards a specific goal.

Students locate and apply Common Core "I Can" statements to their goals. These statements will continue to provide students with self-instruction of what needs to get done. Students rate themselves and engage in the behaviors associated with the statements to write an essay on their own.

## Self-Evaluation

Self-regulated students see the connections between the self-instruction statements, goals, self-efficacy ratings, and self-evaluations. During the performance phase, students spend time entering valuable snapshots of information onto the worksheets (RLW, WLW) to check their progress against the standard (expected outcome) and their set goals. The performance phase provides an opportunity for students write down what is happening during their performance that keeps them focused on their goals. They often ask themselves the following questions:

- "What am I doing right now?"
- "What strategy am I using right now?"
- "Is it working?"

## Help-Seeking

Self-regulated students approach teachers for feedback while they are working on segments of a writing task weeks before the assignment is due. Access to teachers, peers, or another resource is an important part of their planning. These students are not content to remain "stuck" or to write down something to just fill a page; they consistently use resources and assistance from others to move forward with a task independently.

## Self-Regulated Reflection

**Self-reflection:** Students consistently seek out and incorporate feedback from teachers, peers, and others into their assessment of their satisfaction with a completed task. They attribute specific strategies and tools to their successes or failures, making sure they incorporate changes into their planning the next time they are asked to do a similar task. Using self-evaluations and learning outcomes, students make judgments about their effort towards paying close attention to using self-regulatory processes in the three phases of self-regulated learning.

## Modeling

Students share their reflections with peers and model how they used specific strategies to increase their likelihood of successfully completing writing tasks in study groups or with friends. They consistently share with teachers and peers evidence of how they read like a writer to write like a writer using mentor texts and tracking their performance. They also discuss any adaptations they needed to make in order to complete other writing tasks using the same strategies.

## Self-Efficacy

Students describe how strategic planning and preparation have led to increased self-efficacy for writing tasks. Self-regulated students meet challenges to their self-efficacy with learned and practiced solutions, or ask for help.

## Self-Instruction Statements

Self-regulated students spend time looking at past performances and attributing success or failure to specific behaviors, strategies, or errors in judgment. These students see how powerful self-instruction statements can be as a motivational tool and incorporate them into their planning and self-monitoring. Students use strategic planning tools, such as RLW and WLW worksheets, to make modifications to their essays based on newly acquired information about their writing. A self-regulated student demonstrates flexibility and is able to make adaptations as needed.

## Self-Evaluation

Students consistently apply ongoing self-observations and assessments to other areas that require writing proficiency. Students respond to questions about their use of the mentor text to compare their writing sample to and make revisions. Teachers may invite students to cite evidence of difficulties encountered and overcome during the forethought and performance phases that will be helpful to peers when assigned similar tasks in the future.

## Help-Seeking: An Important Strategy for Writing Tasks

Students know that help-seeking outweighs the negative impact help avoidance can have on their performance. Knowing the social implications of needing help, the self-regulated student is willing to take a risk and ask for help in spite of peer pressure to be independent. Help-seekers share resources with others that have helped them to complete writing tasks successfully. The student returns to the teacher or model to give examples of how a teacher, a peer, or an individual helped them move forward with a task rather than persist alone.

## Fostering Self-Regulation

The teacher encourages class discussion and uses the time as an opportunity for students to discuss their challenges and accomplishments. The teacher congratulates students and seeks feedback from them on how well their self-regulated learning was taught. Students share their experiences and read their final essays to each other.

## References

Atwell, N. (1987). *In the middle: Writing, reading, and learning with adolescents*. Portsmouth, NH: Heinemann Educational Books.

Coleman, D., & Pimentel, S. (2012). Revised publishers' criteria for the Common Core State Standards in English language arts and literacy, grades 3–12. Retrieved from the Common Core Standards Initiative at www.corestandards. org/assets/Publishers_Criteria_for_3–12

Culham, R. (2005). *6 + 1 traits of writing for the primary grades*. Portland, OR: Scholastic.

Dembo, M. H., & Eaton, M. J. (2000). Self-regulation of academic learning in middle-level schools. *The Elementary School Journal, 100*, 473–490.

Gallagher, K. (2014). Making the most of mentor texts. *Education Leadership, 71*(7), 28–33.

García-Sánchez, J. N., & Fidalgo-Redondo, R. (2006). Effects of two types of self-regulatory instruction programs on students with learning disabilities in writing products, processes, and self-efficacy. *Learning Disability Quarterly, 29*(3), 181–211.

Graves, D. H. (1983). *Writing: Teachers and children at work*. Exeter, NH: Heinemann Educational Books.

Griffith, R. R. (2010). Students learn to read like writers: A framework for teachers of writing. *Reading Horizons, 50*(1), 5.

Harris, K. R., Graham, S., & Santangelo, T. (2013). Self-regulated strategies development in writing: Implementation, scaling up, and relationships to the work of Barry Zimmerman. In H. Bembenutty, T. J. Cleary, & A. Kitsantas (Eds.), *Applications of self-regulated learning across diverse disciplines: A tribute to Barry Zimmerman* (pp. 59–88). Charlotte, NC: Information Age Publishing.

Holloway, J. H. (2002). Research link: Integrating literacy with content. *Education Leadership, 60*(3), 87–88.

Kane, C. M. K. (2012). *Investigating the impact of a mentor text inquiry approach to narrative writing: Instruction on attitude, self-efficacy, and writing processes of fourth grade students in an urban elementary school*. Doctoral dissertation. Retrieved from http://hdl.handle.net/10211.10/2404

Karabenick, S. A., & Newman, R. S. (Eds.). (2006). *Help seeking in academic settings: Goals, groups and contexts*. Mahwah, NJ: Erlbaum.

Kittle, P. (2008). *Write beside them: Risk, voice, and clarity in high school writing*. Portsmouth, NH: Heinemann.

Lensmire, T. J. (1994). Writing workshop as carnival: Reflections on an alternative learning environment. *Harvard Educational Review, 64*(4), 371–392.

McCarthey, S. J. (2008). The impact of No Child Left Behind on teachers' writing instruction. *Written Communication, 25*(4), 462–505.

McCarthey, S. J., Woodard, R. L., & Kang, G. (2011). Teachers' perceptions of professional development in writing. *60th Yearbook of the Literacy Research Association*. Oak Creek, WI: Literacy Research Association, Inc.

National Center for Education Statistics (2012). *The Nation's Report Card: Writing 2011* (NCES 2012–470). Institute of Education Sciences, U.S. Department of Education, Washington, DC.

National Governors Association Center for Best Practices, & Council of Chief State School Officers. (2010). *Common Core State Standards*. Retrieved from www.corestandards.org

Nolen, P. A., McCutchen, D., & Berninger, V. (1990). Ensuring tomorrow's literacy: A shared responsibility. *Journal of Teacher Education, 41*(3), 63–72.

Orttenburger, R. (2013). Mentor text: Your personal teaching assistant. *Content Literacy Task Force Newsletter, 1*(4). Retrieved from www.ekuwritingproject.org/uploads/5/2/4/0/5240502/febmentortext.pdf

Pajares, F., Johnson, M. J., & Usher, E. L. (2007). Sources of writing self-efficacy beliefs of elementary, middle, and high school students. *Research in the Teaching of English, 42*(1), 104–120.

Palinscar, A. S., & Brown, A. L. (1984). Reciprocal teaching of comprehension-fostering and comprehension-monitoring activities. *Cognition and Instruction, 1*(2), 117–175.

Ray, K. W. (2004). Why Cauley writes well: A close look at what a difference good teaching can make. *Language Arts, 82*(2), 100–109.

Ray, K. (2012). Wondrous words. *The Reading Teacher, 66*(1), 9–14.

Rog, L. J., & Kropp, P. (2004). *The write genre: Classroom activities and mini-lessons that promote writing with clarity, style and flashes of brilliance*. Markham, Ontario: Pembroke Publishers.

Schunk, D. H., & Zimmerman, B. J. (1997). Social origins of self-regulatory competence. *Educational Psychologist, 3*(4), 195–208.

Smith, F. (1992). Learning to read: The never-ending debate. *Phi Delta Kappan*, 432–441.

Stillman, J., & Anderson, L. (2011). To follow, reject, or flip the script: Managing instructional tension in an era of high-stakes accountability. *Language Arts, 89*(1), 22–37.

White, M. (2015, January 22). Why morphemes? (Blog post). Retrieved from http://mariewhiteblog.com/2015/01/22/why-morphemes/

Wulber, A. (2011, June 27). Common core "I can" statements (Updated 5/30) (Blog post). Retrieved from https://turnonyourbrain.wordpress.com/2011/06/27/common-core-i-can-statements/

Zimmerman, B. J. (1994). Academic studying and the development of personal skill: A self-regulatory perspective. *Educational Psychologist, 33*(2–3), 73–86.

Zimmerman, B. J. (1994). Dimensions of academic self-regulation: A conceptual framework for education. In D. H. Schunk & B. J. Zimmerman (Eds.), *Self-regulation of learning and performance: Issues and educational applications* (pp. 3–21). Hillsdale, NJ: Lawrence Erlbaum.

Zimmerman, B. J., & Kitsantas, A. (2002). Acquiring writing revision and self-regulatory skill through observation and emulation. *Journal of Educational Psychology, 94*, 660–668.

Zimmerman, B. J., Kitsantas, A. (2005). Students' perceived responsibility and completion of homework: The role of self-regulatory beliefs and processes. *Contemporary Educational Psychology*, 397–417.

# PART IV
# High School

# 8
# A DIMENSIONAL CROSSWALK
## From the Common Core to Self-Regulation

*Keywords: dimensions, planning, self-monitoring, self-reflection, self-reaction*

The task of helping ninth graders succeed in high school requires serious efforts by educators to work within the framework of the Common Core standards at the kindergarten through eighth-grade levels to prepare students for the academic requirements in the upper grades. High schools have the most immediate responsibility for putting in place the curriculum, school organizational features, and strong teachers who will increase ninth graders' chances of making a good transition to high school. This instructional shift required by the Common Core means that more class time and student writing assignments must be devoted to the analyses of individual texts as well as research projects.

As the students progress through grades K–12, writing in a personal narrative style decreases while argumentative and informative writing increase. Both argumentative and informative writing are tied closely to content-based texts, and explanations are developed with evidence found in the textbook. Most ninth graders enter high school without the prerequisite skills required to write from both nonfiction and fiction sources. College and career readiness requires training in gathering and analyzing data and evidence drawn from both literary and informational texts to answer research questions. The Common Core standards demand significant pedagogical shifts in English Language Arts/Literacy standards for curriculum and classroom instruction, including writing standards that emphasize students be able to read, select, and write from appropriate sources. These pedagogical shifts can be accomplished if training in self-regulated learning is part of the process.

Most critical to the development of writing-from-sources tasks is identifying and gathering relevant information from credible sources that can actually be comprehended and used in science writing projects. In the age of instant information, our ninth and tenth graders have significant amounts of information available to them, but lack the filtering system required to manage and use the information to answer specific research questions. Self-regulatory strategies can be used to organize the search (planning), monitor progress (self-monitoring), and distinguish between accurate and information (self-reflection, self-reaction) before beginning the writing process.

Researchers recognize the challenges that evolve around meeting this standard, considering the writing difficulties that are prevalent among our middle and high school students (Reynolds & Perin, 2009). However, a small body of evidence on the effectiveness of literacy strategies taught in context-specific areas encourages us to focus on training ninth and tenth grade in self-regulatory

**TABLE 8.1** Road Map Research Paper (9–12) Aligned with Common Core and Dimensions of Self-Regulation

| A | B | C | D |
|---|---|---|---|
| *Common Core standards* | *High school target behaviors* | *Skill complexity* | *Self-regulated learning applications* |
| **Ninth and tenth grade basic research skills** | **Ninth and tenth grade level of complexity target behaviors** | **Skill** | **Self-regulation dimensions** |
| W.9–10.7 | Writing a self-generated question | Questioning | (1) When? (Time management) |
| W.9–10.8 | Gathering relevant information | Gathering | (2) What? (Self-monitoring) |
| W.9–10.8 | Using searches effectively | Planning | (3) Where? (Environmental structuring) |
| W.9–10.8 | Assessing the usefulness of each source specific to the task | Planning | |
| W.9–10.8 | Follow a standard for citation | Evaluating | |
| **Activate and reinforce prior knowledge from ninth and tenth grades** ||||
| **Eleventh and twelfth grades introduce new skills** | **Eleventh and twelfth grade level of complexity target behaviors** | **Skills** | **Self-regulation dimensions** |
| W.11–12.7 | Synthesize multiple sources on the subject | Synthesizing | (1) Why? (Goal setting and self-efficacy) |
| W.11–12.7 | Demonstrate an understanding of the subject under investigation | Sorting | (2) What? (Self-evaluation) |
| W.11–12.8 | Integrate information into the text selectively to maintain a flow of ideas, avoiding plagiarism and an overreliance on one source | Integrating | (3) With Whom? (Selective help-seeking) |

*Keywords*: time management, self-efficacy, environmental control strategies for "reading to write" tasks. As depicted in Table 8.1, for the 6–12 Writing strand we have chosen to focus on Research to Build and Present Knowledge, linking the drawing evidence from informational texts to gathering and using relevant information to respond to a research question. Self-regulatory training in planning, self-monitoring, self-reflection, and self-reaction can benefit both proficient and struggling writers by providing them with the necessary tools to become the managers of their writing tasks.

This section explores the connections between self-regulation dimensions and the Common Core standards for grades 9–12. The crosswalk (see Table 8.1) targets learning outcomes (Column A) the Common Core standards clearly expect from high schoolers and aligns them with behavioral dimensions of self-regulation (Column D). What really matters at the high school level is will our students be college ready?

## Project Planning for High Schoolers

College and career readiness require all students to be able to produce a research paper. At the ninth- and tenth-grade level, the standards focus on writing a self-generated research question, gathering relevant information, using searches effectively, assessing the strengths and weaknesses of those sources, and following a standard for citation. At the eleventh- and twelfth-grade level, the standards focus on synthesizing sources, integrating information, and organizing and producing clear and coherent writing through planning, revising, editing, and rewriting. Sustaining motivation and attention for the extended amount of time required to do the research independently is a challenge for most high school students.

The anchor standard requires high school students to develop research skills that mirror real-world research experiences. Short, as well as more sustained, research projects require high school students to structure their environment physically and socially, to manage their time, to self-monitor, and to maintain the motivation to sustain attention over a long period. To meet this standard, students are asked to demonstrate their ability to: (1) explore a specific topic, (2) find multiple sources of information, and (3) create a product that blends that information into a focused study of the subject. They should arrive at colleges and begin careers already having successfully completed projects that evidence a balanced blend of research, analytical skills, and writing skills. In too many educational settings, this area of instruction has not been successful; therefore, for this standard we focus on self-regulatory strategies that can help students sustain motivation to complete short- and long-term research projects by conducting task analysis, managing their time and behavior, and structuring their physical environment.

## Towards Independence

The Common Core initiative recognizes that adolescent learners are cognitively and developmentally able to take on increased levels of independence and personal control. This outcome is dependent on teachers providing opportunities for students to develop and exercise their autonomy, both within and outside the classroom (Feldlaufer, Midgley, & Eccles, 1988). High school students are generally expected to engage in more independent study time, are usually assigned more homework assignments, and must be able to manage different assignments from multiple teachers. Consequently, the Common Core requires students at this level to be given more choices about curriculum activities and opportunities to assume personal responsibility, specifically for short- and long-term research projects. This attempt to encourage greater student independence and self-sufficiency outside the classroom requires students to have a repertoire of study and self-regulation strategies that can be readily accessed and utilized (Zimmerman, 2002; Cleary & Zimmerman, 2004).

## The Struggle

As students transition from middle school to high school, and then from high school to college, many of them struggle to deal with a learning environment that calls for increased independence and greater self-management. This struggle can reduce their motivation to succeed and significantly impact their self-efficacy. Students can be empowered to exert greater control over their learning so that they can become more proactive and self-motivated learners. Students in grades 9–12 still have time to establish a repertoire of effective strategies to conduct sustained research projects. Prior to heading off to college, these students can learn how to select, evaluate, and adjust faulty strategies when they are not working effectively through environmental structuring, time management, self-monitoring, and self-evaluation (Cleary & Zimmerman, 2004; Dembo & Eaton, 2000; Zimmerman, 2002).

## Structuring Independence Through Self-Monitoring

To better demonstrate how self-regulation can help students complete short- and long-term research projects successfully, we focus on lesson planning that helps students self-regulate specific dimensions of the way they function while completing short- and long-term tasks. A project of the magnitude of a research paper is assigned at a time when students experience multiple distractions, the pressure of the college applications process, SAT (Standard Achievement Test) preparation, peer pressure, social media, and opportunities to escape the demands of the learning environment. Self-monitoring logs can assist students with tracking how they manage the demands of a complex project during a very demanding time in their lives.

The structure of project planning at this level depends on how individual students can be trained to manage their time and their behavior, and to control their physical environment consistently for the duration of a short- or long-term project. In addition, students need to sustain motivation, choose the most appropriate strategies and resources, and maintain self-efficacy. We suggest the use of self-monitoring tools to help students manage the challenges that come with working independently. Tracking thoughts, actions, and behaviors while working on a specific task can raise students' awareness of how they structure their learning environment, make use of their time, monitor their progress, and realistically evaluate their performance over short and long periods.

A higher high school dropout rate will predictably accompany projects that require sustained attention unless educators integrate teaching specific self-monitoring strategies into their lesson planning. Self-regulation includes the monitoring of basic psychological functioning, such as motivation (why we do it), method (how we do it), and time (when we do it) (Zimmerman, 1998). Asking students to take more responsibility for managing their own learning is going to require more than lining up teaching and learning methods to Common Core standards to bridge the gaps that now exist.

Valid self-assessments and feedback can help students locate their not-yet-detected strengths and deficiencies in areas that impact learning (McMahon & Luca, 2001). Becoming college and career ready means that students can increase their awareness of how using self-monitoring tools can help complete short- and long-term research projects. Learning to conduct self-assessments of how time is spent and how interruptions are handled can help students track their behavior while on task. Teacher feedback can support their findings, and in turn make recommendations regarding what adjustments need to be made to attain their goals.

## Psychological Dimensions of Self-Regulated Learning

The integrated model provides a framework for the introduction of self-monitoring tools during the development of a research project that can improve self-regulated learning for students beginning at the ninth-grade and continuing through the tenth, eleventh, and twelfth grades. Tables 8.2 and 8.3 highlight the psychological dimensions self-regulated students need to attend to if they are going to successfully manage the complexity of the research projects assigned at the freshmen, sophomore, junior, and senior levels. Our formative approach to developing self-regulatory skills during the high school years begins with focusing on characteristics that vary in each and every high school student and change over time from the freshman through the senior year. Students engaging in self-monitoring at the ninth- and tenth-grade levels will respond to questions about when they will do the task (time management), what they will do to get the task done (behavior), and where they will do the task (physical environment) as detailed in Table 8.2.

Students engaging in self-monitoring at the eleventh- and twelfth-grade levels will respond to questions about why they will do the task (motivation), how they will get the task done (method), and with whom they will do the task (selective use of resources), as detailed in Table 8.3.

**TABLE 8.2** Dimensions of Academic Self-Regulation: Ninth and Tenth Graders (Adapted to include academic delay of gratification and Common Core connection)

| Criteria | Psychological dimensions | Task conditions | Self-regulatory attributes | Self-regulatory processes | Common Core–related outcome |
|---|---|---|---|---|---|
| **When** | Time | Set time limits | Timely, efficient Delay of gratification | Time management | Awareness of time constraints |
| **What** | Behavior | Set goal for outcome behavior | Self-aware | Self-monitoring, self-evaluation, | Awareness of behavior |
| **Where** | Physical environment | Structure environment | Environmentally sensitive/ resourceful | Environmental structuring | Environmentally aware |

**TABLE 8.3** Dimensions of Academic Self-Regulation: Eleventh and Twelfth Graders (Adapted to include academic delay of gratification and Common Core connection)

| Criteria | Psychological dimensions | Task conditions | Self-regulatory attributes | Self-regulatory processes | Common Core–related outcome |
|---|---|---|---|---|---|
| **Why** | Motive | Choose to participate | Self-motivated | Goal setting and self-efficacy | Independent sustained motivation |
| **How** | Method | Choose method | Planned or routinized | Task strategies, self-instruction | Evidence of comprehension of subject under investigation |
| **With Whom?** | Social | Choose partner, model, or teacher | Socially sensitive and resourceful | Selective help-seeking and resource management | Narrow or broaden inquiry using resources appropriate to subject under investigation |

The model integrates strategies that can help students become managers of the areas that so often negatively impact their performance at every level of high school learning, development, and instruction. College and career readiness require all students to sustain motivation and attention for the extended time required to complete both short- and long-term projects independently. The structure of project planning at the high school level depends on how well individual students can be trained to sustain their motivation; select the appropriate strategies; assess social resources; and manage their time, behavior, and physical environment consistently for the duration of a both short- and long-term project. Once goals are in place, controlling all six of the dimensions of academic self-regulation is a significant contributor to academic success (Zimmerman, 1998).

## Generic Project Guidelines: Common Core

The Common Core standards (CCSS W.9–10.7, W.11–12.7) require both short- and long-term research projects to give students opportunities to investigate, read, and comprehend multiple sources and draw their own conclusions using proper research skills to answer a specific research question or solve a problem. Several states have proposed the standard outcome for this type of project to include the following requirements:

- The research project demonstrates college- and career-readiness level of proficiency by addressing Common Core reading and writing standards.
- The research project must have multiple elements such as: (1) conducting research in response to a specific question or problem; (2) gathering relevant information from multiple sources; (3) assessing each source; (4) planning; (5) revising; (6) editing; and (7) rewriting.
- Four informational/literary nonfiction sources gathered from multiple authoritative print and/or digital sources are required.

The research project is designed for students to demonstrate they can synthesize skills, which is something that cannot be assessed by standardized testing. The project is evidence of how students make their way up the staircase of complexity, building on skills learned in the earlier grades. The crosswalk from Common Core requirements to self-regulated learning, found at the beginning of the introduction (see Table 1.1), is a type of roadmap that outlines the complexity of the standards for grades 9–12. Specific skills introduced in the ninth and tenth grade are foundational to the more demanding standards of the eleventh and twelfth grade. Meeting or not meeting the requirements described by the Common Core standards at the eleventh- and twelfth-grade level has a significant impact on high school graduation rates.

## Project Introduction: Self-Efficacy

When introducing the project, the teacher openly shares his own thoughts regarding his self-efficacy regarding the planning, the scope, the overwhelming feelings that can come from attempting this type of assignment, and the level of support he would need to complete the assignment.

Students first observe the teacher in the role of a coping model (one that is not overconfident with the task) who shares the need to manage time, environment, and behavior in order to complete a project of this magnitude.

- The teacher rates his self-efficacy (using a scale of 1–10) responding to the question, "*How confident are you that you can complete this research project within the time constraints?*" He then asks students to hypothesize about their own self-efficacy for completion of the overall project.

- After discussing their self-efficacy beliefs, the students complete a brief questionnaire asking them to rate their use of self-regulatory strategies (Zimmerman & Pons, 1986).

Students are invited to become actively involved in going through the cyclical phases of self-regulated learning (forethought, performance, reflection) while the teacher pays close attention to their development as competent self-regulated learners (observation, emulation, self-control, self-regulation). The training procedure is incorporated into the content of the class, rather than focusing solely on self-regulatory training. Subsequently, both the self-efficacy ratings and self-evaluations are specific to the research project–related assignments and can be used as formative assessments throughout the project. In addition, a task analysis of the specific research-related task is done to help students focus on an expected outcome while learning how to use self-monitoring tools.

## Purpose

The purpose of the following two chapters is primarily to teach high school students how to self-regulate behaviors, thoughts, feelings, and actions found to be critical to successfully completing short- and long-term projects. The sample lessons for the ninth through twelfth grades focus on self-monitoring while working on research project–related tasks that are two of the most significant components of a research paper, though not the entire paper. Chapter 9 focuses on Common Core requirements for ninth and tenth grades, and Chapter 10 focuses on Common Core requirements for eleventh and twelfth grades aligned with underlying dimensions that students self-regulate using specific processes (Zimmerman, 1998).

Before students begin observing how self-monitoring logs can be effective self-monitoring tools for a long-term research project, the teacher should assess the students' level of ability to engage in short- and long-term self-directed learning. Are they developmentally ready and able to work on a long-term research project? If not, students may need to spend more time reviewing how to monitor their self-efficacy, time, environment, and distractions.

## References

Cleary, T. J., & Zimmerman, B. J. (2004). Self-regulation empowerment program: A school-based program to enhance self-regulated and self-motivated cycles of student learning. *Psychology in the Schools, 43*(2), 149–155.

Dembo, M. H., & Eaton, M. J. (2000). Self-regulation of academic learning in middle-level schools. *The Elementary School Journal, 89*(3), 473–490.

Feldlaufer, H., Midgley, C., & Eccles, J. (1988). Student, teacher, and observer perceptions of the classroom before and after the transition to junior high school. *Journal of Early Adolescence, 8*(2), 133–156.

McMahon, M., & Luca, J. (2001). Assessing students' self-regulatory skills. In *Annual Conference of the Australasian Society for Computers in Learning in Tertiary Education, Melbourne, Australia. (ERIC Document Reproduction Service No. ED467960).*

Reynolds, G. A., & Perin, D. (2009). A comparison of text structure and self-regulated writing strategies for composing from sources by middle school students. *Reading Psychology, 30*(3), 265–300.

Zimmerman, B. J. (1998). Academic studying and the development of personal skill: A self-regulatory perspective. *Educational Psychologist, 33*(2–3), 73–86.

Zimmerman, B. J. (2002). Achieving self-regulation: The trial and triumph of adolescence. In F. Pajares & T. C. Urdan (Eds.). *Academic motivation of adolescents* (Vol. 2, pp. 1–27). Greenwich, CT: Information Age.

Zimmerman, B. J., & Pons, M. M. (1986). Development of a structured interview for assessing student use of self-regulated learning strategies. *American Educational Research Journal, 23*(4), 614–628.

# 9

# A STRATEGIC APPROACH TO RESEARCH PROJECTS

## Grades 9 and 10

*Keywords: Dimensions, managing time, structuring environment, adapting behavior, research*

Research skills learned at the ninth- and tenth-grade level include writing self-generated questions, gathering relevant information, using searches effectively, assessing the usefulness of sources specific to the task, and following a standard citation format. For ninth and tenth graders, generating a research question to guide their projects takes a great deal of time, and this is often a place of frustration where students give up before they even begin the process. Research questions need to be revised many times before they become the core component of the research paper or project.

Three weeks before the first class session dedicated to introducing one or more components of a research project, the teacher gives students several topics to choose from for an upcoming project. This activity will give them time to independently explore their personal interests and availability of information before beginning the twelve-week span of research project–related tasks.

Prior to beginning the sequence of the integrated model, the teacher invites the students to participate in casually viewing and discussing specific components of a completed research project that earned a high grade. This brief presentation gives students an overall view of the research project with aligned study logs and invites them to become acquainted with the scope and sequence of the specific tasks related to the research project.

## The Study Log

A study log introduced by Zimmerman, Bonner, and Kovach (1996) has been successfully adapted to diverse educational settings. Later designs of the study log added sections to increase monitoring of independent study habits and other self-regulatory strategic behaviors, including academic delay of gratification. Teachers and teacher educators can affirm that critical to completing any short- or long-term project is the student's ability to postpone giving into immediate and available distractors in order to focus on completing the task at hand (Bembenutty, 2011). How many high school students are able to postpone socializing with friends in person or through social media in order to remain after school to work with their librarian or teacher on a research project that is not due immediately? Or, how many choose not to become distracted by instant messaging and surfing options when using the Internet for research? Ninth and tenth graders can benefit from the use of study logs to self-monitor their behaviors while working on a research-related task.

The study log (see Table 9.1) is the method we have selected to help students monitor their self-efficacy, time management, physical environment, and distractors while they are working on an assignment to generate a research question for an upcoming project. Detailed explanations about the study log are included in the actual lesson plan.

**TABLE 9.1** Study Log

Rows 1–6: To be completed during Forethought phase.
Rows 7–8: To be completed during Performance phase.
Rows 9–11: To be completed during the Self-reflection phase.
A. Teacher model: Can the model (teacher) . . . B. Student model: Can you (student) . . .

| 1 | Can the model (teacher, you) complete the research project–related task? What is he or she saying? Write it down! | | | | |
|---|---|---|---|---|---|
| 2 | Dimensions of Self-regulation | Why? Self-efficacy | When? Time required | Where? Environment required | What to do with distractors? Delay of gratification |
| 3 | Notes: | | | | |
| 4 | Self-monitoring questions | How confident is the teacher? | How much time does the teacher require? | What type of environment does the teacher require? | What are the distractors that could interfere with the teacher meeting the goals? |
| 5 | Write the teacher's measurements of level of confidence, estimate of time, environment structure, and how they plan to deal with distractions. | | | | |
| 6 | Self-monitoring predictions | (Rate 1–10) | Hours to complete | Example: Library, computer, bedroom | Example: Friends, phone, parents, Internet, party |
| 7 | STOP!—After the task has begun and the teacher models adjustments to her original predictions made in Row 4, you will respond to the following questions. Did the teacher meet their expectations? Write if any adjustments were made during the performance or reflection phase. | | | | |

*(Continued)*

**TABLE 9.1** (Continued)

| 8 | Performance phase | Did self-efficacy change? How confident is the model now that the task is in process? | How much time did it take? Does the model need more time than predicted? | Was the environment the correct choice? Does the model need to change environment? | What were the distractions? |
|---|---|---|---|---|---|
| 9 | Self-monitoring outcomes | Self-efficacy (rate 1–10): | Yes/No | Yes/No | Yes/No |
| 10 | Self-reflection phase | Did self-efficacy change? How confident is the model after the task is completed? | How much time was needed? | What were they? | What was done to manage them? |
| 11 | Self-reactions | Self-efficacy (rate 1–10): | Hours/Minutes | Places: | Actions: |
| Self-monitoring comments | | | | | |

## Self-Monitoring Tools

Self-monitoring is not only important for students to evaluate progress; it is also a way for teachers to identify important summative information regarding their progress towards reaching their goals. Students complete self-efficacy reports (see Table 9.2) at specific checkpoints throughout the sessions regarding their confidence in using self-regulatory strategies to plan and manage the writing of a good research question.

**TABLE 9.2** Self-Efficacy Reports

| Self-efficacy | I can use self-regulatory strategies to plan my actions, manage my time and environment, and limit distractions in order to independently write a good research question. Rate here (1–10, with 1 = not confident at all and 10 = very confident): | | |
|---|---|---|---|
| I can use self-regulatory strategies to complete the steps required to write a good research question. Grade yourself in each of the following columns: A (Yes!), C (Ok), or F (No). | | | |
| Self-regulation | Time management | Environmental control | Distractions |
| Self-monitoring | I can manage my time by estimating enough time to complete a research-related task. | I can make the correct choices when planning the environment I need in order to complete a research-related task. | I can manage distractions by using strategies my teacher has modeled. |
| My grade | | | |
| Comments | | | |

## The Plan: The When, Where, and What of Self-Regulation

*Managing Time, Structuring Environment, and Adapting Behavior*

**Objective:** To investigate, read, and comprehend multiple sources and draw conclusions using proper research skills to generate a specific research question for a research paper or project.

**Sessions:** The time frame of the research project–related task conducted using the integrative framework to teach self-regulatory strategies can be shorter or longer than twelve weeks, depending on students' prior knowledge. The suggested twelve-week span allows teachers to spend more time at the observation (modeling) and emulation levels of self-regulatory development and to not increase the level of independent learning until students have evidenced behaviors that indicate self-regulation.

**Materials:** The study log (see Table 9.1) and self-efficacy report (see Table 9.2) are the self-monitoring tools for all levels and phases of this project.

## Observation Level

### Watch It!

### Sessions 1–4

**Observation:** The teacher models ways of thinking through the different phases of self-regulated learning within the larger context of writing a research paper. He demonstrates the use of forethought planning and different performance strategies, followed by checking for understanding at the self-reflection phase. Throughout each of the phases, the teacher models self-monitoring. Self-monitoring provides students with a method of keeping track of one's thoughts and behavior towards reaching the goal of writing a research question. It also provides students with a tool (study log) for comparing one's predicted performance with the outcome performance and making attributions for successes and failures to meet goals.

## Observation of Forethought

### Planning a Strategic Approach to a Research Task

### Session 1

**Forethought:** Students observe as the teacher develops a plan for writing a research question. As outlined later, the teacher models how to use a study log (Table 9.1) to monitor the progress in this phase that precedes writing the actual research question. The teacher not only plans how to do the actual task, but also makes predictions of how much time it will take, as well as other criteria that influence self-regulation. Students' attention is directed to rows 1–6 of the study log as the teacher models how she monitors thoughts, feelings, and actions when preparing to do a task.

### Modeling: What Is the Teacher Doing?

Thinking aloud, the teacher (or competent peer) models behaviors that demonstrate how the study log is used to monitor and evaluate progress of specific self-regulated learning behaviors while writing a research question. Special attention is focused on the study log, as students are reminded for this exercise that the "teacher" is being evaluated, not the student. The teacher models circling the choice of "teacher" on the study log, and students do the same.

> 1. Can the model (teacher, you) complete the research project–related task? What is he or she saying? Write it down!

Throughout the entire forethought phase, students are instructed and reminded to pay close attention to the teacher and to observe everything the teacher is saying and doing.

- Based on observations of the teacher's assessment of his self-efficacy, how he predicts the time required, selects a physical environment, and notes the distractors, students enter the data from their teacher's log into a blank study log in row 6 (Table 9.1).
- Students pay close attention to the teacher's predictions because they will be evaluating how well he was able to meet his own expectations when they fill in the row 9 "Self-Monitoring Outcome" during the performance phase and row 10 "Self-Reactions" during the reflection phase.

The class observes as the teacher asks and responds to the following questions while thinking aloud: *"What do I need to do?"* and *"Do I have the skills to do it?"*

### What Do I Need to Do?

**Task analysis:** Thinking aloud, the teacher analyzes the task and sets realistic, proximal goals. He breaks down the components of an exercise in how to write the question that will guide the research process. It is important for the teacher to evidence a strategic approach to assessing the skills he is asking the students to emulate at the next level.

## Do I Have the Skills to Do It?

**Self-efficacy:** Using a self-questioning strategy, the teacher asks aloud, *"How confident am I that I can write a research question about this topic?"* The students closely observe how the teacher assesses both weaknesses and strengths and arrives at the level of self-efficacy rating by choosing a number from 1 to 10, with 10 being a high rating of self-efficacy and 1 being a low rating.

## How Much Time Will It Take?

**Time management:** Thinking aloud, the teacher predicts (not guesses) how much time it will take to accomplish the self-set goals. The teacher poses questions to assess prior knowledge about the task in order to gain valuable information for predicting how much time it will take to complete the task.

## Does It Matter Where I Study?

**Environmental control:** The teacher thinks aloud as he considers the environment required to get the task done in the amount of time required. As a result, students become aware of how choices are made for where to study by accounting for the resources and distractors of particular learning environments.

- Statements such as, *"The library is the best place to complete this task. I would have the help of the librarian, but then I could not use my phone to talk to my friends,"* can focus students on the importance of structuring an environment that might not be exciting, but will get the task completed in the targeted time required.

## How Will I Stay Focused and Not Get Distracted?

**Distractions:** The teacher thinks aloud about times he has tried to accomplish a goal and a friend calls to invite him over for a party, or to just "hang out." Verbalize how putting off something that is "fun" to accomplish a goal is the better choice, and students should "delay gratification," meaning have fun later, study now!

## Observation of Performance

### Carrying Out

*A Strategic Approach to a Research Task*
### Session 2

**Performance:** The teacher moves into the performance phase, making sure each student is observing and monitoring their performance using the self-regulatory strategies in the study log. The teacher makes sure each student is observing how adjustments are made to the plan. As the teacher works on the task, writing, revising, and rewriting a research question, students fill in the sections of the study log with data gained from their observations of the teacher's behaviors and verbalizations while he is actually demonstrating how self-monitoring is done while working on the task. Students fill in rows 8 and 9 of the study log (Table 9.1).

### *Modeling: What Is the Teacher Doing?*

Thinking aloud, the teacher sequentially demonstrates how to write a research question while using the study log to self-monitor. The class is engaged in monitoring the teacher's performance as he responds to the following questions aloud.

### *What Do I Have to Do?*

**Task analysis:** The teacher demonstrates the actual writing, editing, revising, and completion of a good research question. It is important for the teacher to

**TABLE 9.3** Observation of Performance Rows 7–10

| Enter data after teacher has completed performance phase | | | | |
|---|---|---|---|---|
| 7 Did the teacher meet his/her expectations? Write if any adjustments were made during the performance or reflection phase. | | | | |
| 8 Performance phase | Did self-efficacy change? How confident is the teacher now that the task is in process? | How much time did it take? Does the teacher need more time than predicted? | Was the environment the correct choice? Does the teacher need to change the environment? | What were the distractions? What was done to manage them? |
| 9 Self-monitoring outcome | | | | |

show that he knows how to "chew gum and walk"—in other words, he can self-regulate while working on the task.

### Do I Have the Skills to Do It?

**Self-efficacy:** Using a self-questioning strategy, the teacher thinks aloud: *"Now that I know how to do the task, do I have the self-regulatory skills to complete this task successfully?"* In response to the posed question, the teacher models how one's perceptions of his or her abilities can change once the task is underway.

- The teacher then models what adjustments can be made when one realizes that a task may be more difficult to complete than first thought. For example, *"Writing a research question about his topic is more difficult than I thought; however, I can do it if I have more time."*

### Will I Have Enough Time?

**Time management:** Thinking aloud, the teacher refers to the choices that have been made prior to beginning the task during the "plan it" phase.

- The teacher makes decisions out loud to use specific self-regulatory strategies making better use of the time allotted. He makes statements such as *"If the time for the task is miscalculated, how does one adjust it?"* or *"This task is more difficult than I first thought; I should increase the time I plan to spend on it."*

### Did I Choose the Right Place to Study?

**Environmental control:** The teacher thinks aloud, monitoring the work environment. For example he might ask, *"Did I choose the correct place to focus my full attention on the research project–related task?"*

- Environmental interference might cause the teacher to move from the classroom to the library and then back to the classroom.
- Students pay close attention to how he solves the problems that arise during the performance of the task in order to meet his goals. For example, if the environment is not conducive to learning, how does one change it? If there are distractors, what does one do about them?

### How Do I Stay Focused (Delay Gratification) and Not Get Distracted?

**Delaying gratification:** The teacher thinks aloud as he shares the distracting power of social challenges that can interfere with getting work done on time.

He admits, *"Friends, phone, the Internet, and having fun can easily distract anyone from staying with a plan until the task is completed."* Then he adds, *"Waiting to do things that are more fun until after the task is completed is delaying gratification, an important self-regulatory skill. Work first, and having fun later can be the reward for a well-done research question!"*

**Study log:** After observing the teacher, students are referred to rows 1–9 of the study log making sure they are filled in with enough information to make comparisons between the predicted and actual outcomes of the teacher's performance.

## Observation of Self-Reflection

### Evaluating!

### *A Strategic Approach to a Research Task*
### Session 3

**Self-reflection:** Students observe the teacher model the process of evaluating the work he has done in addition to the strategies used. The main idea of the self-reflection phase is for the teacher to share his self-evaluations in relation to two activities: 1. The planning that is part of any process to remain proactive and in charge of things that could negatively impact his performance. 2. The outcome: Self-regulatory behaviors influencing the successful completion of the task. Students review the completed sections of the study log (Table 9.1) with data gained from their observations of the teacher's behaviors and verbalizations after he has completed the research project–related task.

### *Modeling. What Is the Teacher Doing?*

The teacher thinks aloud while attributing some of his success to the specific self-monitoring strategies that led to successful task completion and how they can be used for future tasks. Students are encouraged to share their observations of the effectiveness of the teacher's use of self-monitoring strategies and self-efficacy ratings for a specific task, such as generating questions about a research topic.

The class observes as the teacher asks and responds to the following questions while thinking aloud.

### *What Was the Most Difficult Part of the Task?*

**Task analysis:** During this time, the students observe the teacher make the connections to behaviors that led to a better understanding of the task and those that did not. For example, the teacher can list specific things he could do to learn more about the task requirements before beginning his research. Information gained from this observation can help students target areas in their task analysis that require improvement.

### Did Monitoring My Self-Efficacy Increase Motivation?

**Self-efficacy:** Thinking aloud, the teacher provides detailed descriptions of how the self-monitoring strategies were related to sustaining motivation and successful task completion to help observers determine what adjustments could be made for future tasks.

### Did I Plan Enough Time to Complete the Task?

**Time management:** The teacher thinks aloud while evaluating his ability to use the self-monitoring tools to manage the time required for the task.

- The teacher verbalizes how he would modify the approach to time management, taking into account the scope and demands of the task that might have been beyond his ability, requiring more assistance than first realized.
- Asking questions aloud about what worked, what did not work, and what adjustments could be made to future attempts at the task provides students with a window into the way a self-regulated learner adjusts strategies to try again instead of giving up on the task.

### Did I Choose the Right Place to Study? What Did I Do with Distractions?

**Environmental control:** The teacher thinks aloud about how he selected where to complete the task and the decisions and distractors that might have contributed to failing to complete the task on time.

- The teacher describes the actions he took to structure, manage, or change the environment to complete the task successfully. What did he do about noise? Friends? Text messaging? Stressors? Invitations to hang out?

## Post-Observation

### Is Our Strategic Approach Working?

#### Session 4

A post-observation assessment is required to determine which of the students are ready to move on to the emulation level. Students will be asked to use the same strategies demonstrated by their teacher to self-monitor and write a good

TABLE 9.4 Self-Evaluation: Post-Observation Report

| Will I be able to repeat the actions the teacher demonstrated to complete the research project–related task? ||||||
|---|---|---|---|---|
| Post-Observation/ Pre- Emulation | Self-Efficacy | Time Required | Environment Required | Distractors |
| Can I write a research question about this topic? | How confident am I that I can copy what the teacher did? | How much time do I require? | What type of environment do I need? | What are the distractors that could interfere with meeting my goals? |
| Self-monitoring predictions | (Rate 1–10) | Hours to complete | Library, computer, bedroom | Friends, phone, parents, Internet |

research question. Teachers can use a quick self-evaluation to assess students for comprehension of self-regulated learning strategy instruction to determine which students are ready to move on to emulation and which students require more observation. At this point, students are grouped according to those who completed the observation level and those who need to observe models again.

## Who's Moving Up?

- Based on the assessment of all of the sections of the study log completed during the observation level and the post-observation report, the teacher groups the students according to those who are ready to imitate modeled behaviors and those who require another cycle of observation.

At the emulation level, the teacher will distribute student-centered study logs and the same task as the one modeled by the teacher. Students are required to use self-monitoring strategies while writing a research question.

## Emulation Level

### Working Together

### Sessions 5–8

**Emulation:** The teacher guides students through tasks that require them to emulate the observed behaviors. The teacher scaffolds students, both individually and in small groups, as they self-monitor and until they demonstrate competency in predicting and assessing the outcome of how well they use self-regulatory strategies during a research task. Within each of the three phases of self-regulated learning, the teacher provides support and guidance for the students. Through extensive practice, the students begin to develop automaticity in self-monitoring their self-efficacy, time, environment, and managing distractions.

## Emulation of Forethought

### Planning

### *A Strategic Approach to Writing a Research Question*
### *Session 5*

**Forethought:** The teacher activates prior knowledge gained from the behaviors observed at the observational level. The teacher divides the class into groups and distributes blank self-monitoring logs and the research task. The teacher then guides the students to use the strategies previously modeled. Throughout the entire forethought phase processes (outlined later), students are instructed and reminded to pay close attention to replicating what was previously modeled at the observation level. The teacher explains to students how they will be using the (now familiar) study log (see Table 9.1), making sure they circle "you" (B) and personalize the statements needed to track their progress towards completing the task of writing a research question over the course of three days.

> Can the model (teacher, you) complete the research project–related task? What is he or she saying? Write it down!

### *Modeling: What Is the Teacher Doing?*

The teacher continues to think aloud, analyzing task components and re-modeling strategies for students who have not retained a visual representation of what they observed. Peer modeling is also used effectively to show students that their classmates with similar abilities are doing what they observed the teacher do during the observation level. Both teachers and students together respond to the following questions.

### *What Do I Have to Do?*

**Task analysis:** The teacher focuses the class's attention on the research question task components, and students are asked to think about how they would use self-regulatory strategies to complete the task.

## Do I Have the Skills to Do It?

**Self-efficacy:** The teacher asks students to refer to the self-monitoring log and to rate themselves on their thoughts and feelings about writing a research question. Students are instructed to be honest and genuine in their responses. Students share with their group members their ratings and why they chose the score they did. Doing this helps students observe their peers' thinking, providing additional modeling opportunities. It also helps students become more self-aware as they talk through their reasoning regarding self-efficacy. The teacher closely monitors each group and individual students and encourages them to discuss their self-efficacy. The teacher monitors and makes note of the students' overall ratings to determine motivation.

## Will I Have Enough Time?

**Time management:** Teachers direct students' attention to the time management cell of the log. Students are asked to think about a time frame for writing the research question. Working in their groups, students discuss their time frames and whether they can manage their time to complete the task. The teacher circulates and closely monitors students' discussion. The teacher may interject if students are setting unrealistic time frames or not taking into account things that can interfere with time management.

## How Do I Choose the Right Place?

**Environmental control:** The teacher instructs the students to think about the physical environment required to complete the research-related task and to make notes of possible distractions. The teacher guides the group discussions in rating the characteristics of which physical environments (in the context of the classroom) might be more conducive to successfully writing a good research question. Students are asked to determine if they have the necessary materials (i.e., Internet access, books, journal articles) in their physical environment to begin the process of writing a research question. If not, where are these items and how and when can they become available?

## What Can I Do to Stay Focused and Not Become Distracted?

**Distractions:** The teacher guides the group discussions now on identifying and managing possible distractions that can interfere with completing the task. Students are encouraged to discuss all possible distractors and to brainstorm on possible ways to eliminate them. Students observe the ways others handle similar distractions and develop a new repertoire of ways to eliminate them by delaying gratification.

# Emulation of Performance

## Practicing
### *A Strategic Approach to a Research Task*
### *Sessions 6 and 7*

**Performance:** Students practice how to write a research question under the close supervision of the teacher. They follow the teacher's strict guidelines demonstrating how to increase self-regulated study habits while working on a research-related task. The class remains in small groups as the teacher reviews with them how to use the self-monitoring logs during this phase. When necessary, the teacher can re-model, advise, redirect, and promote specific behaviors to help students apply self-monitoring skills. Although the writing of a research question is an important outcome, what is more important are the choices that students make regarding how they use their time, where they study, how they manage distractors, and their self-efficacy. The teacher provides constant and consistent feedback and continues to scaffold and move about the room. The teacher can assume questions such as the following will be swirling around in their students' heads as they approach the research task with more independence.

## *What Am I Doing?*

**Task analysis:** Students engage in the strategies outlined in the forethought phase that should be representative of those modeled by the teacher. As students encounter difficulties, the teacher provides support and helps the students work through these challenges. The teacher is constantly monitoring students' progress and helps students identify, articulate, and use self-monitoring strategies modeled earlier.

## *Do I Have the Skills?*

**Self-efficacy:** Using the logs, students discuss and rate their capability of self-monitoring using the self-regulatory strategies modeled by the teacher. The teacher monitors students' discussion and ratings using the information obtained from the logs in the forethought phase. The teacher will provide feedback and encouragement to students who may feel less self-efficacious.

## *How Much Time Is It Taking Me?*

**Time management:** Students keep track of the time they are spending in practicing the writing of a research question. As they do so, they are discussing whether or not they allocated enough time and whether they might need more time in the future when doing this on their own. Students score their time allocation on the self-monitoring logs. Students are encouraged to think about the amount of time the teacher spent and to determine whether more or less time is needed if working independently.

### Did I Choose the Right Place?

**Environmental control:** The teacher instructs students to use the previous demonstration of how to set up one's environment and to make up their own lists of key characteristics of the best classroom environment for writing a research question. The teacher remains attentive to how each student examines the positive and negative effects of specific choices, giving advice to help shape their final decisions. The students set up the environment as the teacher advised and demonstrated.

### What Am I Doing about the Distractions?

**Distractions:** The teacher monitors students' discussions of how to manage distractions noted in the forethought phase and observed by the students when the teacher was modeling. For example, advice can include *"When a friend calls me, I tell them I can come out in three hours, but not until I finish my work!"* Students in groups are asked to help their peers by encouraging management of distractions and to practice using the approaches modeled by the teacher and peers.

**Study log:** Rows 8 and 9 of the study log should be filled out during the performance phase as students become more aware of their time frames, environment, distractors, and task demands.

## Emulation of Self-Reflection

### Reflecting On
### A Strategic Approach to a Research Task
### Session 8

**Self-reflection phase:** This phase follows three sessions of the performance phase. Students should have been monitoring their performance-related activities (study log) and receiving teacher feedback. At this phase, students make evaluations and judgments about their performance. They record their reactions in their self-reflections in rows 10 and 11 of the study log.

The teacher instructs students on how to evaluate the specific self-monitoring strategies that led to task completion and how they can be used for future tasks. Students are encouraged by the teacher to reflect on how useful the logs are in monitoring one's feelings and progress towards a challenging assignment using the patterns of thought observed during the observational level.

## What Was the Most Difficult Part of Self-Monitoring?

**Self-efficacy:** Using the self-monitoring logs, students discuss and rate their self-efficacy for future similar tasks. The teacher monitors the discussion and helps students identify changes in self-efficacy across the three phases. The teacher has previously modeled how to self-reflect on one's self-efficacy and is now scaffolding students to do the same.

## What Did I Do Well? What Would I Change?

**Self-reaction:** The teacher works with the groups to help them assess each step they took in copying the teacher's approach to self-regulating while working on a research project–related task and formulating a research question. Students discuss what worked well and what did not and how closely their self-regulatory behaviors approximate the teacher's. For example, students might say, "*I set my time frame for a longer period than the teacher allotted because I know my research skills are not very strong and I will need help.*" As students evaluate their performance, the teacher and students compare the information on the logs with the outcome of the research-related task. Teachers should be able to attribute stronger performance to self-monitoring strategies.

## Did I Have Enough Time?

**Time management:** Students repeat the approach the teacher took in evaluating the time allocated for writing the research question. Students score their time allocation on the logs and evaluate whether they allocated enough time or too much time.

## Did I Choose the Right Environment?

**Environmental control:** The teacher instructs students on how to determine if the environment used was conducive to writing the research question. Students will copy the method the teacher modeled in conducting this evaluation. The teacher remains attentive and scaffolds as students discuss their environment and determine if changes need to be made in the future.

## How Did I Manage Distractions and Delay Gratification?

**Distractions:** Students are encouraged to use the approach the teacher modeled in evaluating and managing distractions. The teacher monitors students' discussion of whether there were distractions and what their responses were to move forward with the task and not become diverted. Students are also encouraged to practice anticipating distractions and to plan how to manage their responses and learn how to delay gratification until a task is complete.

## Post-Emulation Review

Before moving students to the next level of self-control, the teacher asks students to complete the study log (Table 9.1) and check their self-efficacy ratings (Table 9.2). He uses their self-assessments and other log entries to assess which students are ready to engage in tasks with minimal guidance. At the self-control level, students are competent in working independently, yet some supervision is needed in making adaptations or changes from the strategies modeled by the teacher.

## Self-Control Level

### It's Your Turn

### *Sessions 9–12*

**Self-control:** At this level, the teacher shifts the responsibility of self-monitoring to the student. The students are now expected to work independently while monitoring their self-efficacy, time, and environment and managing their distractions. At the same time, they are expected to take charge of completing the task of writing a research question. The teacher's role changes from providing extensive support to guiding and advising as needed by the students. While working independently, students at this level keep a mental image of how the teacher modeled making choices that led to self-regulation and task completion. Students make similar choices to self-monitor their own behaviors while working on a research project–related task.

## Self-Controlled Forethought

### Planning

### *My Strategic Approach to Writing a Research Question*

### **Session 9**

**Forethought:** Although now working independently, the class remains in groups and the teacher explains to students the next component of the research project. The teacher distributes blank self-monitoring logs (see Table 9.1) and a research project–related task. The teacher discusses the defining behaviors of the self-control level, primarily an increase in behaviors that lead to independent learning. The teacher asks students to think aloud about how difficult it might be to do the research-related task in the allotted time frame and without modifications to the current classroom environment. Students evaluate themselves individually and they enter their ratings into a self-efficacy report (Table 9.2). Students are encouraged to articulate plans for dealing with the challenges that accompany working on research tasks.

### Modeling: What Is the Teacher Doing?

The teacher activates prior knowledge gained from the behaviors observed and practiced in the previous two levels and encourages students to work individually, but to ask peers for help when needed. Using the self-monitoring logs, the teacher models and completes each cell by thinking out loud about the decisions that need to be made to self-regulate their behaviors while planning, writing, and evaluating a research question.

### What Is the Most Difficult Part of the Task?

**Self-efficacy:** Students rate their self-efficacy (Table 9.2), giving the teacher a better understanding of their perceived abilities to do the task with less teacher supervision.

### Will I Use the Study Logs When I Am Not Required to Do So?

**Task analysis:** The teacher monitors as students individually or in small groups break down the steps required to write a research question. At the same time, he instructs students to use the logs to predict and monitor their uses of self-regulatory strategies to complete the task successfully. He remains available to offer insights, correct errors, and provide feedback upon request. He adjusts the level of support and slowly withdraws, providing students with the opportunity to work independently.

### Can I Do The Task Independently?

**Self-efficacy:** Students begin the task by thinking about the task demands and rating their self-efficacy (Table 9.2) for writing the research question with minimal support. They also assess their own use of self-monitoring strategies and express whether or not they can manage time, environment, and distractions without consistent oversight from the teacher.

### Can I Manage My Time Outside of the Classroom?

**Time management:** The teacher monitors discussions and sets checkpoints as reminders for students to be aware of the time it might take to complete the task. Students are reminded to manage distractions to complete the task in the time predicted.

*Can I Control the Environment Where I Choose to Work?*

**Environmental control:** The teacher calls attention to the behaviors of students who are independently planning for where they will work and who are making choices that will assist them in completing the question for their research projects in the allotted amount of time. Students might hear the teacher refer to how much better it might be to work in a specific area of the classroom where it is more secluded, or go to the library.

*Can I Manage Distractions by Delaying Gratification?*

**Distractions:** Managing distractions at this level is the responsibility of the students. Students are encouraged to have a plan to use their time more effectively and not become distracted.

## Self-Controlled Performance

### Practicing

*My Strategic Approach to Writing a Research Question*
*Session 10*

**Performance:** During this phase, students are engaging in the writing of their research question as they use their self-monitoring logs to focus on their ability to manage distractions, time, environment, and set goals. Students are instructed to fill out the logs as they observed and practiced during the previous levels. The teacher reminds the class that assistance can be obtained upon request when they are stuck and cannot move forward without a "hint." Students work based on their recall of what they have observed and practiced during the previous levels. Using a short series of think-alouds, the teacher poses some questions that might be asked to gain clarification during the task. Students are reminded and encouraged to use the self-regulatory strategies learned during the previous levels to take charge of their learning.

*Do I Have the Skills to Self-Monitor During This Task?*

**Self-efficacy:** Self-efficacy is rated individually. Students are encouraged to analyze the task, keeping in mind the successes they experience when successfully managing their time, controlling their environment, and making the correct choices when distracted. Students are encouraged to use the strategies they put in place during the planning phase and to try to make any necessary adaptations on their own if they feel self-efficacious in their ability to do so.

## Can I Use Self-Monitoring Logs When Working Independently?

**Task analysis:** The teacher directs students to use the self-monitoring logs for each of the self-regulation processes during the actual writing of their own research question. They are to focus on managing their thoughts, feelings, and actions in order to produce a research question.

## Can I Manage My Time Better If I Predict and Monitor the Outcome?

**Time management:** Students individually predict the time required to complete the task, keeping in mind how they will self-regulate during the process.

## Do I Make Good Choices for Places to Study?

**Environmental structuring:** Students are reminded that they are in control of their physical environment and should choose to work in a place with the least distractors.

## What Do I Do to Manage Distractions?

**Distractions:** Students choose how to manage distractions; they can change their seats or make a suggestion to the teacher regarding a better work environment

## Self-Controlled Reflection

### Reflecting On

### *My Strategic Approach to Writing a Research Question*
### *Session 11*

**Self-reflection phase:** During this phase, students are reflecting on the process and outcome of self-monitoring logs. They discuss as a class differences between the teacher's self-monitoring behaviors and their own, and the challenges related to their own management of time, environment, and distractions. Students make evaluations and judgments about their performance and record their reactions in their self-reflections in row 10 of the study log. The teacher instructs students on how to evaluate the specific self-monitoring strategies that led to task completion and how they can be used for future tasks. Students are encouraged by the teacher to reflect on how useful the logs are in monitoring one's feelings and progress towards a challenging assignment using the patterns of thought observed during the observational level.

## Students Reflect on the Following Questions As They Review the Outcomes

### How Has Evaluating My Self-Efficacy Helped Me Be More Self-Regulated?

**Self-efficacy:** Students review their predictions and outcomes on their study log and discuss their self-efficacy for future similar tasks. The teacher monitors the discussion and only interjects to clarify a misconception or when asked by students how to explain how self-efficacy changes as one becomes more self-regulated.

### What Do My Self-Reactions Tell Me About My Ability to Self-Monitor?

**Self-reaction:** Working individually, the students decide if they overrated or underrated their self-efficacy and whether their self-efficacy has now changed from what it was in the beginning. As students evaluate their performance, they compare the information on the logs with the outcome of the research-related task. Teachers should be able to attribute stronger performance to self-monitoring strategies.

### What Have I Learned About the Way I Use My Time?

**Time management:** The teacher asks students to use the log to determine if they predicted an accurate amount of time to write the research question and, if not, to discuss what changes they would make in the future. Students compare the time predicted and the actual time it took to complete writing the research question, attributing the outcome to specific choices and time management strategies learned from their teacher.

### What Have I Learned About the Places Where I Choose to Study?

**Environmental control:** Students state the reasons their choice of environment was or was not conducive to writing the research question. The teacher remains attentive and scaffolds as students discuss how their environmental structuring increased or decreased their ability to focus on the research question task.

### What Have I Learned About Delaying Gratification Until I Successfully Complete My Work?

**Distractions:** Students use the approach the teacher modeled in evaluating and managing distractions. Students discuss what they did to move forward with the task and not become diverted from completing their work. Students learn how to delay gratification until a task is complete by setting goals and focusing on them rather than on the fun thing they would rather be doing.

## Post Self-Control Review

### Session 12

Before moving students to the next level of self-regulation, the teacher asks students to complete the following log and uses this along with the study log entries to assess which students are ready for working independently in an unstructured context.

The teacher meets with students individually to provide feedback on their logs and their research questions. The teacher promotes students' self-efficacy by highlighting effort and the self-regulatory processes used by the students in the process of writing a research question.

The teacher talks to each student to obtain feedback on how they felt about writing a research question on their own, and the teacher assesses at this level whether the student is ready to advance to the final level of self-regulated competency. One of the teacher's goals at this level is to prompt students into thinking about how they might make changes in the future when assigned a similar task. The self-regulation level involves being flexible and able to adapt and make changes as needed, even when faced with unanticipated events and in the absence of the teacher.

The teacher assesses which students are ready to self-monitor for short and long-term research projects by evaluating predictions and outcomes entered into the study logs and comparing self-monitoring behaviors with the research question evaluation. Students are grouped according to those who are ready to begin working on their own research question outside of the classroom on another assigned topic or a topic of their choice, and those who may need more time at the self-control level to increase self-monitoring skills.

## Self-Regulation Level

### On Your Own!

#### *Fostering Self-Regulation for Research-Related Tasks*

**Self-regulation:** Students at this level must be able to perform the task when conditions may be somewhat uncertain, such as at home or where teachers or peers may not be readily available. Students are considered to be self-regulated when they are able to make changes or adapt their behavior based on the challenges they may encounter as they work towards reaching their goals and when they feel self-efficacious enough to modify their strategies and plans accordingly. At this level, the responsibility of the work is shifting entirely from the teacher to the student. The students are now expected to be able to work independently and to work through the three phases of self-regulated learning, using study logs to help self-monitor their performance for other tasks. The teacher's role also shifts from providing guidance and advice to being available upon request.

## Self-Regulation of Forethought

### Planning Research-Related Tasks

**Forethought:** Students at this level work independently and readily use study logs to self-monitor their time, environment, and self-efficacy as they make plans to do tasks that require self-regulatory strategies. The teacher provides opportunities for students to use the different planning processes and encourages students to think aloud when working outside of the classroom. Students at this level take charge of their learning and adapt the strategies to new conditions. The teacher remains a model and facilitator of good study habits, always demonstrating and encouraging the use of the newly acquired behaviors in similar types of tasks.

### *Should I Analyze a Task Before I Begin to Work on It?*

**Task analysis:** The teacher often highlights the steps and strategies needed to complete the task outside of the classroom in addition to promoting possible resources students may want to use. He is an example of good planning practices in every area of his lesson presentations and feedback. The teacher often shares with students that good places to study, how to avoid distractions, and tips on time management are a result of good planning.

### *Why Is Monitoring Self-Efficacy Important in Task Preparation?*

**Self-efficacy:** The teacher often stresses the differences between getting the task completed in the context of a classroom or in various other settings that are not structured. He often points out examples when self-efficacy may be different when one is working independently than when one is working with peers or with the teacher. Students are often reminded to evaluate their satisfaction with learning outcomes when completing similar tasks outside of the classroom.

## Why Is Paying Close Attention to Time Frames and Important Part of Task Preparation?

**Time management:** The teacher often reminds students to account for how they use their time and encourages them to make adjustments early in the project so that they will get their work in on time. Students are often reminded of the importance of delaying gratification if an assigned homework task is to be completed within the time frame required. The teacher verbally considers the amount of time it will take to complete the similar research project-related homework task, weighing their motivation, strengths and weaknesses, and availability of resources.

## Why Is It Important to Plan Where I Study?

**Environmental control:** Students are encouraged to identify the characteristics of the environment that would best meet their needs to do a task similar to writing a research question.

## Why Is Delaying Gratification an Important Strategy to Learn for Managing Distractions?

**Distractions:** The teacher often reinforces that distractions will happen and that students should be prepared to manage distractions in ways that will not interfere with working on their task. Students are reminded that postponing fun and more interesting things to do to complete a task or reach a goal is a characteristic of a self-regulated learner.

# Self-Regulated Performance

## Proactive Approaches to Research Tasks

**Performance:** When self-regulated students are engaged in writing a research question for homework, they independently set aside specific time frames, choose the correct environment, manage distractions, and delay gratification. Students make sure they have access to study logs, and are not hesitant to practice self-monitoring strategies outside of the classroom. Students make self-monitoring part of their study process and use study logs, and they work through each phase of the assigned homework.

## How Can a Teacher Influence Students to Self-Monitor?

**Task analysis:** The teacher often includes in his daily teaching how to set up the steps to complete the research-related homework tasks outside of the classroom. He verbalizes the strategies that would be effective and describes the components of the task with the outcome expectations. In addition, he promotes the resources that are available and how to complete a research project–related homework task outside the classroom.

**Self-efficacy:** The teacher sets the stage by describing the differences between getting the task completed in the context of a classroom and in various other settings that are not structured, citing examples from his own experiences. The teacher emphasizes that self-efficacy to work with help readily available and self-efficacy to work independently might be different. At this point, each student evaluates their ability to complete a similar task outside of the classroom.

**Time management:** The teacher is a model time manager. When he commits to a time frame, it is honored or adjusted during the task, not when the bell has rung. Students are rewarded for keeping track of time in and out of class. The teacher often problem-solves with the students possible resolutions to running short on time when working on a long-term project.

**Environmental structuring:** Teachers are transparent when discussing daily distractions that come from doing lesson plans or working with the television on. Students are often asked to share challenges to controlling study environments away from school from a personal perspective. The class brainstorms on ways both teacher and students may handle these challenges.

**Distractions:** Teachers and students keep running records of distractors and share them in class. At times, the teacher can use an example, such as the World Cup soccer games. Helping students choose a study environment away from the soccer matches or setting aside time to watch the matches and then study can limit the mental distraction of the games many high schoolers watched night and day. At the end of the three-day homework task, the teacher requires students to bring to class the homework assignment to use a study log while doing a research project–related task. At this point, the teacher can determine each student's level of self-regulation and continue to encourage the use of self-regulatory strategies in every instructional segment for further growth and development.

## Ongoing Self-Reflection . . .

**Self-reflection:** Self-regulated students conduct ongoing evaluations of how well they can transfer self-monitoring strategies to academic and nonacademic tasks. Students are often encouraged to bring study logs to class and connect any successes or failures to items on their study log entries. The teacher meets individually with each student to review the logs and research questions when requested. Students are often led by the teacher to discuss their experiences and the challenges they face regarding their self-efficacy and managing their time and distractors to their study time.

## What Should Teacher Feedback Include at This Level of Self-Regulation?

**Task analysis:** Feedback from the teacher on any task should include guiding students to evaluate whether or not they adequately prepared for the task requirements by conducting a detailed task analysis. Teachers can provide time in class for students to work in small groups to help each other identify specific demands the tasks will make on their time and the type of environment needed to complete the task successfully.

**Self-efficacy:** Teachers consistently help students accurately evaluate their self-efficacy for managing their time, environment, and distractions.

**Time management, environmental structuring, and distractions:** Self-regulated students account for their time, environmental structuring, and delay gratification so that distractions do not interfere with their study time. Feedback from teachers regarding the effectiveness of good choices on their grades can encourage learners to work towards becoming self-regulated in more than one area. Class discussions about the correct choices that can be made to prepare students for college and careers can encourage others to manage distractions and devote more time and attention to these important areas of self-management.

## Reference

Bembenutty, H. (2011). Meaningful and maladaptive homework practices: The role of self-efficacy and self-regulation. *Journal of Advanced Academics, 22*(3), 448–473.

Zimmerman, B. J., Bonner, S., & Kovach, R. (1996). *Developing self-regulated learners: Beyond achievement to self-efficacy*. Washington, DC: American Psychological Association.

# 10

# BEGINNING A RESEARCH PAPER

## Grades 11 and 12

### Synthesizing Resources

*Keywords: Dimensions, Self-efficacy, motivation, strategic planning, time management*

Research skills learned at the eleventh- and twelfth-grade level build on foundational skills mastered at the ninth- and tenth-grade level. When students enter the eleventh grade, they are expected to already know how to write self-generated questions, gather relevant information, use searches effectively, assess the usefulness of sources specific to the task, and follow a standard citation format. At the eleventh- and twelfth-grade level, students are expected to synthesize sources, to integrate information, and to produce clear and coherent writing by planning, revising, editing, and rewriting. Throughout their high school experience, students are required to acquire a strong foundation to actually write a paper that meets all of the required elements of a Common Core twelfth-grade research project to be completed during the senior year.

The Common Core standards have validated what librarians have always purported to be the key to success in college and beyond: that students have to be able to research a topic and present their findings (Burke, 2013). College and career readiness demands research and media skills that go beyond cutting and pasting to demonstrating an understanding of the subject matter under investigation (Writing Anchor). The designers of the Common Core State Standards agreed that American education should focus on the developing skills of enquiry and critical analysis that can be demonstrated through writing. The Nation's Report Card 2007 (Salahu-Din, Persky, & Miller, 2008) showed only 1 percent of all twelfth graders nationwide could write a sophisticated, well-organized essay. There is little evidence of change from then to now. Other research has shown that 70 percent to 75 percent of students in grades four through twelve write poorly. High schools are still graduating large numbers of students whose writing skills will not sustain them in the workforce or in college.

For those students who enter the eleventh and twelfth grades having had some experience with conducting research projects, the learning curve will not be as steep as for those who enter without such prior knowledge. At this level, students are expected to design and present information learned from informational texts and other sources relevant to the research question. The complexity of the task can be overwhelming to the many students who struggle to read, ponder, paraphrase, and then retool the information into their own language, with the result often being plagiarism (Burke, 2013). In addition, managing the flow of information to include the most important findings in the research project can become overwhelming for students who are not familiar with the strategies needed to complete this type of writing task. Educators realize that the research project is not an easy task for students, but they also believe that it is an essential step to take in modern education (Blaxter, Hughes, & Tight, 1998; Schwegler & Shamoon, 1982).

Training in self-regulatory learning can have a significant impact on how successful students are in developing the necessary skills to meet the demands of the Common Core standards at this level of learning. For many students, self-efficacy in this area will be low, and the motivation to sustain attention over a long period will be challenged. Educators can focus on training students to emulate selected self-regulatory processes used by expert writers, such as environmental structuring, time management, self-instruction, self-monitoring, and assessing the level of difficulty. For this Writing 6–12 strand, we continue to focus on Research to Build and Present Knowledge standards, expanding on what has been learned in the ninth and tenth grades and increasing the level of complexity for research and writing skills.

The "road map" to the research paper (see Table 10.1) revisits the complexity of skill acquisition as students spiral up to becoming good readers, writers, and

**TABLE 10.1** Road Map Research Paper (9–12) Aligned with Common Core and Dimensions of Self-Regulation

| *Common Core standards* | *High school target behaviors* | *Skill complexity* | *Self-regulated learning applications* |
|---|---|---|---|
| **Ninth- and tenth-grade level of basic research skills** | **Ninth- and tenth-grade level of complex target behaviors** | **Skill** | **Self-regulation dimensions** |
| W.9–10.7 | Writing a self-generated question | Questioning | (1) When? (Time management) |
| W.9–10.8 | Gathering relevant information | Gathering | (2) What? (Self-monitoring) |
| W.9–10.8 | Using searches effectively | Planning | (3) Where? (Environmental structuring) |
| W.9–10.8 | Assessing the usefulness of each source specific to task | Planning | |
| W.9–10.8 | Follow a standard for citation | Evaluating | |

*(Continued)*

TABLE 10.1 (Continued)

| Activate and reinforce prior knowledge from ninth and tenth grades ||||
|---|---|---|---|
| **Eleventh and twelfth grades introduce new skills** | **Eleventh- and twelfth-grade level of complex target behaviors** | **Skills** | **Self-regulation dimensions** |
| W.11–12.7 | Synthesize multiple sources on the subject | Synthesizing | (1) Why? (Goal setting and self-efficacy) (2) What? (Self-evaluation) |
| W.11–12.7 | Demonstrate an understanding of the subject under investigation | Sorting | |
| W.11–12.8 | Integrate information into the text selectively to maintain a flow of ideas, avoiding plagiarism and an overreliance on one source | Integrating | (3) With whom? (Selective help-seeking) |

researchers. By the time students enter their senior year of high school, they are asked to demonstrate their ability to: (1) explore a specific topic, (2) find multiple sources of information, and (3) create a product that blends that information into a focused study of the subject. They should arrive at colleges and begin careers already having successfully completed projects that evidence a balanced blend of research, analytical skills, and writing skills.

For eleventh and twelfth graders, gathering and synthesizing sources is an area where students waste time, often surfing the Internet for information that looks good but is not appropriate for the task. Self-monitoring while organizing one's search for sources can help students gain a better comprehension of the importance of motivation, strategies that work, and the availability of resources, all of which can lead to a successful foundation for any research paper or project. Several self-monitoring checklists are found throughout this chapter, yet they all measure the same characteristics of a self-regulated learner for each phase and level of development. Table 10.2 is an example of one of the self-monitory logs students will encounter during the forethought phase of the emulation level as they contemplate specific dimensions of self-regulation that can significantly impact their performance if not managed correctly. Eleventh and twelfth graders focus on the why (motivation), what (strategic planning), and with whom (social/selective help-seeking) dimensions of self-regulation when engaged in a task to gather and synthesize resources in preparation of writing a research paper.

Self-monitoring provides students with a method for tracking thoughts and behaviors while working towards reaching one's goals. It also provides them with a tool for evaluating oneself after the task has been completed. Eleventh and twelfth graders carefully pay attention to how the teacher monitors her self-efficacy: how she initiates the task, chooses appropriate strategies, and selects appropriate social resources for help.

**TABLE 10.2** Student Log

| Can I independently gather and synthesize sources (using a literature review grid) so they can be used to write a good research paper as my teacher did? Give yourself a grade of 1, 2 or 3 (1 = lowest) |||
| Name: _____ |||

| *Self-regulation* | *Self-monitoring outcomes* | *Rate yourself!* |
|---|---|---|
| **Self-efficacy** | I can create the plans to gather and synthesize sources when assigned for homework (literature review grid). | |
| **Motivation** | My plan to help me maintain interest in the research project includes finding great sources to make my research paper interesting when assigned for homework. | |
| **Strategic planning** | When I am doing this type of assignment for homework, I can set short, easy-to-reach goals with targeted dates. | |
| | When I am doing homework I can apply at least two to three strategies I have learned when planning how to do my assignment. | |
| **Social/ selective help-seeking** | If I get stuck doing this type of assignment for homework, I have plans to seek specific people out to help with questions that may arise when doing a similar type of task. | |
| | I know where I can find additional resources for this type of task, when needed. | |
| **Notes:** | | |

**Graphic organizer:** Students are also introduced to a literature review grid, which is a graphic organizer used to synthesize multiple resources (see Table 10.3), a strategic approach to gathering resources for the paper.

**TABLE 10.3** Literature Review: Synthesizing Multiple Resources (Grades 11/12)

| **Purpose: What does it mean to synthesize multiple resources?**<br>1. Combine separate elements from a whole.<br>2. Using multiple resources when researching a paper on a specific topic.<br>3. Making the sources work together to provide a strong research base for the paper. |
|---|
| **Tool:** A graphic organizer tracks information gained from sources when prewriting, writing, and synthesizing. The following instructions complete the planning grid. |
| **Instructions:** In the blank boxes, write down what each author said about each category. Not every box needs to be filled in; however, the more developed the literature review grid, the better developed the final paper. The grid requires the writer to enter categories to guide research about a specific topic. Use the following grid to synthesize resources for a paper on the Civil Rights Movement. |

*(Continued)*

**TABLE 10.3** (Continued)

| Authors' names | Type (article, book, interview) | Historical significance | Political influence | Current impact |
|---|---|---|---|---|
| Author A |  |  |  |  |
| Citation: ||||||
| Author B |  |  |  |  |
| Citation: ||||||
| Author C |  |  |  |  |
| Citation: ||||||
| Author D |  |  |  |  |
| Citation: ||||||
| Author E |  |  |  |  |
| Citation: ||||||
| Author F |  |  |  |  |
| Citation: ||||||

## Grades 11 and 12

### The Plan: The Why, What, and With Whom of Self-Regulation

#### Sustaining Motivation, Making Effective Strategy Choices, and Selecting Social Resources

**Objective:** To self-regulate thoughts, feelings, and actions found to be critical to successfully completing short- and long-term projects.

**Sessions:** The time frame of the research project–related task conducted using the integrative framework to teach self-regulatory strategies can be shorter or longer than twelve weeks, depending on students' prior knowledge. The suggested twelve-week span allows teachers to spend more time at the observation (modeling) and emulation levels of self-regulatory development and to not increase the level of independent learning until students have evidenced behaviors that indicate self-regulation.

**TABLE 10.4** Student Log: Forethought Phase

| Is the teacher able to design a plan to synthesize sources for a research paper? Give your teacher a grade of 1, 2, or 3 (1 = lowest). |||
|---|---|---|
| *Self-regulation* | *Self-monitoring outcomes* | *Rating* |
| **Self-efficacy** | My teacher was confident in her ability to develop a plan to synthesize the five sources in a literature review grid. | |
| | My teacher was confident in her ability set up a good plan to use the literature review grid for writing a research paper. | |
| **Motivation** | My teacher clearly expressed interest in writing about the research topic chosen. | |
| **Strategic planning/ task analysis** | My teacher set a plan for developing short- and long-term goals with targeted dates to work on them. | |
| | My teacher described at least two to three strategies for how she/he plans to use the sources and grid to write a good research paper. | |
| **Social/ selective help-seeking** | My teacher made plans to seek specific people out to help with questions that may arise when gathering and synthesizing sources for the research paper. | |
| **Notes:** | | |

**Materials:** The student logs (see Table 10.2), literature review grid (Table 10.3), and self-monitoring tools for all levels and phases of this project (Table 10.4).

**Pre-Observation:** Three weeks before the first class session dedicated to introducing one or more components of a research project, the teacher gives students several topics to choose from. This activity will give them time to independently explore their personal interests and availability of information before beginning the twelve-week span of research project–related tasks.

## Observation Level

### Watch It!

#### Sessions 1–4

**Observation:** The teacher models how she thinks through the different phases of self-regulated learning within the context of doing a specific assignment for a research project. Throughout each of the phases, the teacher models self-monitoring for specific dimensions of self-regulated learning. The teacher demonstrates useful planning strategies and different performance strategies, followed by checking for understanding during the self-reflection phase.

## Observation of Forethought

### Session 1

*A Strategic Approach to Synthesizing Resources Planning*

**Forethought:** Students observe as the teacher develops a plan for one component of a long-term research project. It is during the forethought phase that students confront the task demands and create a plan towards successful completion, knowing adjustments can be made during the performance phase. Following the plan can be difficult, especially for students who do not account for their self-efficacy, motivation, task strategies, and availability of resources. Students who begin to monitor these psychological dimensions before they begin a project are more likely to successfully complete long-term projects than their classmates who just do it.

*Modeling: What Is the Teacher Doing?*

The teacher introduces the self-monitoring log (Table 10.4) and thinks aloud, demonstrating how each section is used to record information about personal study habits while working on the research project. The students pay close attention to the teacher's actions and think-alouds as she makes planning decisions during the forethought phase that will guide her behaviors in the performance phase. These entries will help them compare the teacher's predicted performance with the outcome performance and make attributions for which behaviors led to success and which led to failure.

- When the teacher has completed modeling how she would use the self-monitoring log to monitor her approach to the research task, students rate the teacher on the effectiveness of the modeled self-monitoring strategies.

*Do I Have the Skills to Do It?*

**Self-efficacy:** Using a self-questioning strategy, the teacher asks aloud: "*How confident am I that I can develop a plan to synthesize my sources in ways that make sense?*" and "*How confident am I that I can use my sources for writing my paper?*" Students closely observe how the teacher assesses both weaknesses and strengths and arrives at the self-efficacy rating for gathering and synthesizing sources.

*Why Am I Doing This Task? Am I Interested?*

**Motivation:** Thinking aloud, the teacher describes the level of self-interest in the task—for example, questions and statements such as "*Am I even interested in the topic I chose?*" or "*I am very excited to learn more about my topic.*" Responses to both are valuable clues for predicting how motivated the teacher feels about working on the assignment.

## What Is Strategic Planning?

The teacher activates prior knowledge by questioning students about their experiences with research tasks, specifically how they gathered and organized their sources. They respond to the questions, *"Did you have a plan?" "What did you do?"*

- The teacher emphasizes that setting realistic goals, selecting strategies, and choosing resources now will save a great deal of time and frustration once work on the research task begins.
- The teacher thinks aloud about the short- and long-term goals, describing the elements of each. The teacher makes a list of both types of these goals to organize and develop a plan with checkpoints.
- The teacher reminds students that a research paper requires specific strategies, such as how to identify a topic; gather, synthesize, and cite the sources; and organize the paper by developing an outline.
- The teacher introduces the literature review grid as a strategy for organizing and synthesizing the sources.

**With Whom Will I Be Working?** The teacher thinks aloud, considering possible choices for help, such as a teacher, peers, librarians, friends, or others who move the completion of the task forward. This helps students become aware of the choices made regarding whom to study with or where to seek help and whether working with others presents another series of challenges.

- The teacher also thinks aloud about the availability of resources and how to obtain them. This highlights for students the issue of limitations of resources. For example, if they don't have access to the Internet at home, the library may be closed in the evening hours when students begin to gather resources for their papers.

## Give Your Teacher a Grade!

After observing the teacher, students are given a worksheet (see Table 10.4) and asked to grade their teacher's demonstration of the self-monitoring skills needed to develop a plan to synthesize sources and plan the process of writing a research paper. The students grade their teacher, while the teacher gives herself a grade. The teacher models how to assess self-efficacy, motivation, strategic planning, and help-seeking, making sure students are aware that they will be grading themselves at the next level. In each of the cells, the teacher substitutes "my teacher" with "I" as she models how to use the log.

## Observation of Performance

### Carrying Out

#### A Strategic Approach to Synthesizing Resources
#### Sessions 2 and 3

**Performance:** The teacher demonstrates how to gather, organize, and use the literature review grid (Table 10.3) to synthesize sources. The teacher continues to use the self-monitoring log while working through the processes in the performance phase and the steps involved in gathering and synthesizing resources for a research paper. The teacher is making sure each student is observing and monitoring as she is making adjustments to the original plan and remains focused on the task.

*Modeling: What Is the Teacher Doing?*

Students observe the teacher modeling the process of gathering and synthesizing sources for the larger task of writing a research paper. This process may involve several steps following the identification of a topic and collection of five sources. For example, using the literature review grid, the teacher can first organize the citations around individual subtopics and then write an outline. Further lessons can focus on the teacher modeling the various methods used to write the research paper from beginning to end. At the same time, the teacher is tracking her self-efficacy, checking her motivation, and sticking to the plans she made at the forethought phase.

*Do I Have the Skills to Do This?*

**Self-efficacy:** Using a self-questioning strategy, the teacher thinks aloud: "*Now that I know more about what I need to do to synthesize resources for a research paper, do I have the skills to do it successfully?*"

- This is a good opportunity for the teacher to model how one's confidence level may improve with planning, using a graphic organizer, and self-monitoring.
- Alternatively, the teacher may model how to deal with challenges without losing one's confidence when one realizes that the task may be more difficult than first thought: "*Synthesizing resources gathered for this topic is more difficult than I thought, but I know enough to get started and I know where to get help if I need it.*"

*Why Am I Doing This? How Will I Keep Going?*

**Motivation:** The teacher thinks aloud and describes challenges that make the process more difficult than initially thought. The trick here is for the teacher to be able to identify challenges that may threaten motivation and interest in completing the task and to express ways of sustaining motivation.

*What Do I Know About This Task? Are My Plans Working?*

**Strategic planning/task analysis:** The teacher demonstrates and explains a systematic approach to gathering and synthesizing resources to write a good research paper. The teacher thinks aloud as she explains how using a graphic organizer (literature review grid) allows writers to organize and make adaptations while working on a project.

- It is important for the teacher to show how the task is done, particularly the strategies used. Teachers try to relay to the students as they think aloud the strategies, both good and bad, for gathering resources for a good research paper.

*Who Am I Working With? Am I On My Own?*

The teacher simulates situations using students and peers such as the librarian to demonstrate how it would be to work with others. The teacher thinks aloud about how to engage others in the task and the challenges that may come up in doing so. The teacher also models appropriate methods of help-seeking and considers the effectiveness of this strategy for having the correct resources for the paper.

## Give Your Teacher Another Grade!

After observing the teacher, students are given a worksheet (see Table 10.5) and asked to grade their teacher's ability to model the synthesizing of sources and writing of a research paper. The students grade their teacher, while the teacher

**TABLE 10.5** Student Log: Performance Phase

| Is the teacher able to write a good research question? Give your teacher a grade of 1, 2 or 3 (1 = lowest). | | |
|---|---|---|
| *Self-regulation* | *Self-monitoring outcomes* | *Rating* |
| **Self-efficacy** | My teacher was confident in her ability to synthesize the five sources in a literature review grid. | |
| | My teacher was confident in her ability to gather and synthesize resources when faced with challenges. | |
| **Motivation** | My teacher clearly expressed interest in searching for resources about the research topic chosen. | |
| **Strategic planning/ task analysis** | My teacher worked through the short- and long-term goals and made adjustments as needed. | |
| | My teacher used at least two to three strategies for how she/he plans to use the resources to write a research paper. | |
| **Social/selective help-seeking** | My teacher sought others out, which proved to be helpful in gathering and synthesizing resources. | |
| | My teacher used additional resources when needed, such as the librarian, peers, or the Internet. | |
| **Notes** | | |

gives herself a grade. The teacher models how to assess self-efficacy, motivation, strategic planning, and help-seeking, making sure students are aware that they will be grading themselves at the next level. In each of the cells, the teacher substitutes "my teacher" with "I" as she models how to use the log.

## Observation of Self-Reflection

### Evaluating!
*A Strategic Approach to Synthesizing Resources*
*Session 4*

**Self-reflection phase:** Students are observing the teacher model the processes of evaluating the work done. The teacher describes aloud the thoughts about the sources she has gathered for the research paper. The main idea of the self-reflection phase is for the teacher to model evaluating herself in relation to two activities: (1) the process of synthesizing sources and planning and writing the research paper, and (2) the outcome: a literature review grid for writing a good research paper. This is helpful because it provides information about what to continue doing or what to change in future similar tasks. As the teacher works through this last phase, the teacher thinks aloud as she evaluates her forethought and performance phase measures. In this phase, the teacher continues to use the self-monitoring log and is asking questions such as:

- Am I satisfied with my choice of resources?
- Was the topic as interesting once I began to research it?
- Did I set realistic and attainable short- and long-term goals?
- Did I seek help from others who could really help me?
- Did I use other resources available to me, or should I have done something a little differently?
- What worked? What didn't work?
- Are there things I should do differently next time?
- Do I feel more confident in my ability to gather and synthesize the best resources next time?

### *Modeling: What Is the Teacher Doing?*

The teacher models her reactions to the entire process and outcome. The teacher is focused in particular on the processes that were used and whether or not changes or adjustments needed to be made along the way.

**Self-Efficacy:** Using a self-questioning strategy, the teacher thinks aloud: *"Now that I have gathered and synthesized sources for my research paper, do I have the skills needed to do it again with less assistance from the teacher?"*

- The teacher also thinks aloud: "*If I have a similar project next year, am I capable of gathering the correct resources that can be used to write a research paper?*" This is a great opportunity for the teacher to model how one's confidence level may improve with planning and self-monitoring.

**Did I Maintain a Level of Interest?** The teacher thinks aloud about the challenges that lowered her motivation. The teacher describes the strategies used to help sustain motivation and remain focused on the task, and also evaluates whether these were correct choices or not.

## Did My Strategic Planning and Task Analysis Work?

At this phase, the teacher is modeling how reactions can impact future planning and performance. The teacher does this by evaluating whether or not she has accomplished the task of gathering and synthesizing resources for a good research paper and if she is satisfied with the final result. For example, "*Is my literature review grid the best it can be? Is there something I could have done to make it stronger? More clear? Better planning?*"

- The teacher also thinks aloud and forms attributions. Attributions involve articulating the strategies used that may have caused the results. For example, if not satisfied with the way the resources were synthesized, the teacher may say: "*My literature review grid is ok, but I kind of rushed to get it done, and it does not include details to help me write a good research paper. Next time I need to set more realistic short-term goals and keep better track of which ones I get done.*"
- This will result in the teacher making the transition to the next step in the cycle, which is done to inform the forethought phase for the next time the task is assigned: "*Next time, I will be more aggressive in reaching my goals earlier in the process and then I will have more time to gain a stronger comprehension about the sources available.*"
- At this point, the teacher focuses on specific strategies that can be controlled. For example, the teacher cannot control the due date for the literature review grid, but the teacher can control the pacing of the work and the setting of her checkpoints for reaching goals.
- The teacher also reflects on the use of the self-monitoring log and the literature review grid. If these were helpful, what modifications could be made to make them even better in the future?

## Who Did I Work With? Was It Helpful to Work With Someone?

The teacher thinks aloud while evaluating the study partners and peers sought to help with synthesizing multiple resources.

- The teacher describes specific situations in which help was sought and discusses whether or not this strategy was used effectively. The teacher also reflects on the resources used and evaluates whether there was an adequate number of resources or if more were needed.

## How Did Your Teacher Do?

After observing the teacher, students are given a worksheet and asked to grade their teacher's ability to reflect on the effectiveness of her self-monitoring while synthesizing sources in preparation to writing a research paper. In each of the cells (see Table 10.6), the teacher substitutes "I" for "my teacher" as she fills out her personalized version of the student log.

TABLE 10.6 Student Log: Reflection

| Now that the sources have been synthesized and you are ready to write the research paper, let's think about what we did from the beginning. Did the teacher have good plans in place, and did the teacher do a good job self-monitoring while gathering and synthesizing resources for a good research paper? Give your teacher a grade of 1, 2, or 3 (1 = lowest). |||
|---|---|---|
| *Self-regulation* | *Self-monitoring outcomes* | *Rating* |
| **Self-efficacy** | My teacher seemed confident about integrating the five sources in a literature review grid. | |
| | My teacher seemed confident about using the synthesized resources to write a good research paper. | |
| | I think next time, my teacher will feel even more confident to do a better job. | |
| **Motivation** | My teacher kept her interest even when faced with challenges and seemed very motivated to gather resources to write a good research paper. | |
| | My teacher described things she will do in the future to help sustain motivation. | |
| **Strategic planning/ self-reactions** | My teacher evaluated the planning and performance processes as well as the final result. | |
| | My teacher identified specific changes to the planning and performance processes to write an even better paper in the future. | |
| **Social/selective help-seeking** | My teacher reflected on the benefits and drawbacks to working with others to synthesize and use the resources found. | |
| | My teacher identified things she will do differently next time regarding working with others to synthesize and use resources. | |
| **Notes:** | | |

## Post-Observation Review

Before moving students to the next level of emulation, teachers need to assess whether the students are ready. The following log will help teachers determine if students are ready to begin imitating what they observed the teacher do, or if students need to observe additional examples of how to write a research question. Students fill out the log without teacher modeling.

**TABLE 10.7** Study Log: Review Observation Level/Three Phases

| Forethought | | |
|---|---|---|
| I can (or cannot) do what my teacher did the way she did it! See Column A for rating scales. | | |
| *A* | *B* | *C* |
| *Self-regulation* | *Self-monitoring outcomes* | *Rating* |
| **Self-efficacy** 1 = not confident at all and 10 = very confident | How confident am I that I can develop a plan to synthesize my sources? | |
| | How confident am I that I can develop a plan to use my sources in the writing of a research paper? | |
| **Motivation** Y/N | I can sustain my interest in gathering and synthesizing resources for a research project. | |
| **Strategic planning** Y/N/Maybe | I can set short, easy-to-reach goals with targeted due dates. | |
| | I can develop two to three strategies as I observed my teacher do to gather and synthesize resources for a research paper. | |
| **Social/selective help-seeking** Y/N/Maybe | I can seek out specific people to help in gathering and synthesizing sources for a research paper. | |
| | I can develop a plan for using additional resources when needed. | |
| **Performance** | | |
| I can (or cannot) do what my teacher did the way she did it! See Column A for rating scales. | | |
| *A* | *B* | *C* |
| *Self-regulation* | *Self-monitoring outcomes* | *Rating* |
| **Self-efficacy** 1 = not confident at all and 10 = very confident | How confident am I that I can synthesize the resources for a research project? | |
| | How confident am I that I can use the literature review grid to make an outline for the research paper? | |

*(Continued)*

**TABLE 10.7** (Continued)

| Motivation Y/N/Maybe | I can maintain a high level of interest in my research topic as I gather and synthesize sources. | |
|---|---|---|
| Strategic planning/task analysis Y/N | I can set short- and long-term goals with targeted dates and work toward accomplishing them. | |
| | I can use at least two to three strategies for how to work on the research paper. | |
| Social/selective help-seeking Y/N/Maybe | I can seek out the appropriate help-givers when I need some help in gathering and synthesizing sources that I can use to write a research paper. | |
| | I can locate additional resources when needed. | |

**Reflection**

I can (or cannot) do what my teacher did the way she did it!
See Column A for rating scales.

| A | B | C |
|---|---|---|
| *Self-regulation* | *Self-monitoring processes and outcomes* | *Rating* |
| **Self-efficacy** Y/N/Maybe | I am confident that the final product will be similar to my teacher's. | |
| **Motivation** Y/N/Maybe | I can keep my interest and sustain my motivation in order to create a literature review grid that can be used to write a good research paper. | |
| **Strategic planning** Y/N/Maybe | I can evaluate the planning and performance processes as well as the final result. | |
| **Social/selective help-seeking** Y/N/Maybe | I can reflect on the benefits and drawbacks to working with others and on using social resources to improve my performance. | |
| **Notes:** | | |

## Emulation Level

## Working Together!

### Sessions 5–10

**Emulation:** The teacher guides students individually and in small groups through tasks that require them to emulate the observed behaviors. The teacher scaffolds students as they self-monitor and until students demonstrate competency in completing the logs and using the literature review grid to gather and synthesize sources for a research paper. Within each of the three phases of self-regulated learning, the teacher provides support and guidance to the students. Through extensive practice, the students begin to develop levels of automaticity in repeating what they observed in the earlier observation level.

## Emulation of Forethought

### Planning

### *A Strategic Approach to Synthesizing Sources*
### *Sessions 5–6*

**Forethought:** The teacher activates prior knowledge gained from the behaviors observed at the observational level. She divides the class into groups and distributes blank student logs and the research project task with a blank literature review grid. The teacher then guides the students in adopting the strategies previously modeled. The blank literature review grid is provided to help students keep a record of gathering and synthesizing the five sources required before they can begin to write a research paper.

### *Modeling: What Is the Teacher Doing?*

Throughout the entire forethought phase process, students are instructed and reminded to pay close attention to replicating what was modeled at the observation level. The teacher explains to students that they will be using the logs to monitor their self-efficacy, motivation, strategies, and use of social resources. For each of the processes described next, students are filling out the logs and using the literature review grid as directed.

### *Do I Have the Skills to Do It?*

**Self-efficacy:** The teacher asks students to rate their self-efficacy to gather and synthesize five sources on a literature review grid to be used for writing the research paper.

- Students are encouraged to discuss their self-efficacy ratings with one another while the teacher remains involved, moving around the room to closely observe how accurately students are rating their self-efficacy.

**Why Am I Doing This Task?** The teacher asks students to recite the steps she demonstrated when thinking aloud about her interest in performing the tasks.

- Students are instructed to individually complete the self-monitoring logs.

### *How Am I Going to Do It?*

**Strategic planning:** The teacher works with each group as they recite the specific steps modeled at the observation level about self-monitoring, using the literature review grid, and setting goals for how the task of gathering and synthesizing resources will be done.

- As students reconstruct the actions of the teacher, the teacher remains actively engaged and provides feedback and guidance as needed.

## Will I Be Working with Anyone?

**Social (with whom):** The students think aloud (discuss with their group members) as their teacher had done on the benefits and drawbacks of working with others on the research project.

- The students also think aloud about the availability of resources and how to obtain them. Students discuss what the teacher used and how to obtain similar methods to gather and synthesize their own resources.

Note: Students evaluate themselves (see Table 10.8) indicating their readiness to move on to the performance phase.

**TABLE 10.8** Student Log: Forethought Emulation

| \multicolumn{3}{l|}{**Student Log—Can I Do It?** Can I set up plans for how to synthesize my sources so they can be used to write a good research paper as my teacher did? Give yourself a grade of 1, 2 or 3 (1 = lowest). Name: _____} |
|---|---|---|
| *Self-regulation* | *Self-monitoring outcomes* | *Grade yourself!* |
| **Self-efficacy** | I can use the plans my teacher set to synthesize my sources (literature review grid). | |
| | I can plan to gather and synthesize sources so that I can write a good research paper. | |
| **Motivation** | My plan to maintain interest in the research project includes finding great sources to make my research paper interesting. | |
| **Strategic planning** | I am setting short, easy-to-reach goals with targeted dates to work on them for gathering and synthesizing the sources used for writing my research paper. | |
| | I can describe at least two to three strategies on how to work on my research project. | |
| **Social/selective help-seeking** | I have plans to seek out specific people to help with questions that may arise in gathering and synthesizing sources that can be used for writing the research paper. | |
| | I have a plan for using additional resources when needed. | |
| **Notes:** | | |

## Emulation of Performance

### Carrying Out

#### *A Strategic Approach to Synthesizing Resources*
#### *Sessions 7–9*

**Performance:** Students practice how to gather and synthesize the five sources using the literature review grid. Under the close supervision of the teacher, they must be able to explain how sources contribute to the actual writing of the research paper. The use of the literature review grid should be an almost exact replica of the teacher's originally modeled one, but differ slightly in content. For example, students may be working on a topic suggested by the teacher, with sources that the teacher previously obtained, and sorting them based on categories the teacher suggested.

**Modeling: What Is the Teacher Doing?** The class remains in small groups as the teacher reviews with them how to use the self-monitoring logs and literature review grid during this phase. When necessary, the teacher re-models, advises, redirects, and promotes specific behaviors to help students better understand and apply self-monitoring skills. The teacher displays visual images of the grid and the self-monitoring log, as well as constant and consistent feedback as she continues to scaffold and evaluate students' progress.

### *Do I Have the Skills to Do This?*

**Self-efficacy:** Using the logs, students discuss and rate their capability of gathering and synthesizing the sources that can be used to write a research paper.

- The teacher monitors students' discussions about the information obtained from their ratings in the logs following the forethought phase. The teacher provides feedback and encouragement to students who may feel overwhelmed.

### *Why Am I Doing This? How Will I Keep Going?*

**Motivation:** The teacher encourages small group discussions and closely attends to how each student assesses his or her own interest level. Students are encouraged to discuss ways of making the project exciting by forming groups with common topics and sharing information to sustain motivation.

- Students rate their motivation on the self-monitoring log now that they have a better idea of their interest in actually completing the task.

## Are My Plans Working? Do I Know More About the Task Now Than I Did When We Started?

**Strategic planning/task analysis:** Students engage in the strategies that will help them understand the task complexities as outlined in the forethought phase.

- As students encounter difficulties, the teacher provides support and helps students work through these challenges. Further modeling of how to use the literature review grid to record information from sources can help students who have difficulty recalling what they first observed.
- The teacher is constantly monitoring students' progress and helps students identify, articulate, and use strategies modeled earlier.

## Have I Found Helpful Resources? Peers? Teacher? Librarian?

**Social (With Whom):** The teacher instructs students to list and discuss the appropriate methods of help-seeking from several types of resources that would increase the likelihood of successfully completing the research project.

- The students also discuss the use of possible resources beyond those found in the classroom and share which ones the teacher recommended using.

Note: Students are encouraged to evaluate themselves and fill in "Student" (Table 10.9) indicating their readiness to move on to the self-control level.

**TABLE 10.9** Student Log: Performance Emulation

| **Student log: How am I doing?** Now that I am doing it, can I gather and synthesize my sources as my teacher demonstrated and use them to write a good research paper? Give yourself a grade of 1, 2 or 3 (1 = lowest). <br> Name: _____ ||||
|---|---|---|---|
| *Self-regulation* | *Self-monitoring outcomes* || *Rate Myself!* |
| **Self-efficacy** | I am confident that I am synthesizing and using sources appropriately to write a good research paper. || |
| **Motivation** | I am maintaining interest in the research project. || |
| **Strategic planning** | I am first working on the short, easy-to-reach goals, followed by the more challenging ones, as my teacher did. || |
| | I am using two to three strategies that my teacher used on how to gather and synthesize sources for my research paper. || |

| Self-regulation | Self-monitoring outcomes | Rate Myself! |
|---|---|---|
| **Social/selective help-seeking** | I am aware of where I can find specific people and resources to help with questions that may arise in gathering and synthesizing sources. | |
| | I am using additional resources such as a model of a research paper with a good list of sources about a topic similar to mine. | |
| **Notes:** | | |

## Emulation of Self-Reflection

### Looking Back: How Did I Do?

### Session 10

**Self-reflection:** Students are instructed to use the self-monitoring log to evaluate the effectiveness of their planning and performance on the research project tasks. Students are encouraged to share their evaluations of the effectiveness of using the self-monitoring log and the literature review grid. They can share their individual ratings with each other as they reflect on the entire process.

### *Modeling: What Is the Teacher Doing?*

The teacher reminds students to model for each other as they discuss any adaptations they needed to make to their plans as they were working through the process of gathering and synthesizing their sources. Students demonstrate the changes they would suggest that might improve the teacher's model.

**Self-efficacy:** Students rate their self-efficacy and look for any changes that took place from when they began the tasks. Students are encouraged to share what their ratings tell them about their self-efficacy and check for accuracy in underestimating and overestimating their skills.

- Students discuss how their self-efficacy beliefs could influence their motivation to attempt similar types of tasks in the future.

### *Did I Remain Interested?*

**Motivation:** Students give examples of specific statements made by the teacher that increased or decreased her motivation to continue with the task even when it became challenging.

## Did My Strategic Planning and Task Analysis Work?

**Strategic planning/task analysis:** Students evaluate the usefulness of the literature review grid, self-monitoring log, and self-regulatory processes they engaged in.

- Students reflect on their learning outcomes and discuss ways to improve or modify the process to gather and synthesize sources for a research paper.

## Who Did I Work With? Did I Benefit from Help-Seeking?

**Social resources:** The teacher instructs students to list and discuss the key characteristics of the most useful social resources that led to a successful completion of the task. The teacher poses questions that focus students on both positive and negative outcomes when not having a specific plan to obtain assistance, and provides recommendations for future choices.

Note: Students evaluate themselves, indicating their readiness to move on to the self-control level (see Table 10.10).

**TABLE 10.10** Student Log: Emulation/Self-Reflection

| **Looking back: Student log** Now that you have gathered and synthesized your sources to write a research paper, let's evaluate what we did from the beginning. Did good planning and self-monitoring help you gather and synthesize the sources needed to write a research paper? Give yourself a grade of 1, 2 or 3 (1 = lowest). |||
|---|---|---|
| *Self-regulation* | *Self-monitoring outcomes* | *Ratings* |
| **Self-efficacy** | I am confident that I gathered and synthesized sources that can be used to write a research paper. | |
| | I am confident that my literature review grid will help me write a good research paper. | |
| | I will be even more confident when given tasks similar to this one in the future. | |
| | I will be even more confident when asked to gather and synthesize sources because I know how to use a literature review grid and self-monitor my actions. | |
| **Motivation** | I maintained a strong interest in the research project. | |
| | I have identified some things I can do next time to make my research task more interesting. | |
| | In the future, I will identify some things I can do with a little help from my teacher and/or peers. | |

| Self-regulation | Self-monitoring outcomes | Ratings |
|---|---|---|
| **Strategic planning** | I am satisfied with the way I planned my research-related goals, which I modeled after my teacher's. | |
| | I am satisfied with way I planned my use of strategies in writing the research paper, which I modeled after my teacher's. | |
| | Next time on my own, I will be able to set the short- and long-term goals with due dates with a little help from my teacher and/or peers. | |
| | Next time on my own, I will be able to identify and use additional strategies in writing the research paper with a little help from my teacher and peers. | |
| **Social** | I am able to evaluate the benefits and drawbacks to working with others as my teacher did. | |
| | I am able to evaluate the benefits of obtaining additional resources as my teacher did. | |
| | I am able to identify things I will do differently next time regarding working with others and the use of resources as my teacher did. | |
| | I am able to identify things I will do differently next time regarding the use of resources as my teacher did. | |
| **Notes:** | | |

## Post-Emulation/Pre Self-Control Review

Before moving students to the next level of self-control, the teacher reviews the information from the three phases of the self-regulation self-monitoring log entries to assess which students are ready to engage in tasks with less supervision. At this next level, while some students are competent in working independently, other students need some supervision and are not yet capable of making adaptations or changes to their planning and strategy choices. In a long-term project such as this one, students require constant monitoring until they demonstrate more self-directed competency. The teacher uses the data from students' responses on the self-reflection ratings review to assess whether students are ready to work independently. Students at this level should be able to simulate what they observed and practiced during the previous sessions. The teacher maintains a watchful eye, but at the self-control level, will slowly remove the scaffolding as students become more self-sufficient.

## Self-Control Level

## It's Your Turn!

### Sessions 11–18

**Self-control:** At this level, the teacher is encouraging independence by shifting the responsibility of the process to the students. Students are now expected to work independently or with a peer to replicate the original task. The teacher's role also shifts from providing extensive support to guiding and advising as needed by the students. Although working independently, the students at this level are not yet ready to deviate from the original modeling, and the product is representative of what they originally observed and emulated.

## Self-Controlled Forethought

### Planning

### *My Strategic Approach to Synthesizing Sources*

### Session 11

**Forethought:** Although now working independently, the class remains in groups and the teacher explains the task. She distributes blank self-monitoring logs and the research project task, the literature review grid (blank), selected topics, and materials to be used for writing the research paper outline. The teacher uses every opportunity to activate prior knowledge gained from the behaviors observed and practiced in the planning phases of the previous two levels. Students are encouraged to work individually and cooperatively using their peers for support when needed.

### *Modeling: Who Is Modeling?*

The teacher asks students to model for each other the defining behavior of the self-control level, primarily independent learning and thinking aloud. The teacher encourages students to think aloud about how difficult it might be to do the research task and discusses possible remedies to these challenges. Using the self-monitoring logs, the students complete each cell by thinking out loud about the decisions that need to be made in planning to gather and synthesize sources for a well-organized research paper.

### Do I Have the Skills to Do This Task with Less Teacher Monitoring?

**Self-efficacy:** Students are asked to rate their self-efficacy for developing plans to synthesize sources and to write the research paper using the self-monitoring logs. The teacher reminds the class to think aloud about the potential demands of the task and how they influence their self-efficacy.

### How Will I Remain Interested with Less Teacher Supervision?

**Motivation:** Students are instructed to indicate their true level of interest in working on the research project and to rate their motivation on the logs.

- Students are encouraged to think about ways in which they will sustain motivation when faced with challenges and to recall what they observed and practiced in the previous two levels.

### Do I Have a Plan to Work Independently?

**Strategic planning:** Students are instructed to develop short- and long-term goals and strategies for synthesizing the five sources and for writing the research paper. They are encouraged by the teacher to use the literature review grid as a strategy for synthesizing their sources.

### Do I Know Where to Get the Help I Need to Work Independently?

**Social:** Students are reminded that although sitting in groups, they should try to work independently and use available resources as needed. Students should help each other recall methods observed during the original observation and practice sessions while working. The teacher also reminds them of the list of social resources discussed at earlier levels that can be used if they become "stuck."

- As the teacher circulates the room and listens to the students' discussions in the groups, she listens and reinforces students' decisions about working with peers and how they are making choices about resources to use.

Note: Students evaluate themselves (see Table 10.11) indicating their readiness to move on to the performance phase.

TABLE 10.11 Student Log: Forethought/Self-Control

**Student log: I can do it!**
Can I independently gather and synthesize sources (using a literature review grid) so they can be used to write a good research paper as my teacher did? Give yourself a grade of 1, 2 or 3 (1 = lowest).
Name: _____

| *Self-regulation* | *Self-monitoring outcomes* | *Rate yourself!* |
|---|---|---|
| **Self-efficacy** | I can create the plans to gather and synthesize my sources (literature review grid). | |
| **Motivation** | My plan to help me maintain interest in the research project includes finding great sources to make my research paper interesting. | |
| **Strategic planning** | I am setting short, easy-to-reach goals with targeted dates to work on them for gathering and synthesizing the sources used for writing my research paper. | |
| | I can describe at least two to three strategies on how to work on my research project. | |
| **Social/selective help-seeking** | I have plans to seek out specific people to help with questions that may arise in gathering and synthesizing sources that can be used for writing the research paper. | |
| | I have a plan for using additional resources when needed. | |
| **Notes:** | | |

## Self-Controlled Performance

## Practicing

### *My Strategic Approach to Synthesizing Resources*

### *Sessions 12–16*

**Performance:** The teacher reminds students to continue filling out the self-monitoring logs while working independently to gather and synthesize sources for the upcoming research paper. Although students are seated with their groups, they are instructed to work individually on their literature review grids, requesting assistance from both teacher and peers if needed. Students are encouraged to replicate what they had previously practiced,

**Modeling:** Using a short series of think-alouds, the teacher poses questions to help clear up any uncertainty or confusion students may still have. They should be following the plans they set up in the forethought phase and try to work as independently as possible, using resources and peers selectively.

### Do I Have the Skills to Complete This Task?

**Self-efficacy:** Students are encouraged to weigh weaknesses and strengths during the performance phase in order to make the correct evaluation of the skills they have to do the research-related tasks independently. They are encouraged to openly share their challenges with their peers and assist each other in areas where one is weak and the other is stronger.

### Will I Be Able to Maintain Focus?

**Motivation:** Students are encouraged to verbalize the challenging components of the task and how these challenges affect motivation. Students should keep in mind the original observation of the teacher and what was done to sustain motivation. Students are encouraged to strive for this. When diverting from the task, students should be encouraged to use self-talk or ask the teacher for help to get back on task.

### How Effective Are My Plans?

**Strategy planning/task analysis:** Students work individually on their short- and long-term goals. They should be using the literature review grid or other similar strategies to assist them with the synthesis and writing of the research paper outline.

- Students should also be thinking about their strategies in terms of whether or not it is a "good fit" for their personal use or whether it needs to be changed or adapted in the future. The teacher encourages students to closely monitor their performance and ask for feedback regarding their progress.

### What Resources Are Available If I Need Help?

**Social (with whom):** The students are encouraged to seek help from individuals or an array of available resources to help complete the research-related task. The teacher closely monitors how and from whom they seek assistance to check for behaviors that show an effective use of social resources.

Note: Students evaluate themselves (see Table 10.12) indicating their readiness to move on to the self-reflection phase.

TABLE 10.12 Student Log: Performance/Self-Control

**Student log: How am I doing now?**
Now that I am doing it, can I gather and synthesize my sources as my teacher demonstrated and use them to write a good research paper? Give yourself a grade of 1, 2 or 3 (1 = lowest).
Name: _____

| *Self-regulation* | *Self-monitoring outcomes* | *Rate myself!* |
|---|---|---|
| **Self-efficacy** | I am confident that I am synthesizing and using my sources appropriately so they can be used to write a good research paper. | |
| **Motivation** | I am maintaining interest in the research project. | |
| **Strategic planning** | I am first working on the short, easy-to-reach goals, followed by the more challenging ones as my teacher did. | |
| | I am using two to three strategies that my teacher used on how to gather and synthesize sources for my research paper. | |
| **Social/selective help-seeking** | I am aware of where I can find specific people and resources to help with questions that may arise in gathering and synthesizing sources. | |
| | I am using additional resources, such as a model of a research paper with a good list of sources about a topic similar to mine. | |
| **Notes:** | | |

# Self-Controlled Reflection

## Reflecting On

### *My Strategic Approach to Synthesizing Sources*
### Session 17

**Self-reflection:** Students are instructed to evaluate their planning and performance on the research project task based on the outcomes and teacher feedback. Students should consult their self-monitoring logs (student logs—all levels and phases) and the completed literature review grid to realistically reflect upon their monitoring skills and their use of the literature review grid. This phase is pivotal, because if students are able to work through the research tasks with little or no support from the teacher, they are ready to move on to the next level, where they will apply their newly acquired strategic approach to this type of task to completely independent situations.

### Modeling: Who Is Modeling?

The teacher encourages students to model for each other what is expected during reflection. They are reminded to share with each other how they use self-monitoring logs to self-evaluate. The students demonstrate for each other how to make comparisons of their work to the teacher's, as well as to the ones they practiced at the previous level, and to look for any discrepancies. They discuss in small groups differences found, as well as any challenges related to the processes that may have unexpectedly come about, and are briefly instructed on how to complete this portion of the self-monitoring log or the literature review grid.

### How Has Evaluating My Self-Efficacy Helped Me Self-Regulate My Actions?

**Self-efficacy:** Working individually, yet in earshot of the teacher, students share examples of over- or underrating their self-efficacy from the beginning of the task.

- Students are instructed to examine if their self-efficacy rating changed and, if so, how.
- Students begin to feel competent in their ability to self-monitor and complete a challenging task successfully. They enter their outcome ratings in the self-monitoring log.

### Was I Able to Maintain Interest in My Topic and Completing the Task?

**Motivation:** The teacher provides feedback based on observations of how well each student was able to remain motivated to complete the research project task in spite of some challenges.

- Students are asked to identify specific times during the task when they began to feel as if they did not want to continue and to share this with their peers, along with what they did to remain focused and on task.

**Strategic planning/task analysis:** The teacher provides feedback and instructs students to compare their completed task with the model presented at the beginning of the lessons on self-monitoring and using the literature review grid to gather and synthesize sources.

- Working individually, students list the strategies that are now familiar and those that need re-modeling.

## Who Did I Work With? Did I Benefit from Help Seeking?

**Social resources:** Students are asked to evaluate the effectiveness of selected social sources of help, as well as the resources they may have used. The students are encouraged to lead discussions of what worked best and what presented more obstacles to completing the task.

Note: Students evaluate themselves (see Table 10.13) indicating their level of self-regulation in the areas of motivation, strategic planning, and using social resources effectively.

**TABLE 10.13** Student Log: Self-Reflection/Self-Control

| **Looking back: Student log** Now that you have independently gathered and synthesized your sources to write a research paper, let's evaluate what we did from the beginning. Did good planning and self-monitoring help you gather and synthesize the sources needed to write a research paper? Give yourself a grade of 1, 2 or 3 (1 = lowest). |||
| --- | --- | --- |
| *Self-regulation* | *Self-monitoring outcomes* | *Ratings* |
| **Self-efficacy** | I am confident that I gathered and synthesized sources that can be used to write a research paper. | |
| | I am confident that my literature review grid will help me write a good research paper. | |
| | I will be even more confident when given tasks similar to this one in the future. | |
| | I will be even more confident when asked to gather and synthesize sources because I know how to use a literature review grid and self-monitor my actions. | |
| **Motivation** | I maintained a strong interest in the research project. | |
| | I have identified some things I can do next time to make my research task more interesting. | |
| | In the future, I will identify some things I can do with a little help from my teacher and/or peers. | |
| **Strategic planning** | I am satisfied with the way I planned my research-related goals, which I modeled after my teacher's. | |
| | I am satisfied with the way I planned my use of strategies in writing the research paper, which I modeled after my teacher's. | |
| | Next time on my own, I will be able to set the short- and long-term goals with due dates with a little help from my teacher and/or peers. | |
| | Next time on my own, I will be able to identify and use additional strategies in writing the research paper with a little help from my teacher and peers. | |

| Self-regulation | Self-monitoring outcomes | Ratings |
|---|---|---|
| **Social** | I am able to evaluate the benefits and drawbacks to working with others as my teacher did. | |
| | I am able to evaluate the benefits of obtaining additional resources as my teacher had done | |
| | I am able to identify things I will do differently next time regarding working with others and the use of resources as my teacher did. | |
| | I am able to identify things I will do differently next time regarding the use of resources as my teacher did. | |
| **Notes:** | | |

## Evaluation

The teacher collects all logs from the self-control level to provide feedback during individual sessions with each student. The logs from each level so far are formative assessments that can be used to determine which students are most likely to independently apply self-regulated strategies when not in an accompanying assignment or supervised setting. The teacher meets with students individually to provide feedback on their logs and their literature review guides. The teacher promotes students' self-efficacy by highlighting effort and the self-regulatory processes used by students in the process of working on the research task.

The teacher invites students to share how they felt about gathering and synthesizing sources as a precursor to the actual writing of a research paper. One of the teacher's goals at this level is to prompt students to think about how they might make changes in the future when assigned a similar task and where else they might use what they have learned. Self-regulation competency involves being flexible and able to adapt and make changes as needed, even when faced with unanticipated events and in the absence of the teacher.

## Self-Regulation Level

### On My Own!

#### *Fostering Self-Regulation to Synthesize Resources*

Not every student is going to be ready to take charge of their learning, yet teachers can encourage strategies during daily classroom learning experiences that foster self-regulation. Teachers can use the data from students' responses on the student logs to evaluate their growth and development as self-regulated learners, specifically in their understanding of self-monitoring strategies. The teacher's job now is to provide opportunities for students to apply the newly acquired strategies to other areas of learning and spend more time with students who need more practice.

**Self-regulation:** At this level, the teacher challenges students to adapt their self-regulated learning strategies to varying conditions and watch as they begin to independently self-regulate their behavior. Acting on requests from students, the teacher can provide minimal assistance and redirect learning when necessary. At this point, the students are grouped according to those who are ready to begin working on the next research task and those who require more time at the self-control level working on the current task.

## Planning Research-Related Tasks

**Forethought:** Self-regulated students independently include self-monitoring logs and the literature review grids as they make plans to gather and synthesize the next five sources for their research paper, or for a similar task in another class. Students at this level are expected to take charge of how they will adapt the strategies to new conditions, such as homework. The teacher is a facilitator, providing opportunities and encouraging good planning and goal setting for all types of tasks.

**Modeling:** The teacher consistently models what self-regulated learning "looks like" by thinking aloud when she is using a strategy and self-monitoring. In addition, the teacher incorporates self-monitoring logs and graphic organizers into the class routines, encouraging the development of self-regulation in her students.

**Self-efficacy:** The teacher listens while students set the stage, verbalizing the differences between getting a task complete in the context of the classroom and in various other unstructured settings. The teacher emphasizes that self-efficacy to work independently and self-efficacy to work alongside a teacher will be very different. Each student evaluates their ability to complete a similar task outside of the classroom and enters their self-efficacy ratings into the self-monitoring log.

**Motivation:** The teacher encourages students to use "self-talk" as a strategy to sustain motivation when working independently. As the teacher observes students planning the task, she listens for statements that indicate self-praise for each accomplishment (no matter how small) that leads to successful planning of any task.

**Strategic planning/task analysis:** The teacher listens as students verbalize how to "own" a strategy to complete a similar research project–related task independently. Working with the literature review grid, the students demonstrate the adjustments that can be made to the graphic organizer in order to use it more effectively.

**Social resources:** The teacher closely observes as students discuss the challenges that arise when working with a partner or attempting to seek help from appropriate resources. An emphasis is put on when to decide it is time to seek help rather than persist alone and knowing what/who is available.

## Proactive Approach to Research Tasks

**Performance:** The teacher puts the class through a simulation requiring them to complete research tasks outside of the classroom for homework. The focus of the independent work is to raise students' awareness of how adaptations can be made when using the learned self-regulatory processes. Both the self-monitoring logs (for all three phases) and the literature review grids are readily available for students to access when needed. Self-regulated students will seek help to plan the next component of the research project from a peer, the teacher, or the librarian.

### Modeling

Over time, the teacher practices self-monitoring and the use of graphic organizers to sustain motivation and complete complex tasks. The teacher uses several types of graphic organizers and routinely includes self-monitoring of her self-efficacy, motivation, and social resources so the students can become increasingly familiar with how self-regulation is applied inside and outside of the classroom.

### How Can the Teacher Influence Students to Self-Monitor?

**Self-efficacy:** The teacher encourages students to express doubts about their abilities to do the task independently and set realistic goals. Self-regulated students consistently review the requirements of the homework assignments and rate their self-efficacy to do the research task outside of the classroom. They are encouraged by the teacher to maintain this practice.

**Motivation:** The teacher consistently models setting goals for her own work. Students are encouraged to set goals for work to be done outside the context of the classroom. Each time an assignment is given, the teacher can ask students who are self-regulated in that particular area to share their experiences regarding task completion. They can share how they handle the challenges that interfere with task completion outside structured learning environments.

**Strategic planning/task analysis:** Self-regulated students find a specific strategy that works for them and adopt it when required to gather and synthesize sources for another class. As the teacher consistently models her own methods for strategic planning, students are encouraged to adopt her strategies as well. Self-regulated students make adjustments to their performance to fit the task demands to personal areas of strength and weakness.

**Social resources:** The teacher sets aside time during class for students to share how they selected help in the past and evaluate their choices. The teacher guides students in discussing how to take advantage of accessible resources (e.g., library, online journals and publications, books, websites) as they work through the research tasks.

## Ongoing Reflection Requires Teacher Feedback...

**Self-reflection:** Self-regulated students conduct ongoing evaluations of how well they self-monitor during tasks. They consistently reflect how processes and outcomes connect and attribute success and failure to specific actions. Their entries in self-monitoring logs help them evaluate their planning and reflect upon their planning and performance, looking for what worked and what did not work.

**Modeling:** Self-regulated students have consistent and strong educators who at times evidence proficiency and at other times are coping models. Their teachers consistently and honestly reflect on their teaching performances when they evaluate students' learning progress. Modeling at this level should encourage students to investigate areas where they excel and other areas where they might need help, teaching them to self-evaluate and reflect on their performances as a step towards improvement.

### *What Should Teacher Feedback Include at This Level of Self-Regulation?*

**Motivation:** The teacher gives students choices of topics and areas of interest from which they can conduct their research projects. Students who are given choices are more likely to pursue completing the task with higher motivation than those who are not given choices. Class discussions often include students sharing what they did to sustain motivation when a task became challenging or confusing and they needed help. What specific actions did they take to sustain motivation in spite of setbacks?

**Strategic planning/task analysis:** Self-regulated students seek out feedback from their teachers to review their planning and completion of tasks. Teachers should schedule regular individual sessions to provide each student with the opportunity to get feedback on a project, task, or idea they are working on. During these sessions, students are welcome to discuss their reflections of the challenges they face when working on the planning and doing a specific task.

Students also discuss and evaluate the effectiveness of the strategies to self-monitor and to complete research-related tasks for homework. Self-evaluations of strategy use and adjustments made can be recorded in the self-monitoring log and shared with the teacher for feedback.

**Social resources:** Teachers can encourage students to evaluate how effectively they choose and utilize resources. Self-regulated students learn to make good choices by evaluating the resources before they invest their time in using them. Knowing when the library is open is not enough—checking to see if the librarian is available during those hours is a more effective strategy than just going to the library because it is a good resource. Self-regulated learners learn to investigate when resources are available, as well as their appropriateness to the task.

## References

Blaxter, L., Hughes, C., & Tight, M. (1998). Writing on academic careers. *Studies in Higher Education, 23*(3), 281–295.

Burke, B. A. (2013). Up close with close reading. *Library Sparks, 11*(3), 14.

Salahu-Din, D., Persky, H., & Miller, J. (2008). The Nation's Report Card: Writing 2007 (NCES 2008–468). National Center for Education Statistics, Institute of Education Sciences, U.S. Department of Education, Washington, DC.

Schwegler, R. A., & Shamoon, L. K. (1982). The aims and process of the research paper. *College English, 44*(8), 817–824.

# INDEX

academic language, defined 109, 112
academic language acquisition (elementary school) 107–52; *see also* context clues; "I Can" statements; morpheme clues; sessions in academic language acquisition; words; complexity of 109, 112–13; deliberate practice required for 109; emulation level in 132–40; emulation of forethought in 133–5; emulation of performance in 135–7; emulation of self-reflection in 138–9; fostering self-regulation in 152; goal attainment in 130–1, 138, 146, 151; goal setting and 110; instructional components for 118–22; observation level in 123–32; observation of forethought in 123–5; observation of performance in 127–8; observation of self-reflection in 130–1; ongoing reflection in 150–1; post-emulation of performance in 137–8; post-observation of forethought in 126–7, 126*t*; post-observation of performance in 128–30, 129*t*; post-observation of self-reflection in 132; self-controlled forethought in 141–2; self-controlled performance in 143–4, 144*t*; self-controlled reflection in 145–6; self-control level in 140–7; self-monitoring and self-evaluation during 110–11, 114; self-regulated forethought in 148–9; self-regulated learning for 110, 111*t*, 114–17; self-regulated performance in 149–50; self-regulated reflection in 151–2; self-regulation level in 147–52; shifting to be college ready 111, 111*t*
adaptive response 13
annotating 42, 44, 49, 51
attention focusing 13

career ready, defined 4
CCSS *see* Common Core State Standards (CCSS)
CCSSO *see* Council of Chief State School Officers (CCSSO)
close reading: in emulation of forethought 88; in emulation of self-reflection 53; help-seeking and 32, 33, 35–6, 43, 45, 53; monitoring strategies and 36; in observation of performance 43, 80; in observation of self-reflection 45; in post-observation of forethought 80; in self-controlled forethought 96; in self-controlled performance 98; in self-controlled reflection 61; self-reactions and 45, 53, 61; in self-regulated writing 202; teacher modeling and 35–6; in writing from informational texts 73, 78, 80, 88, 96, 98
College and Career Readiness anchor standards: for language vocabulary acquisition and use 108*t*; motivational variables and 13; overview of 4–5; project planning and 216; for reading 108*t*; research paper and 213

# Index

college readiness; *see also* crosswalk from Common Core to self-regulated learning: help-seeking and 33; ready for college, defined 4; self-regulated writing and 165–6*t*; writing from informational text and 71–2, 71*t*

Common Core State Standards (CCSS); *see also* crosswalk from Common Core to self-regulated learning: for all students 4–6; overview of 3–4

complexity: of academic language 109, 112–13; of research projects 215, 217, 247; spiral staircase of 3–4, 6, 10, 111, 247; of text 3–4, 14, 103, 107, 124–5, 151; of writing 68, 163, 178, 180

context clues: to find word meaning to improve comprehension 137, 140; in "I Can" Statements 125*t*; inferring meaning from 114; in learning progress goals for guiding student actions 144*t*; in Outside/Inside strategy 119*t*, 127; in self-efficacy ratings and goal attainment 115*t*, 116*t*, 136, 150; in self-evaluation/reflection ratings 117*t*; in teacher actions and student engagement aligned with learning process 129*t*; in Teacher Performance Rating checklist 126–7*t*; Vtrix and 119*t*, 125, 127

contextual analysis 113, 114; *see also* context clues

coping model 40, 123, 124, 168, 179, 217, 278

corrective feedback 22

Council of Chief State School Officers (CCSSO) 4

crosswalk from Common Core to self-regulated learning: in academic language acquisition (grades 4–5) 108, 108*t*; dimensional (grades 9–12) 211–18, 212*t*; in help-seeking (grades K–1) 29, 30*t*; overview of 6–7; in self-regulated writing (grades 6–8) 158, 158–9*t*; in writing from informational text (grades 2–3) 67, 67*t*

defensive response 13
deliberate practice 109, 114, 118, 144
"Did I" questions 85, 93, 130–1
difficulty level, goals and 70
dimensional crosswalk 211–18, 212*t*; Common Core standards 217; independence structured through self-monitoring 214–15; project planning for high schoolers 213; psychological dimensions of self-regulated learning 215–16, 216*t*; purpose 218; Road Map Research Paper and 212*t*; self-efficacy in project introduction 217–18; struggle in 214; towards independence 213–14

dimensions of self-regulated learning 215–16, 216*t*, 251–60; see also dimensional crosswalk; time management

distal goals 70, 76

elementary school (grades K–5): academic language acquisition 107–52; help-seeking 29–64; writing from informational text 66–106

emulation level: in academic language acquisition 132–40; in beginning a research paper 260–7; forethought in 9*f*; in help-seeking 47–54; overview of 9*f*, 10, 11, 15; performance in 9*f*; self-reflection in 9*f*; in self-regulated writing 186–93; in self-regulatory competence 11; in strategic approach to research projects 230–6; in writing from informational text 86–95

emulation of forethought: in academic language acquisition 133–5; in beginning a research paper 261–2; in help-seeking 47–9, 48–9*t*; in self-regulated writing 187–9; in strategic approach to research projects 231–2; in writing from informational text 87–9

emulation of performance: in academic language acquisition 135–7; in beginning a research paper 263–5; in help-seeking 49–51, 50–1*t*; in self-regulated writing 189–90; in strategic approach to research projects 233–4; in writing from informational text 89–92

emulation of self-reflection: in academic language acquisition 138–9; in beginning a research paper 265–7, 266–7*t*; in help-seeking 51–4, 52–3*t*; in self-regulated writing 191–3; in strategic approach to research projects 234–6; in writing from informational text 92–3

environmental control: in emulation of forethought 232; in emulation of performance 234; in emulation of self-reflection 235; in observation of forethought 225; in observation of performance 227; in observation of self-reflection 229; in self-controlled forethought 238; in self-controlled

reflection 240; in self-efficacy reports 222t; in self-regulated forethought 243
environmental structuring 13, 212t, 214, 216t, 247, 247t; in ongoing self-reflection 245; in self-controlled performance 239; in self-controlled reflection 240; in self-regulated performance 244
evidence from text 71, 91, 99, 103, 105, 106, 166t, 167

feedback: in beginning a research paper 278–9; benefits of 25; corrective 22
feedback loops, interdependent strategic 8, 9f
forethought: in academic language acquisition 123, 133, 141, 148; in beginning a research paper 251–2, 261, 268; in help-seeking 39, 47, 55, 62; overview of 9f, 12, 13; in planning research-related tasks 276; in self-regulated writing 179, 187, 194, 201; in strategic approach to research projects 223–4, 231, 236–7, 242; writing from informational text 77, 87, 95–6, 102–3
fostering self-regulation: in academic language acquisition 152; in beginning a research paper 275–6; in self-regulated writing 206; in strategic approach to research projects 241–2

goal attainment: in academic language acquisition 130–1, 138, 146, 151; aligning self-efficacy and 81, 114, 115t, 116t; in emulation of performance 90; in emulation of self-reflection 93, 138, 193; linking self-efficacy with learning process goal attainment 130, 138, 146, 151; in observation of performance 81; in observation of self-reflection 85, 130–1; partnering self-efficacy and 85, 104, 105; planning and self-monitoring linked with 85, 93, 94, 101, 105–6; rating progress towards 117t; in self-controlled performance 98; in self-controlled reflection 101, 146, 199, 200; in self-regulated forethought 202; in self-regulated performance 104; in self-regulated reflection 105–6, 151; in self-regulated writing 193, 199, 200, 202; in writing from informational text 81, 85, 90, 93, 94, 98, 101, 104, 105
goal orientation 12

goal progress and task performance: in emulation of performance 90; in emulation of self-reflection 93; in observation of performance 81–2; in self-controlled performance 98; in self-control of forethought 97; in self-regulated performance 104
goal properties 70
graphic organizer 73, 74, 75–6t; in information map 73, 74, 73–4t, 77; in observation level 76–7; in observation of forethought 77; in observation of performance 83; in observation of self-reflection 86; Progress Monitoring Chart (PMC) 118–19, 118t; in self-regulated forethought 103; in self-regulated performance 104, 105; in self-regulated reflection 106

help-avoidance 163
help-seeking (elementary school) 29–64; *see also* sessions in help-seeking; benefits of 33–5, 266; beyond classroom 62–3; close reading in 35–6; college readiness and 33; comprehension of informational text in 38; crosswalks from Common Core standards to self-regulated learning 30t; developing 31–2; emulation of forethought in 48, 49–50t, 188–9; emulation of performance in 50, 50–1t, 190; emulation of self-reflection in 52, 52–3t, 193, 266; encouraged by teacher 21–2; evaluating help-seeking strategies in 57, 58t; explained 40, 43; for goal attainment 193, 200; to help-avoidance 163; monitoring 50, 50–1t, 59, 60t; observation of forethought in 40, 41t, 181; observation of performance in 43, 43t, 184; observation of self-reflection in 44, 45, 45t, 185–6; overview of 13; plan, overview of 38; practicing strategies of 56; promoting in classroom 64; rating teacher's help-seeking strategies 43, 45; self-controlled forethought in 56, 56t, 196; self-controlled performance in 57, 58t, 198; self-controlled reflection in 59, 60t, 200; self-monitoring logs for increasing 36–7, 37–8t; self-regulated forethought in 62–3, 203; self-regulated performance in 63, 204; self-regulated reflection in 64, 205; in self-regulated writing, overview of 163, 173; as social dimension of self-regulation 31–2; speaking and listening in 29–32, 31t,

## 284  Index

39; thinking about 48; for writing proficiency 203

high school (grades 9–12): dimensional crosswalk 211–18, 212*t*; research paper, beginning 246–79; research projects, strategic approach to 220–45

"I Can" checklists: Self-Efficacy for Learning Process Goals: Student Ratings checklist (With "I Can" Statements) 115, 116*t*, 132, 133, 134, 135, 136, 137, 138, 139–40, 143, 147, 148, 149; Self-Efficacy for Learning Process Goals: Teacher Ratings checklist (with "I Can" statements) 115, 115*t*, 125, 127, 128, 131, 132; Self-Instruction and Self-Efficacy Ratings: All Phases 170*t*

"I Can" statements: in emulation of forethought 87, 88, 133, 134; in emulation of performance 89, 90, 136; in emulation of self-reflection 92, 93, 138, 139; in goal setting 72; in observation of forethought 77, 79, 123, 124, 125*t*; in observation of performance 80, 81, 83, 128, 183; in observation of self-reflection 84, 85, 130–1; in post emulation of forethought 89; in post-emulation of performance 92; in post-emulation of reflection 139–40; in post observation of forethought 80; in post-observation of performance 83; in post-observation of self-reflection 86; in post-observation student self-efficacy evaluation 86, 89, 92, 139–40, 145, 147; in post self-controlled performance 145; in promoting self-regulated learning experiences 102, 104, 149, 150; in self-controlled forethought 141, 142; in self-controlled performance 144; in self-controlled reflection 101, 146; in self-efficacy 75, 75*t*, 114, 115*t*, 116*t*, 121*t*, 124, 125*t*; in self-efficacy ratings 75, 75*t*, 170*t*, 181, 183; in self-instruction 170*t*, 181, 183; as self-instruction statements 164–5, 164*t*, 183, 204; in self-regulated forethought 148–9; in self-regulated performance 104, 150, 204; to set learning process goals 111*t*, 114, 115–16*t*; in worksheets/rating sheets/checklists 122*t*

identify words: in "I Can" Statements 125*t*; in self-efficacy ratings and goal attainment 115*t*, 116*t*, 150; in self-evaluation/reflection ratings 117*t*; in teacher actions and student engagement aligned with learning process 129*t*; in Teacher Performance Rating checklist 126–7*t*

imagery 13

independence *see* help-seeking (elementary school)

informational text *see* reading informational text; writing from informational text (elementary school)

information map; *see also* graphic organizer; self-monitoring logs: all phases self-efficacy/"I Can" checklist 73, 74, 73–4*t*, 77, 78–9; in emulation of forethought 87–9; in emulation of performance 89–92; in emulation of self-reflection 92–4, 94*t*; in observation of forethought 77–80; in observation of performance 80–3; in observation of self-reflection 84–6, 85*t*; overview of 73–6, 75–6*t*; in post-emulation of performance 92; in post-emulation of reflection 95; in post-observation of self-reflection 86–7; in post self-controlled reflection 102; in post self-control of forethought 97; in self-controlled performance 98–100; in self-controlled reflection 101; in self-control of forethought 95–7; in self-regulated forethought 103; in self-regulated performance 104–5; in self-regulated reflection 106

instructional components for self-regulated learning; *see also individual components*: goal setting 169; help-seeking 173; learning process goal setting 114; self-efficacy 114, 115*t*, 116*t*, 169, 170*t*; self-evaluation 115, 117, 117*t*, 171–3*t*; self-instruction 169, 170*t*; self-monitoring 114, 115

intrinsic interest 12

learning process goals; *see also* goal attainment; learning process goals, setting: in academic language acquisition 110–11, 111*t*, 114; in emulation level 132; in emulation of forethought 133–4; in emulation of performance 135–6; in emulation of self-reflection 138, 139; evaluate and setting 121–2*t*, 125; in fostering self-regulation 152; "I Can" statements incorporated into 114, 115, 115*t*; in observation level 123; in observation of forethought 123, 125; in observation of performance 127,

128; in observation of self-refection 130–1; in ongoing evaluations 149; in post-emulation of forethought 135; in post-emulation of performance 137–8; in post-emulation of reflection 139, 140; in post-observation of self-refection 132; in post self-controlled forethought 143; in post self-controlled performance 145; in post self-controlled reflection 147; in self-control 140; in self-controlled forethought 141–2; in self-controlled performance 144; in self-controlled reflection 146; self-efficacy for 114, 116*t*, 121–2*t*, 128; in self-regulated forethought 148–9; in self-regulated performance 150; in self-regulated reflection 151, 152; in self-regulation level 147; teacher actions and student engagement aligned with 128–30, 129*t*; in teacher performance rating 126–7*t*
learning process goals, setting 132, 133–4, 136, 141–2, 144, 145, 148, 150; in emulation level 132; in emulation of forethought 133–4; in emulation of performance 136; modeling and 148; in post self-controlled performance 145; in self-controlled forethought 133, 141–2; in self-controlled performance 144; self-efficacy aligned with 128, 136, 144, 150; in self-regulated forethought 148; in self-regulated performance 150; thinking about 133, 141–2
levels of SRL development; *see also individual levels*: emulation 9*f*, 10, 11; observation 9*f*, 10–11; overview of 10–12; self-control 9*f*, 10, 11–12; self-regulation 9*f*, 10, 12; in self-regulatory competence 10–12
literature review grids 249, 249*t*; in emulation of forethought 261, 262*t*; in emulation of performance 263, 264; in emulation of self-reflection 265, 266, 266*f*; in observation of performance 249, 249*t*, 253–4, 255*t*; in observation of self-reflection 256, 257, 258*t*; in planning research-related tasks 276; in post-observation review 259*t*, 260*t*; in proactive approach to research tasks 276; in self-controlled forethought 268, 269, 270*f*; in self-controlled performance 270, 271; in self-controlled reflection 272, 273, 274*f*
loaded words 176
long-term goals 70, 76

mentor texts: in emulation of forethought 187, 188; in emulation of performance 190; in emulation of self-reflection 192; for evolving writer 165, 167; in help-seeking 173; instructional components for using 173–8, 175*t*, 177*t*; modeling 173–4; in observation of forethought 180, 181; in observation of performance 182, 183, 184; in observation of self-reflection 184–5, 186; overview of 161–2; persuasive techniques 176; read like a writer 174, 175*t*; in self-controlled forethought 194, 195; in self-controlled performance 197; in self-controlled reflection 200; self-efficacy and 162, 163; in self-evaluations 165, 171–3*t*; in self-instruction 169, 170*t*; in self-regulated forethought 201, 202; in self-regulated performance 203; in self-regulated reflection 205; in self-regulated writing 165, 169, 178; uses of 162*t*; write like a writer 174, 176
middle school (grades 6–8) *see* self-regulated writing (grades 6–8)
modeling; *see also* peer modeling: in academic language acquisition 118; in close reading 35–6; in emulation of forethought 47, 87, 133, 187, 231, 261; in emulation of performance 49, 89, 136, 189–90, 263; in emulation of self-reflection 51, 93, 138, 191–2, 265; in mentor texts 173–4; in observation of forethought 39, 77–8, 123–4, 179–80, 224, 252; in observation of performance 42, 80–1, 127, 182, 226, 254; in observation of self-reflection 44, 84, 130, 184–5, 228, 256; in planning research-related tasks 276; in proactive approach to research tasks 277; in self-controlled forethought 55, 96, 141, 194–5, 237, 268; in self-controlled performance 57, 98, 143–4, 197, 270–1; in self-controlled reflection 58–9, 101, 146, 199, 273; in self-regulated forethought 62, 103, 148, 202; in self-regulated performance 63, 104, 150, 203; in self-regulated reflection 151, 205; in self-regulated self-reflection 64, 105; in self-regulated writing workshops 168*t*; as self-regulatory learning strategy 72; teacher feedback and 278
morpheme clues: to find word meaning to improve comprehension 137, 140; in "I Can" Statements 125*t*; inferring

meaning from 114; in learning progress goals for guiding student actions 144*t*; in Outside/Inside strategy 119–20*t*, 127; in self-efficacy ratings and goal attainment 115*t*, 116*t*, 136, 150; in self-evaluation/reflection ratings 117*t*; in teacher actions and student engagement aligned with learning process 129*t*; in Teacher Performance Rating checklist 126–7*t*; Vtrix and 119–20*t*, 125, 127; word consciousness and 113, 120–1

morphology 113, 114; *see also* morpheme clues

motivation: in beginning a research paper 247, 248, 249*t*, 250, 251*t*; college and career readiness and 216; in emulation of forethought 134, 232, 261, 262*t*; in emulation of performance 263, 264*t*; in emulation of self-reflection 265, 266*t*; goals and 70, 110; help-seeking and 34; modeling and 174; in observation of forethought 252, 253; in observation of performance 254, 255, 255*t*; in observation of self-reflection 229, 257, 258*t*; in planning research-related tasks 276; in post-observation review 259*t*, 260*t*; in proactive approach to research tasks 277; project planning for high schoolers and 213; in self-controlled forethought 141, 269, 270*t*; in self-controlled performance 271, 272*t*; in self-controlled reflection 273, 274*t*; self-efficacy and 178; self-monitoring and 214–15; in self-regulated forethought 243; of self-regulated student 24; self-regulation and 69; in self-regulation of forethought 103; teacher feedback and 278; transitioning into high school and 214; transitioning into middle grades and 157, 158

National Governors Association (NGA) 4
NGA *see* National Governors Association (NGA)

observation level: in academic language acquisition 123–32; in beginning a research paper 251–60; forethought in 9*f*; in help-seeking 39–46; overview of 9*f*, 10–11, 14; performance in 9*f*; pre-observation, in forethought phase 250; self-reflection in 9*f*; in self-regulated writing 178–86; in self-regulatory competence 10–11; in strategic approach to research projects 223–30; in writing from informational text 76–86

observation of forethought: in academic language acquisition 123–5; in beginning a research paper 251–3; in help-seeking 39–41, 40–1*t*; in self-regulated writing 179–81; in strategic approach to research projects 223–5; in writing from informational text 77–80

observation of performance: in academic language acquisition 127–8; in beginning a research paper 253–5, 255*t*; in help-seeking 42–3, 42*t*, 43*t*; in self-regulated writing 182–4; in strategic approach to research projects 226–8, 226*t*; in writing from informational text 80–3

observation of self-reflection: in academic language acquisition 130–1; in beginning a research paper 256–8, 258*t*; in help-seeking 44–6, 44*t*, 45*t*, 46*t*; in self-regulated writing 184–6; in strategic approach to research projects 228–9; in writing from informational text 84–6, 85*t*

ongoing reflection: in academic language acquisition 150–1; teacher feedback and 278–9; in writing from informational text 105–6

outcome expectations 12, 13, 166, 244
Outside-Inside strategy 119

peer modeling; *see also* modeling: in emulation of performance 136; in self-controlled forethought 141, 194–5; in self-controlled performance 98, 143–4, 197; in self-controlled reflection 101, 146; in self-regulated performance 150; in self-regulated reflection 151

performance: in academic language acquisition 127, 135–6, 143, 149; in beginning a research paper 253–4, 263, 270, 277; in help-seeking 42, 42*t*, 43*t*, 49, 50–1*t*, 56, 57–8*t*, 63; overview of 9*f*, 12, 13; in self-regulated writing 182, 189, 190, 196, 197, 203; in strategic approach to research projects 226, 233, 238, 243; writing from informational text 80, 89, 104; in writing from informational text 97–8

phases of SRL development; *see also individual phases*: forethought 12, 13; motivational variables in 12–13; overview of 9*f*, 12–14; performance

12, 13; self-efficacy and 12–13; self-reflection 12, 13
PMC *see* Progress Monitoring Chart (PMC)
post-emulation challenge 54
post-emulation of performance: in academic language acquisition 137–8; in self-regulated writing 191; in writing from informational text 92
post-emulation review: in beginning a research paper 267; in help-seeking 54; in strategic approach to research projects 236
post-observation challenge 46
post-observation of forethought: in academic language acquisition 126–7, 126*t*; in help-seeking 41; in self-regulated writing 181; in writing from informational text 80
post-observation of performance: in academic language acquisition 128–30, 129*t*; in self-regulated writing 184; in writing from informational text 83–4, 84*t*
post-observation of self-reflection: in academic language acquisition 132; in self-regulated writing 186; in writing from informational text 86
post self-control challenge 61
post self-control review: in help-seeking 61; in strategic approach to research projects 241
pre-self-control review, in beginning a research paper 267
production and distribution 66, 67*t*, 158, 159*t*
Progress Monitoring Chart (PMC) 118–19, 118*t*, 124
proximal goals 70

read-alouds; *see also* close reading: in emulation of forethought 48; help-seeking and 35, 36, 48, 62; in self-regulation 62
reading informational text: in emulation of forethought 133–5; in emulation of performance 135–7; in emulation of self-reflection 138–9; K–5 standard for 107–8, 108*t*; in observation of forethought 123–5; in observation of performance 127–8; in observation of self-reflection 130–1
Read Like a Writer (RLW) worksheet: in emulation of forethought 187–8; in emulation of performance 189–90; in emulation of self-reflection 191–2; in observation of performance 182–3; in observation of self-reflection 184–4; overview of 181; in post self-controlled performance 198; in self-controlled forethought 194, 195; in self-controlled performance 197; in self-controlled reflection 199; in self-control level 194; in self-regulated forethought 201, 202; in self-regulated performance 204; in self-regulated reflection 205
ready for college, defined 4; *see also* college readiness
research paper, beginning (high school) 246–79; *see also* sessions in beginning a research paper; student logs; emulation level in 260–7; emulation of forethought in 261–2; emulation of performance in 263–5; emulation of self-reflection in 265–7, 266–7*t*; fostering self-regulation in 275–6; observation level in 251–60; observation of forethought in 251–3; observation of performance in 253–5, 255*t*; observation of self-reflection in 256–8, 258*t*; ongoing reflection in 278–9; overview of 246–50; plan, overview of 250; post-emulation review in 267; pre-self-control review in 267; Road Map Research Paper 212*t*, 247, 247*t*; self-controlled forethought in 268–70, 270*t*; self-controlled performance in 270–2, 272*t*; self-controlled reflection in 272–5, 274–5*t*; self-control level in 268–75; self-regulated forethought in 276; self-regulated performance in 277; self-regulated reflection in 278–9; self-regulation level in 275–9; teacher feedback in 278–9
research projects, strategic approach to (high school) 220–45; *see also* sessions in strategic approach to research projects; emulation level in 230–6; emulation of forethought in 231–2; emulation of performance in 233–4; emulation of self-reflection in 234–6; fostering self-regulation in 241–2; observation level in 223–30; observation of forethought in 223–5; observation of performance in 226–8, 226*t*; observation of self-reflection in 228–9; plan, overview of 223; post-emulation review in 236; post self-

control review in 241; self-controlled forethought in 236–8; self-controlled performance in 238–9; self-controlled reflection in 239–41; self-control level in 236–41; self-efficacy reports in 222*t*; self-monitoring tools in 222–3; self-regulated forethought in 242–3; self-regulated performance in 243–4; self-regulated reflection in 244–5; self-regulation level in 241–5; study log in 220–2, 221–2*t*
RLW worksheet *see* Read Like a Writer (RLW) worksheet
Road Map Research Paper 212*t*, 247, 247*t*

Scientific Method 120*t*
self-controlled forethought: in academic language acquisition 141–2; in beginning a research paper 268–70, 270*t*; in help-seeking 55–6, 55*t*, 56*t*; in self-regulated writing 194–6; in strategic approach to research projects 236–8; in writing from informational text 97
self-controlled performance: in academic language acquisition 143–4, 144*t*; in beginning a research paper 270–2, 272*t*; in help-seeking 56–8, 57*t*, 58*t*; in self-regulated writing 196–8; in strategic approach to research projects 238–9; in writing from informational text 97–100
self-controlled reflection: in academic language acquisition 145–6; in beginning a research paper 272–5, 274–5*t*; in help-seeking 58–61, 59*t*, 60*t*; in self-regulated writing 198–200; in strategic approach to research projects 239–41; in writing from informational text 100–1
self-control level: in academic language acquisition 140–7; in beginning a research paper 268–75; forethought in 9*f*; in help-seeking 54–61; overview of 9*f*, 10, 11–12, 15; performance in 9*f*, 13; self-reflection in 9*f*; in self-regulated writing 193–201; in self-regulatory competence 11–12; in strategic approach to research projects 236–41; in writing from informational text 95–102
self-efficacy; *see also* self-efficacy ratings: defined 8; in doing challenging task 51–2; in emulation of forethought 47–8, 88, 133, 134, 135, 188; in emulation of performance 49–50, 50*t*, 90, 190;

in emulation of self-reflection 51–2, 52*t*, 93, 138, 139, 192; evaluating 131, 139, 146, 240, 273; explained 39–40, 78–9, 124; goal attainment aligned with 69–70, 81, 85, 85*t*, 90, 93, 98, 101, 104, 105, 114, 128, 130–1, 136, 138, 144, 146, 150, 151, 199; in "I Can" statements 75, 75*t*, 114, 115*t*, 116*t*, 121*t*, 124, 125*t* (*see also* "I Can" checklists); in middle school writing performance 162–3; monitoring 42, 42*t*, 49–50, 59, 59*t*, 197, 229, 242; motivation and 229; in observation of forethought 78–9, 124, 125*t*; in observation of performance 128, 182–3, 255*t*; in observation of self-reflection 44, 44*t*, 85, 85*t*, 130–1, 185, 229, 256–7, 258*t*; in planning research-related tasks 276; in post-emulation of forethought 135, 137; in post-emulation of reflection 140; in post-observation 230*t*; in post-observation of reflection 139–40; in post-observation of self-reflection 132; in post-observation review 259*t*, 260*t*; in post self-controlled forethought 143; in post self-controlled performance 145, 197; in post self-controlled reflection 147; in project introduction 217–18; reports 222, 222*t*; in self-control 140; in self-controlled forethought 55, 55*t*, 96, 141, 142, 195; in self-controlled performance 57, 57*t*, 98, 144; in self-controlled reflection 59, 59*t*, 101, 146, 199, 240, 273; in Self-Evaluation: Post-Observation Report 230*t*; self-monitoring logs for increasing 36–7, 37–8*t*; in self-regulated forethought 62, 103, 148, 149, 202; in self-regulated learning 8–9, 12–13; in self-regulated performance 63, 104, 150, 203; in self-regulated reflection 64, 105, 151, 205; self-regulated teacher and 19; in self-regulated writing 180, 182–3, 185, 188, 190, 192, 195, 197, 199, 202; as self-regulatory learning strategy for second and third graders 72; in students built by teacher 19; in task preparation 242; in task requirements 96, 103; in teacher 19; in "Teacher Can" Checklist 75, 76*t*; thinking about 47–8, 88, 134, 142
Self-Efficacy for Learning Process Goals(With "I Can" Statements): Student Ratings checklist 115, 116*t*, 132, 133, 134, 135, 136, 137, 138, 139–40,

Index **289**

143, 147, 148, 149; Teacher Ratings checklist 115, 115*t*, 125, 127, 128, 131, 132
self-efficacy ratings: checklist 169, 170*t*, 178, 181, 182, 183, 185, 186, 187, 188, 190, 192, 194, 195, 197, 198, 199; in emulation of forethought 48, 88, 187, 188, 261; in emulation of performance 136, 190; in emulation of self-reflection 94, 192; goal attainment aligned with 81, 114, 115*t*, 116*t*; for "I Can" goals 75, 75–6*t*, 79, 81, 86, 89, 94, 97, 114, 115*t*, 116*t*, 131, 135, 136, 143, 145, 149; in observation of forethought 79, 181; in observation of performance 81, 182, 183; in observation of self-reflection 86, 131, 185, 228; in planning research-related tasks 276; in post-emulation of forethought 89, 135; in post-emulation of self-reflection 194; in post-emulation review 236; in post-observation of self-reflection 186, 187; in post self-controlled forethought 97, 143; in post self-controlled performance 100, 145, 198; in research project-related assignments 218; in self-controlled forethought 195; in self-controlled performance 197; in self-controlled reflection 59, 199; in self-efficacy reports 222*t*, 236; in self-regulated forethought 102–3, 149, 202; in self-regulated performance 204; in self-regulated reflection 151
self-evaluation: in academic language acquisition, overview of 110–11; in emulation of forethought 134–5, 188; in emulation of performance 137, 190; in emulation of self-reflection 139, 192; in observation of forethought 125, 181; in observation of performance 128, 183; in observation of self-reflection 131, 185; in post observation 230*t*; in self-controlled forethought 142, 195; in self-controlled performance 144, 144*t*, 197; in self-controlled reflection 146; Self-Evaluation/Reflection Ratings 117*t*, 138, 139–40, 142, 145, 146, 149; as self-management strategy 165; in self-regulated forethought 149, 202; in self-regulated performance 150, 204; in self-regulated reflection 152, 205; in self-regulated writing, overview of 115, 117, 165, 171–3*t*

self-instruction; *see also* self-instruction statements: in emulation of performance 190; in observation of forethought 180–1; overview of 163–5, 164*t*, 169, 170*t*; in self-controlled forethought 195
Self-Instruction and Self-Efficacy Ratings: All Phases 170*t*
self-instruction statements: in emulation of forethought 188; in emulation of self-reflection 192; in observation of performance 183; in observation of self-reflection 185; in self-controlled performance 197; in self-controlled reflection 199–200; in self-regulated forethought 202; in self-regulated performance 204; in self-regulated reflection 205
self-judgments 13
self-management strategies 163–5; *see also individual strategies*; self-evaluation 165; self-instruction 163–5, 164*t*
self-monitoring: in academic language acquisition, overview of 110–11; in emulation of forethought 88–9, 134–5; in emulation of performance 92, 137; in emulation of self-reflection 93, 139, 235; of help-seeking in forethought phase 41*t*, 48–9*t*, 56*t*; of help-seeking in performance phase 43*t*, 50–1*t*, 58*t*; of help-seeking in self-reflection phase 45*t*, 52–3*t*, 60*t*; independence structured through 214–15; in observation of forethought 79–80, 125; in observation of performance 83, 128; in observation of self-reflection 85, 131; of reactions in self-reflection phase 46*t*, 53*t*, 60*t*; in self-controlled forethought 97, 142; in self-controlled performance 100, 144, 144*t*; in self-controlled reflection 101, 146; of self-efficacy in forethought phase 40*t*, 48*t*; of self-efficacy in performance phase 42*t*, 44*t*, 50*t*, 55*t*, 57*t*; of self-efficacy in self-reflection phase 44*t*, 52*t*, 59*t*; in self-regulated forethought 104, 149; in self-regulated performance 150; in self-regulated reflection 105–6, 152; tools 222–3, 222*t*; in writing from informational text, overview of 73
self-monitoring logs; *see also* student logs: in emulation of forethought 231, 261; in emulation of performance 233, 234, 263; in emulation of self-reflection 235; of help-seeking 36–7, 37*t*; for ongoing

reflection and teacher feedback 278; in planning research-related tasks 276; in proactive approach to research tasks 277; in self-controlled forethought 236–7, 268, 269; in self-controlled performance 238, 239, 270; in self-controlled reflection 239, 272, 273; of self-efficacy 36–7, 37*t*, 48; of self-reactions 36–7, 37*t*, 64; in structuring independence 214

self-reactions: evaluating 45; overview of 13, 14; performance evaluations and 53, 60–1; self-monitoring 36, 37–8*t*, 38, 64, 224, 240, 258*t*; self-monitoring logs for increasing 36–7, 37–8*t*

self-reflection: in academic language acquisition 130, 138, 145, 151; in beginning a research paper 265, 272; in help-seeking 44, 51, 58; overview of 9*f*, 12, 13; in self-regulated writing 184, 191, 198–9, 204; in strategic approach to research projects 228, 244; teacher feedback and 278; in writing from informational text 84, 92–3, 100–1, 105

self-regulated forethought: in academic language acquisition 148–9; in beginning a research paper 276; in help-seeking 62–3; in self-regulated writing 201–3; in strategic approach to research projects 242–3; in writing from informational text 102–4

self-regulated learning (SRL); *see also* crosswalk from Common Core to self-regulated learning: academic language acquisition through 110; instructional components for 114, 115, 117, 169–73; levels of 9*f*, 10–12; phases of 9*f*, 12–14; psychological dimensions of 215–16, 216*t*; theory-based instruction and 8–15

self-regulated performance: in academic language acquisition 149–50; in beginning a research paper 277; in help-seeking 63; in self-regulated writing 203–4; in strategic approach to research projects 243–4; in writing from informational text 104–5

self-regulated reflection: in academic language acquisition 151–2; in beginning a research paper 278–9; in help-seeking 64; in self-regulated writing 204–5; in strategic approach to research projects 244–5; in writing from informational text 105–6

Self-Regulated Strategy Development (SRSD) model 163

self-regulated student 23–5; environment managed by 24; feedback for benefiting 25; motivation of 24; overview of 23; proactive 23; time managed by 24

self-regulated teacher 18–23; as agent of change 20; choices given by 19–20; corrective feedback provided by 22; goals set by, realistic and attainable 21; help-seeking encouraged by 21–2; as model 18; self-efficacy and 19; self-monitoring used by 18; self-reflective 21; SRL process and 20

self-regulated writing (grades 6–8); *see also* sessions in self-regulated writing: college readiness and 165–6*t*; craft of writing and 161; crosswalk from Common Core to self-regulated learning 158, 158–9*t*; emulation level in 186–93; emulation of forethought in 187–9; emulation of performance in 189–90; emulation of self-reflection in 191–3; evolving writer and 165, 167; fostering self-regulation in 206; goal attainment in 193, 199, 200, 202; goal setting in 169; help-avoidance in 163; help-seeking in 163, 173; instructional component for 169–73; mentor texts in 161–2, 162*t*, 173–6; models for, accessible 159–60; observation level in 171–2*t*, 178–86; observation of forethought in 179–81; observation of performance in 182–4; observation of self-reflection in 184–6; post-emulation of performance in 191; post-observation of forethought in 181; post-observation of performance in 184; post-observation of self-reflection in 186; self-controlled forethought in 194–6; self-controlled performance in 196–8; self-controlled reflection in 198–200; self-control level in 193–201; self-efficacy and 162–3, 169, 170*t*; self-evaluation in 169; self-instruction in 170*t*; self-management strategies in 163–5; self-regulated forethought in 201–3; self-regulated performance in 203–4; self-regulated reflection in 204–5; self-regulation level in 171–3*t*, 201–6; shared responsibility for literacy development in 160–1; standardized tests and 167; writing workshops and 167–8, 168*t*

self-regulation and writing process 68–70; goal properties in 70; goal setting and self-efficacy in 69–70

self-regulation in classroom context 17–25; self-regulated student in 23–5; self-regulated teacher in 18–23

self-regulation level: in academic language acquisition 147–52; in beginning a research paper 275–9; forethought in 9*f*; in help-seeking 61–4; overview of 9*f*, 10, 12, 15; performance in 9*f*; reflection in 9*f*; in self-regulated writing 201–6; in self-regulatory competence 12; in strategic approach to research projects 241–5; in writing from informational text 102–6

self-regulation skills 29–32, 39, 160

self-regulatory competence 10–12; *see also* levels of SRL development

self-regulatory learning strategies, overview of 72–3; *see also individual strategies*; goal setting 72; information map 73–4*t*, 73–6; self-efficacy 72; self-monitoring 73; task analysis 73; "Teacher Can" Checklist 76*t*

self-satisfaction 13–14

sessions in academic language acquisition: emulation level (sessions 10–18) 132–40; emulation of forethought (sessions 10–12) 133–5; emulation of performance (sessions 16–18) 135–8; emulation of self-reflection (sessions 16–18) 138–40; observation level (sessions 1–9) 123–32; observation of forethought (sessions 1–3) 123–7; observation of performance (sessions 4–6) 127–30; observation of self-reflection (sessions 7–9) 130–2; overview of 122; self-controlled forethought (sessions 19–21) 141–3; self-controlled performance (sessions 22–24) 143–5; self-controlled reflection (sessions 25–27) 145–7; self-control level (sessions 19–27) 140–7

sessions in beginning a research paper: emulation level (sessions 5–10) 260–7; emulation of forethought (sessions 7–8) 261–2; emulation of performance (sessions 10–12) 263–5; emulation of self-reflection (session 11) 265–7; observation level (sessions 1–4) 251–60; observation of forethought (session 1) 251–3; observation of performance (sessions 2–3) 253–5; observation of self-reflection (session 4) 256–8; overview of 250; post-emulation review (session 10) 267; post-observation review (session 4) 258–60; pre self-control review (session 10) 267; self-controlled forethought (session 11) 268–70; self-controlled performance (sessions 12–16) 270–2; self-controlled reflection (session 17) 272–5; self-control level (sessions 11–18) 267–75

sessions in help-seeking: emulation level (sessions 8–14) 47–54; emulation of forethought (sessions 8–9) 47–9; emulation of performance (sessions 10–11) 49–51; emulation of self-reflection (sessions 12–13) 51–4; observation level (sessions 1–7) 39–46; observation of forethought (sessions 1–2) 39–41; observation of performance (sessions 3–4) 42–4; observation of self-reflection (sessions 5–6) 44–6; overview of 38; post-emulation review (session 14) 54; post-observation challenge (session 7) 46; post self-control review (session 21) 61; self-controlled forethought (sessions 15–16) 55–6; self-controlled performance (sessions 17–18) 56–8; self-controlled reflection (sessions 19–20) 58–61; self-control level (sessions 15–21) 54–61; self-regulated forethought (sessions 22–23) 62–3; self-regulated performance (sessions 24–25) 63; self-regulation level (sessions 22–27) 61–4

sessions in self-regulated writing: emulation level (sessions 16–30) 186–93; emulation of forethought (sessions 16–20) 187–9; emulation of performance (sessions 21–25) 189–91; emulation of self-reflection (sessions 26–30) 191–3; observation level (sessions 1–15) 178–86; observation of forethought (sessions 1–5) 179–81; observation of performance (sessions 6–10) 182–4; observation of self-reflection (sessions 11–15) 184–6; overview of 178; self-controlled forethought (sessions 31–35) 194–6; self-controlled performance (sessions 36–40) 196–8; self-controlled

reflection (sessions 41–45) 198–201; self-control level (sessions 30–45) 193–201
sessions in strategic approach to research projects: emulation level (sessions 5–7) 230–6; emulation of forethought (session 5) 231–2; emulation of performance (sessions 6–7) 233–4; emulation of self-reflection (session 8) 234–6; observation level (sessions 1–15) 223–30; observation of forethought (sessions 1–3) 223–5; observation of performance (session 2) 226–8; observation of self-reflection (session 3) 228–9; overview of 223; post-observation (session 4) 229–30; self-controlled forethought (session 9) 236–8; self-controlled performance (session 10) 238–9; self-controlled reflection (session 11) 239–41; self-control level (sessions 9–11) 236–41
sessions in writing from informational text: emulation level (sessions 13–24) 86–95; emulation of forethought (sessions 13–16) 87–9; emulation of performance (sessions 5–8) 89–92; emulation of self-reflection (sessions 21–24) 92–5; observation level (sessions 1–3) 76–7; observation of forethought (sessions 1–4) 77–80; observation of performance (sessions 5–8) 80–4; observation of self-reflection (sessions 9–12) 84–6; overview of 76; self-controlled forethought (sessions 29–32) 95–7; self-controlled performance (sessions 29–32) 97–100; self-control level (sessions 25–36) 95–102
short-term goals 70
social cognitive theorists 8, 9
social cognitive theory 8, 17
social resources: in beginning a research paper 249, 250, 251$t$; in emulation of forethought 261; in emulation of self-reflection 266, 267$t$; in planning research-related tasks 276–7; in post-observation review 260$t$; in proactive approach to research tasks 277–8; in self-controlled forethought 269, 270$t$; in self-controlled performance 271, 272$t$; in self-controlled reflection 274, 274$t$; teacher feedback and 279
speaking and listening 29–32, 31$t$, 39, 160
specific goals 70
spiral staircase of complexity 3–4, 6, 10, 111, 247

SRL *see* self-regulated learning (SRL)
SRSD model *see* Self-Regulated Strategy Development (SRSD) model
standardized test relevance 73, 167
strategic planning: in beginning a research paper 249$t$, 250$t$ (*see also* research paper, beginning (high school)); in emulation of forethought 261–2, 262$t$; in emulation of performance 264, 264$t$; in emulation of self-reflection 266, 267$t$; in observation of forethought 79, 252–3; in observation of performance 254, 255$t$; in observation of self-reflection 257, 258$t$; in planning research-related tasks 276 (*see also* research projects, strategic approach to (high school)); in post-emulation of forethought 88; in post-observation review 259$t$, 260$t$; in proactive approach to research tasks 277; in self-controlled forethought 96–7, 269, 270$t$; in self-controlled performance 272$t$; in self-controlled reflection 273, 274$f$; in self-regulated forethought 103; as self-regulatory learning strategy 72; teacher feedback and 278
student *see* self-regulated student
student logs: in emulation of forethought 262$t$; in emulation of performance 264–5$t$; in emulation of self-reflection 266–7$t$; in forethought phase 251$t$; in observation of performance 255$t$; in observation of self-reflection phase 258$t$; overview of 248, 249$t$; in self-controlled forethought 270$t$; in self-controlled performance 272$t$; in self-controlled reflection 274–5$t$

task analysis: in beginning a research paper 251$t$; in emulation of forethought 231, 264; in emulation of performance 233; in emulation of self-reflection 266; in observation of forethought 79, 124, 224–5; in observation of performance 226, 254–5, 255$t$; in observation of self-reflection 228–9, 257; in ongoing self-reflection 245; in planning research-related tasks 276; in post-emulation of forethought 88; in post-observation review 260$t$; in proactive approach to research tasks 277; in project planning 213, 218; in self-controlled forethought 96, 237; in self-controlled performance 239, 271; in self-controlled reflection

273; self-efficacy and 218; in self-regulated forethought 103, 242; in self-regulated performance 243–4; as self-regulatory learning strategy 72; teacher feedback and 278

task strategies 13, 216t, 252; in emulation of performance 90–2; in observation of performance 82–3; in self-regulation of performance 104–5

teacher *see* self-regulated teacher

"Teacher Can" Checklist 75, 76t

teacher feedback 278–9; *see also* feedback

theory-based instruction 8–15; feedback loops and 8, 9f; integrated framework of 14–15; levels of development in 10; self-efficacy and 8–9; self-regulatory competence and 10–12

think-alouds: in emulation of forethought 47, 88; in observation level 76, 123, 178; in observation of forethought 252; in observation of performance 82; in post-observation of forethought 80, 127, 181; in post-observation of performance 184; in self-controlled forethought 194–5; in self-controlled performance 238, 270–1

time management: in dimensions of self-regulated learning 215, 216t; in emulation of forethought 231, 232; in emulation of performance 233–4; in emulation of self-reflection 235; in observation of forethought 225; in observation of performance 227; in observation of self-reflection 229; in Road Map Research Paper 212t; in self-controlled forethought 237; in self-controlled performance 239; in self-controlled reflection 240; in self-efficacy reports 222t; in self-regulated forethought 243; in self-regulated performance 243; by self-regulated student 24; study logs for 221; in transitioning from middle school to high school 214; writing errors and 158

triarchic reciprocal causality 8, 9f

Vtrix 119–20t, 120–1, 125, 127; in emulation of forethought 133–4; in emulation of performance 136, 137; in emulation of self-reflection 138, 139; in observation of forethought 124, 125; in observation of performance 127; in observation of self-reflection 130, 131; overview of 119, 119–20t, 120–1, 122t; in post-emulation of performance 137, 138; in post-emulation of self-reflection 140; in post-observation of forethought 126, 127; in post-observation of performance 129t; in post self-controlled performance 145; in self-controlled forethought 142; in self-controlled performance 144t; in self-control level 140; in self-evaluation 125; in self-monitoring 125; in self-regulated forethought 148, 149; in self-regulation level 147

WLW worksheet *see* Write Like a Writer (WLW) worksheet

word consciousness 113, 120–1

words; *see also* context clues; identify words; morpheme clues: loaded 176; meanings of 113; parts of 112–13; tiers of 112

Write Like a Writer (WLW) worksheet: in emulation of forethought 187–8; in emulation of performance 189–90; in emulation of self-reflection 191–2; in observation of performance 182–3; in observation of self-reflection 184–4; overview of 181; in post self-controlled performance 198; in self-controlled forethought 194, 195; in self-controlled performance 197; in self-controlled reflection 199; in self-control level 194; in self-regulated forethought 201, 202; in self-regulated performance 204; in self-regulated reflection 205

writing from informational text (elementary school) 66–106; *see also* sessions in writing from informational text; college readiness and 71–2, 71t; emulation of forethought in 87–9; emulation of performance in 89–92; emulation of self-reflection in 92–4, 94t; goal properties in 70; goal setting in, self-efficacy and 69–70; informational writing and 72; information maps in 73, 74, 73–4t, 75; linking Common Core and self-regulation 67t; materials 74–6; observation of forethought in 77–80; observation of self-reflection in 84–6; overview of 66–7; planning 68; prior knowledge and lesson requirements in 73; self-controlled forethought in 95–7;

self-controlled performance in 97–100; self-controlled reflection in 100–1; self-regulation and writing process in 68–70; self-regulatory learning strategies in 72–3; standardized test relevance and 73; "Teacher Can" Checklist 75, 76*t*; writing complexity and 68

writing from sources; *see also* writing from informational text (elementary school): informational writing 72, 73; objective 75–6; prior knowledge and lesson requirements 73; shifting to be college ready 71, 71*t*; standardized test relevance 73